CU01558630

Published by Drinks Enthusiast, UK www.drinksenthusiast.com

Printed by Book Printing UK www.bookprintinguk.com

Remus House, Coltsfoot Drive, Peterborough, PE2 9BF

Printed in Great Britain

ISBN 978-1-0369-1934-4

Foreword

Saint Lucia's history is steeped in rich traditions, vibrant cultures, and remarkable craftsmanship, none more so than in the story of its rum. This spirit, both literally and figuratively, has been woven into the fabric of our island's identity for centuries. From the earliest sugarcane plantations to the current distillery producing world-class rums, this journey is one of resilience, innovation, and deep cultural significance.

In *Saint Lucia: A Sugarcane and Rum History*, Dave Marsland has embarked on an extraordinary mission: to meticulously document the evolution of rum in Saint Lucia. His extensive research, passion for spirits, and commitment to uncovering the island's rum heritage have culminated in this essential volume—a book that not only tells the story of our rum but also preserves an important piece of our national history.

Through this book, readers will be transported back in time to the days when sugarcane dominated the landscape, to the rise and fall of plantations, and ultimately, to the birth of the iconic rums that define Saint Lucia today. It is a tale of craftsmanship and dedication, of tradition and progress. More than just a drink, rum has been a witness to our struggles and triumphs, a symbol of celebration, and a reflection of our island's spirit.

This book is not just a historical account—it is a tribute. A tribute to the generations of Saint Lucians who cultivated the land, mastered the art of distillation, and carried forward the legacy of rum-making. It is a work that will inspire pride, curiosity, and a newfound appreciation for what lies in every bottle of Saint Lucian rum.

To those who have a passion for history, for rum, or simply for the beauty of our island's heritage, this book is an invaluable treasure. I invite you to turn the pages and immerse yourself in the remarkable journey of Saint Lucian rum—one that continues to shape our culture, our economy, and our identity.

Margaret Monplaisir
CEO, St. Lucia Distillers

Contents

Foreword
The Idea
Acknowledgements

1: Saint Lucia, 5
2: The Arrival of the Sucrérie, 9
3: The Growth of Labour, 18
4: The Brigand Wars, 27
5: 1874: The Central Sugar Factories, 37
6: The Death of Sugar, 52
7: Formation of St. Lucia Distillers Ltd, 57
8: Sugar Production and Export: An Overview, 73
9: Sucrérie and Slave Conditions, 84
10: The Sucrérie Today, 89
11: Saint Lucian Rum, 110
12: The Rum Brands of Saint Lucia, 120
13: Saint Lucia Production Figures, 155
14: Saint Lucia Export Figures, 223

Bibliography
Index

THE IDEA

My love affair with all things Saint Lucia really began when I purchased a bottle of Chairman's Reserve Original Rum back in 2009 for a bar I was bar manager for in Knutsford, United Kingdom. It stood out to me due to its shorter, wider bottle look compared to its taller competitors, and although I lacked any sort of brand knowledge of Chairman's Reserve Rum (these were the days before immersive social media channels and brand websites that offered more than just the basic information), my natural instinct to try new spirits meant the willingness to embrace. Back then, rum as a category was very small in terms of its United Kingdom offerings, with Barbados (Mount Gay), Jamaica (Appleton Estate and Wray & Nephew), Cuba (Havana Club), Puerto Rico (Bacardí) and Guyana (El Dorado) the main staples for most, alongside Gosling's, Matusalem, Myers's, Planteray, Captain Morgan's, Lamb's, Sailor Jerry and Pusser's, with the odd brand outside of these attempting to make a splash into the United Kingdom market that was gearing up for its gin renaissance.

Chairman's Reserve Rum though came to me at the right time in my own personal journey, as a bartender eager to learn more and experience new approaches to the norm. I found the rum very easy to enjoy as the flavours waved around my palate, and flexible to mix with a chilled cola or as part of the classic rum cocktails that the bar was serving up at that time. Fast forward to 2013 and I was eager to prove that Manchester is just as good as London for the bar scene. With my work at Northern Restaurant and Bar trade show in Manchester, I was after a great brand to host a cocktail competition for the bartenders of the north for the 2014 edition, and Chairman's Reserve Rum came to mind straight away as one that could offer a twist in the rum tail of bartenders. After showing the head of the brands United Kingdom importer, James Rackham of Emporia Brands, around Manchester and introducing him to a wide range of suggested venues who I'd be aiming to have entries from for the proposed cocktail competition, James didn't only agree to get involved but saw the opportunity to really immerse Chairman's Reserve Rum into the north of England. With that, he offered me the opportunity to bring the brand to the next level. From hosting consumer masterclasses to bartender training sessions and working with famous rum bars in the north, and of course hosting the wildly successful cocktail competition, I found myself visiting Saint Lucia for the first time in 2014 – and instantly fell in love with the island.

My inaugural visit to the Caribbean was exactly as expected – sun, sea sand and a whole load of rum! Bringing with me a set of bartenders from across Manchester and London as part of the latest leg of what was then coined as the *'Chairman's XI'*, the trip enlisted the group to host training sessions for the island bartenders in some of the most prestigious resorts in Saint Lucia, including Sugar Beach Viceroy that nestles itself between the iconic Pitons. No trip can be complete though without a visit to the Roseau Valley Distillery, the home of Chairman's Reserve and *St. Lucia Distillers Ltd.* It's here that I started to really immerse myself into the brand identity, listening to everything our tour guide, Ian John, had to say as well as taste some history with the, at that time, available 1931 rum range.

Fast forward to 2025 and I'm still very much a part of *St. Lucia Distillers Ltd* and its family. But it was in 2020 that I first formulated the idea of diving into the more historical aspects of our company rum history, and indeed Saint Lucia. After the enforced United Kingdom wide lockdowns due to the Covid-19 pandemic, the hours normally spent travelling and promoting the *St. Lucia Distillers Ltd* range meant I took the opportunity to update the United Kingdom brand training programmes for Chairman's Reserve, Bounty and Admiral Rodney rums. By bringing together multiple presentations used over the years from *St. Lucia Distillers Ltd*, I realised that although we could go into great transparency and detail for the production methods of the rums and the historical origins of each, there was only ever a short brief mention of the company history, with even less highlighted when talking pre-1972 and the formation of *St. Lucia Distillers Ltd.* Knowing that we mention a handful of rum distilleries in Saint Lucia from around the early 1900's within some of our presentations, I started to research each one and quickly realised that each were light on details when it came to rum production, and the wider articles solely focused on the current *St. Lucia Distillers Ltd.* Knowing that in 2007, the year of the fire at the Roseau Valley Distillery that destroyed the historical records and surrounding buildings, I decided to preserve as much as I could of anything I could find that related to Saint Lucian rum, and sugar production as a whole and build an 'unofficial' reference guide that we could use to highlight. Scouring books on Saint Lucian history, postcards and historical imagery of the island, and conversations with past and current workers of *St. Lucia Distillers Ltd*, it became clear that a small guide could turn itself into a comprehensive reference book.

So here we are, five years after the initial idea, from a small guide to a full book, diving into the history of Saint Lucia's sugarcane introduction, decline, then re-introduction. *St. Lucia Distillers Ltd* itself is covered, as well as a brief guide on rum production methods both past and present, and a comprehensive guide to the rum bottlings available around the world. You'll find a good amount of data too, from export volumes and values to production levels, numbers of cane fields and rum distilleries alongside much more that historical records allow.

I'm hoping this book offers a fascinating insight into Saint Lucia and its sugarcane and rum offerings as much as I've enjoyed tumbling down the rabbit hole and putting it all together.

David Marsland

ACKNOWLEDGEMEMTS

Thank you to all who have helped contribute, verify and support me on this journey. To the team at *St. Lucia Distillers Ltd,* thank you Margaret, Michael, Lennox, Deny, Ian and Eleonor for the valuable support in not only this book, but in myself since 2013. Thank you to Sam Boulton for the advice on going from an idea to print, to Tony Joseph for his unwavering commitment to document and present the history of Saint Lucia, and to Jolien Harmsen, Guy Ellis and Robert Devaux for starting me down this rabbit hole of learning not just about rum, but Saint Lucia's incredible history. To Melisa Cherubin-James at National Archives Authority of Saint Lucia for pointing me in the right direction, David Kelly of Carvid Books for taking the time to reach out and supply me with fascinating historical texts on Saint Lucia, to Uta and Verena Lawaetz of Balenbouche Estate for the support, insight and historical guide in to Saint Lucia's sugar history within Laborie and beyond, and to Connor and Kayleigh for convincing me over dinner in Rodney Bay that people would want to read about this niche topic.

Finally, thank you to my wife, who has supported me endlessly in all my endeavours.

CHAPTER 1

Saint Lucia

Saint Lucia as an island, offers as much in politics and war, as it does with weather and culture when it comes to discussing her place in the world. Although many books have been written about her history, with probably the finest piece of literature to dive into such coming from Jolien Harmsen, Guy Ellis and Robert Devaux's *'A History of St Lucia'*, sugarcane plantations mark a deep impact that is still felt and seen to this day. To understand sugar's introduction to Saint Lucia though, you must immerse yourself into what created Saint Lucia as a key target for planters, and the tussle between France and Great Britain to rule this small island in the Caribbean.

Saint Lucia was first known as *"Louanalao"* by the Arawak Indians in 200 AD, meaning *"Island of the Iguanas",* and then *"Hewanorra"* in 800 AD when the Carib Indians arrived and assimilated their culture into Saint Lucia. The Caribs lived on Saint Lucia until the 1600's, when in 1605 the first known attempt at settlement was made when the ship *Olive Branch*, driven off course when en route for French Guiana, landed its 67 passengers under command of Captain Nicholas St. John. On the ship's departure the colonists were attacked by the Caribs and after several days of severe fighting, the 19 survivors took to their boat. The island was included in the grant made to the Earl of Carlisle by Charles I in July 1627, and a more determined attempt at settlement was made in 1638 when 130 colonists arrived from Bermuda and Major Judge was appointed Governor. Though reinforcements arrived in 1639 and 1640, colonists were unable to withstand the Carib attackers, and the island was abandoned in 1641.

Meanwhile the French developed an interest in the island, which they claimed was included in a grant made by Cardinal Richelieu to M. d'Esnambuc in October 1626. In 1643, M. du Parquet, Lieutenant-General of Martinique, appointed M. Rousselan Governor of Saint Lucia. M. Rousselan, who married a Carib, maintained his authority until his death in 1654, but his successors had brief and tragic careers. In 1660, however, local treaties were negotiated by the French Governors of St. Christopher and Guadeloupe alongside the British Governors of Nevis, Antigua and Montserrat on the one hand and between the French and Caribs on the other; these treaties left the French in possession of Saint Lucia and the possibility of peaceful co-existence arose. But in 1663 Francis Lord Willoughby reached Barbados as Governor and as heir to the English Patent whilst also to alleviate the problem he had of finding further accommodation for Barbados' surplus population. Barbados not being party to the 1660 treaty, he utilised the serves of 'Indian' Warner to purchase Saint Lucia from the Caribs and the following year, 1664, sent an expedition under Colonel Carew to occupy the island, the French Governor capitulating without a shot being fired. The settlement proved a failure and, on the English withdrawal from the island early in 1666, the French resumed occupation. But the wars of 1673 and 1688, the attacks of the English, and the lack of assistance received by the settlement from Martinique, forced a French withdrawal in turn.

In 1718 a fresh grant of the island was made by the French regent, the Duke of Orleans, to Marechal D'Estrees, who attempted to settle it with refugees. British objections were raised to this grant and in 1772 George I granted Saint Lucia and St. Vincent to the Duke of Montagu. An expedition under Nathanial Uring was fitted out at great expense to consolidate this grant; but local French opposition proved too strong, and the expedition was forced to withdraw early in 1723 on the signature of an agreement that subsequent to the British withdrawal the French would also evacuate and leave the island in its former state until a decision could be reached between the two Crowns. The next attempt at settlement was made in 1744, when England and France being once again at war, the Marquis de Champigny, Governor of Martinique, established a garrison under M. de Longueville as military commandment. The Treaty of Aix la Chapelle in 1748 in theory once more restored the status quo; in practice, however, M. de Longueville remained as civil commandant until his death in 1761, when he was succeeded by his nephew. Meanwhile English and French commissaries disputed at length the respective rights of their nations to the island.

In February 1762, war having once again broken out, the island surrendered to Captain Hervey, one of Lord Rodney's staff; but at the Treaty of Paris in 1763 the island was fully assigned to France. With security of tenure at last, apparently, assured, the French proceeded rapidly with its development and fortification. The fortifications were strengthened by the construction of the huge forts on Morne Fortune, and the capital was moved to its present site from Le Petit Carenage in the Castries Harbour on the Vigie peninsular. But the island was not yet due for a period of peaceful progress; with one of the finest small harbours in the Caribbean its military importance was such that it immediately became a target when war broke out, and its improved defences only ensured that subsequent fighting would be bloodier. In December 1778 a strong British expedition surprised and captured the island and French relieving forces under Count d'Estaing were beaten off. Lord Rodney was so impressed by the strategic potentialities of the island as a naval base that he wrote at length in May 1778 to the Earl of Sandwich stressing the importance of retaining the island, and it was from Saint Lucia that he sailed in 1782 to win his great Battle of the Saints over the French under François Joseph Paul De Grasse. But in 1783 it was agreed in the Treaty of Versailles that the island should once again be restored to France, though the British continued in possession until January 1784.

When war broke out again, an expedition was sent from England to the West Indies under Admiral Jarvis. This force surprised the French and captured Saint Lucia in April 1794. France at this time was in the throes of its revolution and in February 1794 a decree had been promulgated for the abolition of slavery in the French Antilles. On the surrender of Saint Lucia many of the ex-slaves and several French soldiers escaped into the woods when, with the aid of planters of republican sympathies, they harassed the British. In June 1794 Victor Hugues arrived in Guadeloupe as representative of the National Convention, and he succeeded in organising and inspiring the disaffected that they compelled the depleted British garrison to withdraw in 1795. A strong British force under General Abercrombie reconquered the fortifications after severe fighting in the summer of 1796; but it was not till the end of 1797 that guerilla warfare ceased and the "*Armee francais dans les bois*" surrendered at discretion.

By the Treaty of Amiens in 1802 the island was yet once more returned to France. But with the resumption of hostilities, it again became the object of British attack, and it was captured in June 1803. Since then, Saint Lucia has remained without interruption under British rule, and it was finally ceded to Britain by the Treaty of Paris in 1814. Until 1838 Saint Lucia was administered as a separate administrative, its Governor being in direct correspondence with the Colonial Office. In 1838 it was annexed to the Government of the Windward Islands, then comprising Barbados, Grenada, St. Vincent and Tobago with the seat of government in Barbados. Although from time to time since the composition and the seat of government of the Windward Islands has changed, Saint Lucia has always remained a member. An important event in Saint Lucia's history was the establishment of two United States bases under the 1940 Anglo-American agreement. In 1950 one of these bases, at Beane Field, was 'de-activated' and the Government assumed control by agreement. This base was brought back into use and is now home of the Hewanorra International Airport. When the French claim to the island was conceded in 1763, their first aim was to develop the colony as an entrepot centre. But estates were also planted with coffee, cocoa and cotton; sugar gradually obtained pre-eminence in the colony's economy. As British annexation came when talk of emancipation was in the air (followed by the Emancipation Act in 1833), economic development was slow but later in the century, with the advent of steamships, the colony became an important coaling station, an activity which reached its peak during the 1914-18 war. However, with the changeover to oil-burning vessels this trade declined. Saint Lucia gained independence from the United Kingdom on 22nd February 1979.

This book will investigate sections of historical moments of the island in more detail as it pertains to sugar and its wider impact to the economy, starting with the 1600's and the beginning of the Saint Lucian agricultural journey.

CHAPTER 2

The Arrival of the Sucrérie

Saint Lucia appears to have remained wholly uncultivated until about the middle of the seventeenth century. According to '*St. Lucia: Historical, Statistical, and Descriptive*', authored by Englishman Henry Hegart Breen in 1844, the settlers in those days, few and moderate in their wants, led very basic livelihoods until the year 1651. As the population began to increase, the cultivation of tobacco, ginger, and cotton were introduced and continued to be the chief resources of the island until the commencement of the eighteenth century, when they were almost entirely displaced by the more lucrative commodities of coffee and cocoa. At this period agricultural enterprise was confined to the leeward (west) side of the island, and it was not until 1736 that a handful of adventurers from Martinique, allured by the impressive fertility of the soil, came and settled in the windward (east) quarters. With Saint Lucia back under French control in 1744, and with the establishment of coffee and cotton plantations soaring, it bought an expansion of population rising from 463 persons (175 of them slaves) in 1730 to 3,455 persons (2,573 as slaves) in 1745. The first grant of land was made by Governor de Longueville in 1745 - a measure which was soon followed by the apportionment of large tracts of land amongst the more influential settlers. This policy had the effect of strengthening the confidence of all classes and the island soon rose to such a degree of prosperity that the inhabitants of Martinique procured the passing of an ordinance whereby it was enacted, *"that any ship or vessel, found within three miles of the coast of St. Lucia, should be held liable to seizure and confiscation"*.

Only 4 years passed until the Treaty of Aix-la-Chapelle (1748) declared Saint Lucia as neutral once again. By *de facto*, the island remained under French possession as it headed into the start of the Seven-Year-War (1756) between France and England that saw England conquering Martinique in 1762 and subsequently took Saint

Lucia in the aftermath. Just one year later though, Saint Lucia was ceded back to France under the Treaty of Paris and brought with them a host of French and Creole planters from Martinique to settle into the burgeoning agricultural industry. French planters from Grenada and St. Vincent also made their way over to Saint Lucia after fleeing from the British takeovers of their islands and brought with them their slaves, resulting in a great influx of not only people, but capital and resources that in 1763 brought a rise in development of Saint Lucia's plantation economy. It was in this year that the beginnings of sugar start to be claimed and recorded.

With this, and with kind permission from Jolien Harmsen, the next several chapters have been extracted and adapted from 'A History of St Lucia' unless highlighted otherwise.

Vieux Fort, on the south of the island, lays claim to being the first sugar estate of Saint Lucia in the month of April 1763, founded by two planters, Levacher and le Bond. The flat piece of land stretched from La Ressource to Beausejour, St Urbain and Aupicon, and located on the Le Chemin Royal (or now locally known as the Royal Road, as well as le Grand Chemin on early maps) that wound itself between Gros Islet to Micoud and had started its construction in 1763. Madame Dubuc Roche in the now former quarter of Praslin (within the district of Micoud. Saint Lucia changed from using the term *Quarters or Quartiers* to the term *District*, first seen in the 2001 Census of Saint Lucia) founded her estate next, with other sugar estates quickly following that by 1767, five sugar plantations (or *sucrérie*) were in operation, with Vieux Fort accounting for fifty percent of the total acreage under sugar cane. Come 1769 there were 16, by 1771 there were 33 (with Vieux Fort now only accounting for fourteen percent of the total acreage under sugar cane), in 1779 the total had risen to 44 and up to as many as 73 in 1784 and a further 83 in total by 1785. These *sucréries* were almost exclusively found close to a river and covered every district of the island. The quick expansion of *sucréries* meant that the acreage of land used for sugarcane production increased rapidly alongside, from eighteen *carrés* (square, equivalent to about 3 ⅓ acre) in 1764 to 1,040 *carrés* in 1771; 2,003 *carrés* in 1777, and 3,271 *carrés* in 1784.

An example of one of the earliest planters of Saint Lucia is the Devaux family who owned various lands in Saint Lucia at one time or another, but that of Morne Coubaril, at Soufrière, is the only one which remained in the hands of the family for more than two centuries, a factor no other Saint Lucian estate can claim. The following has been extracted from the *'Morne Coubaril History'* courtesy of the Morne Coubaril Historical Adventure Park, which offers a fascinating insight into the movement of each family member, but also their wider impact into the investment of Saint Lucia as an island.

"In the 1740's the sugar planters of Martinique suffered a decline in prosperity. Some of them sought to improve their fortunes by selling their sugar estates and establishing coffee plantations, which required less capital expenditure on slaves and on equipment. Several planters moved from Martinique to St Lucia, which was still largely unoccupied, so that land could be obtained for little more than the cost of clearing the forest and bush. Among these planters were Philippe de Vaux and his brothers Guillaume-Andre de Vaux des Rivieres and Henry de Vaux de Bellefond. They obtained a concession of land in the Soufriere valley, which was thought to be the most fertile part of St Lucia. (According to an account written by the chief government surveyor of St Lucia about forty years later, the soil of the Soufriere district was perhaps the best in the islands, and certainly the best in St Lucia.)"

This reflects upon the influx of planters coming over from Martinique to Saint Lucia and bringing their families and agricultural experience with them. It also highlighted Vieux Fort and its integral standing within cultivation, with no huge surprise of it being the first to grow sugar.

"It was in the 1740's that the French authorities established an administrative system in St Lucia. A map of the island, which seems to have been made at this time, shows the various plantations which were scattered about the island. One was the "Devaux" establishment at Soufrière. The brothers supported the new administration, and helped by providing labour for the construction of ports and other public buildings, and boats for transport. Other prominent colonists were reluctant to help, perhaps because they knew that effective government

would control trade and perhaps introduce taxation. In a letter to the Minister in France, the commander of the colony complained that he was not receiving much help from the colonists. Of those who did help, the brothers de Vaux surpassed all the rest. They had spared no effort for the advancement or the colony. They had continually provided slaves and boats for the King's service. Without them, progress would have been much slower. After receiving this letter, the Minister wrote to the three brothers in February 1746, acknowledging their assistance. Philippe de Vaux, already a captain in the militia in Martinique, was given the command of the Soufrière district. In addition to commanding the colonists who formed the defence force, he was the local representative of government and local magistrate. His brothers both became captains. After Philippe's early death in 1752, Henry became the commander or the district, and later he was made a Chevalier of the military order of St Louis. In the forty years after 1746, the colony became fairly prosperous, notwithstanding disruptions caused by hurricanes and invasions, and a chronic shortage of labour. In the latter part of this period, the produce of each hectare. of canes was worth from £30 to £60 (depending on variations in yield and in sugar prices). While the net profit of the grower was rather less than this, it is apparent that it was not necessary to own a large estate in order to make a comfortable living."

The three brothers looked to be the entrepreneurs of Saint Lucia, seeing the opportunity to not only make a living, but to improve their social standing and working relationship with the government and make use of their military background for local prosperity.

"The three brothers divided the land between them. The three resulting estates came to be called Soufrière, Soufreuse or Terre Blanche, and Morne Coubaril. They are clearly shown on a map of the Soufrière district made in 1770. Henry, the youngest brother, had Soufrière Estate, which was situated along the Soufrière River. At first it was a coffee plantation, but it became a sugar estate before 1770. For this purpose, a portion of a stream flowing from the Soufriere Volcano down to the Soufrière River was diverted to drive a sugar mill. At that time the area of the estate was about 80 hectares, but before Henry's death in 1785 it was increased to 120 hectares by the incorporation of some land on the other side of the river. (In 1770 this land had

belonged to a certain Widow Izaac.) Henry died childless. By his will he left his property mainly to some of his great-nephews and great-nieces. Some of these were the children of his niece Marie-Anne de Vaux, wife of the Comte de Micoud. It was arranged that she should take the estate and should compensate the other legatees for their shares. That is why the estate appears under her husband's name in a list of owners annexed to a map of St Lucia made in 1786.

Guillaume-Andrè had Soufreuse or Terre-Blanche, which surrounded and included the constantly active Soufrière Volcano. The estate took its names from the pale deposits of sulphur which encrusted the area of the volcano. In 1770 the area of the estate was 90 hectares, By 1786 the 20 hectares immediately surrounding the volcano had been acquired by Henri Loyo, a coloured man who had been manager of the Soufrière Estate for Henry de Vaux, who had spoken well of him in his will. According to the list of owners annexed to the map of 1786, Guillaume-Andre owned other lands in the Soufrière district, but-it has not been possible to locate them. Guillaume-Andre died childless in 1791. By his will of 1788 he left his property equally between his nephews Philippe-Henry and Jean-Baptiste (or rather, since the latter was dead, his children).

Soufrière and Terre Blanche soon passed wholly out of the family. The former stayed for a time with the descendants of Marie-Anne de Vaux (Madame de Micoud). It was being worked in 1810 by her son and her son-in-law, and in the 1830's by her granddaughter's husband. In 1843 the owner was said to be one G. H. Todd, a recent arrival in St Lucia, and by 1858 the estate had passed into the hands of Belisle Cornibert du Boulay; since then it has remained with his descendants. As for Terre Blanche, two of the sons of Jean-Baptiste de Vaux, who are known to have been planters at Soufrière in 1810, were perhaps working that estate; one, a second Henry Devaux de Bellefond, appears to have owned a small estate further inland which has retained the name Bellefond or Belfond to this day. In 1833 Terre-Blanche (which by then had almost certainly left the family) was sold by court order (it was only a portion of its former self, having been reduced to only 37 or 40 hectares); ten years later it was again sold by court order.

Philippe de Vaux, eldest of the three brothers who settled in St Lucia in the 1740's, had Morne Coubaril. This estate took its name from the courbaril, or West Indian locust tree (Hymenaea courbaril). When Philippe died in 1752 it was still a coffee plantation, but by 1785 it had become a sugar estate. Its 85 hectares extended from the shore of Soufrière Bay, which formed its northwestern boundary, to a 1200 foot hill on the southeast. Its fertile but uneven surface was well suited to intensive cultivation by slave labour, although not to modern machinery. The principal house, built on a piece of flat land high up overlooking the bay, was accompanied by the usual buildings of a sugar estate, including a house for the manager, Jean Olivier, a number of slave huts, a hospital for sick slaves, various barns, workshops and other outhouses, and a sugar mill. The mill was driven by water from an artificial lake."

The early function of the *sucrérie*: production, labour and choice of power

Up-to the 1870's, the initial function of the *sucrérie* was the use of basic equipment to grind juice out of the sugarcane, boil into a syrup then allow to crystalize into sugar. Due to the small-scale operation, this resulted in almost every estate manufacturing the crude variety of sugar known as muscovado (from the Spanish word *mascabado* meaning 'lowest quality'). The sugarcane itself was planted during the wet season of July to November and not touched until mature around twelve to eighteen months later. It would then be harvested by hand during the dry season of January to May with the stalks of the sugarcane replanted every two to five years, each stalk one foot long and buried in holes three feet square and one foot deep. The yield of such work meant 30 field slaves could plant approximately two acres in a day. As found across much of the Caribbean, once harvested, the leaves were cut and the stalks bundled together, loaded onto ox carts and taken to the mill. Cane trash was collected separately and used for fuel, manure and bedding in the stables. Each *sucrérie* would have its own mill, usually fitted with three or five heavy rollers with sufficient power to grind and crush the harvested stalks, releasing the juice from within. These rollers, connected with cogs, were often set in motion by horses or oxen (the easiest method of power to construct), fixed with

14

long sweeps and would walk in circles. It's also worth noting that mobile animal mills were in use from the earliest days of Saint Lucian sugarcane cultivation. These were dragged from field to field by oxen, mules, horses or donkeys and rented on shares to adjoining plantation owners. Other estates utilised mobile mills for extended periods of time, and for some, even after permanent mills were built. Due to Saint Lucia's positioning and the elevated area between Choiseul and Soufrière, the wind from the Atlantic coast meant that windmills were a common sight to power the mills. Ruins of the stonework bases are still evident to this day, themselves a design of the Dutch style that was brought to Brazil by Sephardic Jews, on from there to Barbados and eventually Saint Lucia. The third model of power went to the water wheel mill, which offered the most constant power, but required elaborate aqueducts to channel the water from a point that was higher than the mill itself.

With the sites of the *sucrérie* often chosen carefully, and close to the rivers, location was key. A gentle slope worked best, with the mill at the top where the harvested canes were unloaded onto a stone platform beside the mill house. After being pushed through the mill and squeezed dry, the left-over pressed stalks (known as bagasse) would be used for fuel for the ovens, whilst the cane juice drained into a gutter and ran downslope towards the first, and largest, of five large copper vessels within a boiling house. The boiling of the cane juice thickened and reduced the juice, in which the scum was skimmed off and the liquid ladled into the further vessels of decreasing size until thick syrup remained. The skimming from the third and fourth vessels were mixed with molasses and distilled twice to make high strength rum, whilst the skimming from the first and second pots were discarded. The five copper vessels were heated by ovens underneath the boiling house, connected to a series of vent pipes that led to a tall stone chimney. The boiling juice was then clarified using lime or ashes, alongside the addition of water. The sweltering heat of the boiling house meant that teams of slaves had to be relieved every four hours. A specialist role was that of the boiler, who watched the fifth and last copper vessel. He had to know when the brew was ready to crystallize, and when the time came, the bubbling liquid would be carried in great two-handled ladles to the cooling cistern and poured into tapering wooden barrels known as hogsheads. These hogsheads were sixteen inches square at the top and twenty-six or twenty-eight inches deep and would be left to cool in the filling-room. Once two days had gone by, they were tested by rapping the outside; a ringing sound meant good sugar, a dead sound meant a bad load. The hogsheads had small drain holes in the bottom, that after four weeks in the curing-house, the molasses would then be allowed to drain from the sugar crystals. In comparison, in modern times, the same result can be achieved in minutes by spinning to apply centrifugal force. The resulting molasses would then be exported or used to produce rum. The curing-house was kept as airtight and warm as possible, with coal fires lit when necessary.

The impact of this crude process is telling in that, due to raw sugar juice spoiling quickly, during crop season the fires were doused for just one full day per week: from Saturday midnight until 1am on Monday morning. Otherwise, it was a continuous day and night process during the harvest.

Jolien Harmsen offers an insight within her book, '*Sugar, slavery and settlement: A social history of Vieux Fort St. Lucia, from the Amerindians to the present'*, of what a sugar estate would have looked like before the abolition of slavery in 1838, including the layout of the buildings, mills and living quarters.

"*In the Vieux Fort area, plantations tended to be located, wherever possible, near rivers for water power, drainage and irrigation purposes. In a central position in order to facilitate transportation of cane from the cane lands surrounding were one or two mills, the boiling house, curing house, trash house and, possibly, a distillery. Close by were the cattle pens, tradesmen shops, houses of the white employees, stables, a small hospital and on the larger plantations maybe a prison, and even a chapel. In close proximity were the slave barracks, grouped in straight rows and normally composed each of two rooms of between sixteen to twenty feet long and twelve feet wide. The owner's house, generally on a hillock facing the sea, was built some distance away so as not to inconvenience the proprietor or manager with the noises and odours of the industrial buildings and other residences. All the plantations in the Vieux Fort region possessed a canal.*
A small percentage of the rest of the land served as slaves' ground

provision plots, usually on hilly land unfit for cane cultivation. However, the major portion of the land remaining was preserved for pasturage and, principally, for woodlands which fed the boiling houses' furnaces and also served as a source of timber and reserve land in case of extension".

CHAPTER 3

The Growth of Labour

The 1770's onwards saw the production of sugarcane in Saint Lucia use an average of three times the labour force needed compared to the traditional crops of coffee, cotton, or cocoa. Unfortunately, though, as the amount of land required for sugarcane cultivation grew, so did the slave population. It's mentioned that between 1772 and 1789, more than 5,000 new slaves were imported in Saint Lucia (predominantly from neighbouring sugar colonies of Barbados, Martinique, Antigua, St. Vincent and Grenada where they had originally arrived from Africa or had been born into slavery): an average of almost 300 people per year. For stark contrast, in 1764, there were 5,069 slaves out of a total population of 6,336 (with 18 hectares in sugarcane, 717 in coffee and 621 in cotton). Just five years later in 1769, the number of slaves doubled to 10,278 out of a total population of 12,794, with 16 *sucréries* in production, then by 1779, there were 16,003 slaves from a total population of 19,230 and 53 *sucréries*. Come the end of 1784, the previous two decades of sugarcane cultivation had seen the Saint Lucian slave population triple from 6,000 to 18,000 persons, with the number of slave owners increasing by one-third: from 2,468 in 1765 to 3,227 in 1779 (an increase of just 759 persons). For even more stark context, as a percentage of the total Saint Lucian population, slaves increased from 73 to 84 per cent, whilst slave owners decreased from 27 to 16 per cent. In 1765, there were 3.7 slaves to each slave owner, but by 1779, this had increased to 6.25.

In-comparison to Barbados, Martinique, Guadeloupe and Antigua, Saint Lucia came to the plantation economy quite late and tended to attract free people of colour (*mulâtre libre*) - the Floissacs from Senegal in Africa for example, and poor whites (*petits blancs*) who lacked any capital to buy their own plantation in the established colonies across the Caribbean. Although no whites were ever slaves, it was recorded that people of mixed African/European descent found themselves on both sides of the divide, as slaves and slave owners. By 1787, 1,500 free people of colour (*gens de couleur libres*) owned 170 of the 881 plantations operational in Saint Lucia, counting towards approximately one-seventh of the total land available. Although there is a lack of information to be found on this topic of conversation, as mentioned, like their white counterparts, they owned and managed the agricultural estates on which a range of crops were harvested, including sugarcane, and employed slave labour. Indeed, the number of free people of colour as a proportion of the total planter's class increased over time by which in 1779, free people of colour outnumbered whites in Saint Lucia by 1,364 to 1,195. It is mentioned though that despite the majority, the land owned by the free people of colour in 1787 amounted to one-seventh of the island, despite forming only one-fifth of the total population. Although come the late eighteenth and early nineteenth century, the balance of ownership tipped in their favour.

It's also worth noting that whilst the free people of colour did own plantations and slaves, they were generally employed as personal slaves rather than field slaves, and much fewer than the white plantation owners. Free people of colour are also attributed towards the agricultural development of Saint Lucia from the early days, including a free person of colour named Nouet, of the Compagnie de Pichery estate in the Castries area, who in 1745 became the second-largest slave owner in Saint Lucia. Nouet owned *"46 negres, 24 negresses, and 23 negrillons"*, making for a total of 93 slaves across men, women and children. At this time, there was only one white man who had a larger plantation: Dubuq Letang, who owned Dezincher in Trois Islets (within what was the quarter of Praslin, now of the Micoud District) and had 109 slaves (50 men, 23 women and 36 children). Both men were also eighteen years prior to the first harvest of sugarcane, meaning the practice of slaves was well established in Saint Lucia through cotton, cocoa and coffee cultivation.

In 1771, then Governor-General Baron de Micoud ordered surveys to be drawn up that would specify land ownership per district (*quartier*), in which there were 33 *sucréries* and 1,040 *carrés* of sugarcane. The following shows highlights from each district on land ownership by free people of colour (across all types of plantations, not just sugarcane).

- *Quartier du Carénage (Castries), (2)*

- *La négresse* Charlotte owned 1 *carré* of land (in what is now Rodney Bay).
- The *famille libre* (free family) Dugue owned 30 acres at Choc/Marisule, adjacent to land owned by Dugue de la Touche.

- *Quartier de l'Ance la Raye (Anse la Raye)*

No free coloured landowners.

- *Quartier de Soufrière, (5)*

- Francois, *mulâtresse libre* (a free person of mixed white and black ancestry), 7 *carrés*
- Stanislas, *mulâtre libre* (a free person of mixed white and black ancestry), 20 *carrés*
- the widow of Martin, *mulâtresse libre*, 27 *carrés*
- Budin, *mulâtre libre*, 20 *carrés*
- the widow of Duc, *mulâtresse libre*, 15 *carrés*

It was stated that Soufrière had three sugarcane plantations during this period: Belfond estate immediately east of the town, owned by Devaux (65 *carrés*) and two along the coast just south of the Canaries River, owned by Prevost (96 *carrés*) and Ferret Marnoux (35 *carrés*).

- *Quartier Choiseul, (2)*

- Lizoni, *mulâtre*, 5 1/3 *carrés* on the L'Ivrogne river
- Marie Rose, *mulâtresse*, owned 4 1/3 *carrés*
- Rabaca, Zabeth and Marianne owned 2, 3 and 11 2/3 *carrés* respectively in an area known today as Pointe Caraïbe.

The report mentioned that Choiseul had two free coloured landowners (Lizoni and Marie Rose), and three landowners (Rabaca, Zabeth and Marianne) indicated as *Caraïbes* that showed that a few individual Caribs continued to survive on the island.

- Quartier de l'Islet Caret (Laborie)

No free coloured landowners.

- Quartier de Vieux Fort

No free coloured landowners.

- Quartier de Micoud, (24)

24 *gens libre* (free people), all with land between 2 ½ and 10 *carrés* and one with 25 *carrés*. All were clustered together in three sections located at the mouth of the Anse Ger River, just south of Ti Rocher at Des Blanchard and around Rameau/Latille.

- Quartier Praslin

No free coloured landowners.

- Quartier de Dennery (3)

      - la Garde, *mulâtre*, 35 *carrés*,
      - Francois *mulâtre*, 15 *carrés*
      - the widow of Louison, *mulâtresse*, 10 *carrés*.

Two of who had either died or abandoned their estates at the time of recording.

- Quartier de Gros Islet (4)

      - Marie Rose and Francois Martininq, *libre*, 10 *carrés*
      - Elisabeth Brisefer, *libre*, 33 1/3 *carrés*
      - Mimy Ridier, *libre*, 33 1/3 *carrés*
      - Rigout, *libre*, 29 *carrés*

- *Quartier du Dauphin (16)* all of whom were indicated in the records as *libre*.

  - Duhamal, 10 *carrés*
  - La Norrat, 15 3/5 *carrés*
  - Louise Soyer, 10 *carrés*
  - Dubernay, 10 *carrés*
  - Francois Grand Champ, 21 2/3 *carrés*
  - Colas Dada, 6 *carrés*
  - Frambourg, 32 ¾ *carrés*
  - Ferol Lacour, 10 *carrés*
  - Bernard 3 2/3 *carrés*
  - La Diorant 22 ¾ *carrés*
  - Marie Magdeleine, 12 *carres*
  - Remond Dampierre, 20 ¾ *carrés*
  - Blancherot 20 1/3 *carrés*
  - Charles Dada, 10 *carrés*
  - Boniface Gaud, 30 *carrés*
  - Toussaint Blancherot, 12 *carrés*

In 1773, a further report by de Nozière and de Tascher on the situation in Saint Lucia highlighted that *"The plantations in sugar cane occupy 1,120 quarrés of lands divided between 39 sugar estates"*.

The American War of Independence and hurricanes

The American War of Independence that started in 1776 cut off the regular trade routes from North America and resulted in widespread famine and disease across the West Indies, with slaves heavily affected due to the lack of imported flour and salt fish that they relied upon. Between this, relocation and the hurricane of 1780 it decimated the islanders, with a total 5,000 (mostly slaves) persons out of the 14,000-population dead or moving on to other islands. Britain occupied Saint Lucia once again in 1778 after the Grand Battle of Cul de Sac during the American Revolutionary War after France had entered the war on the side of the rebels opposing British rule in America. This severely hampered the planters on the island as they lost their line of credit to Martinique and under the terms of the capitulation, they were obliged to pay fines and lend out their slaves as labourers to British military construction sites. Combined with the hurricane that destroyed crops across the island, the sugarcane seasons were all but gone. It's worth noting that it is during this time that British Admiral George Rodney built Fort Rodney from 1779 to 1782, the ruins you can still see today within Pigeon Island. The economy though was reported to have had 300 plantations that lay abandoned with only a few working estates near the coast remaining in 1784, 68 of those being to produce sugar.

By 1784, Baron de Laborie was Governor of Saint Lucia after the Treaty of Versailles re-instated the island to France a year earlier. To drive his campaign towards the Martinique Government of allowing Saint Lucia financial independence from the French colony and re-instate free trade of goods (believing this would bring in an estimated seventeen to eighteen million pounds in sugar crops annually), he appointed Arpenteur Générale Jean François Lefort de Latour to put together a *General and Descriptive Report* of Saint Lucia. He mentions a range of opinions for each district, with highlights below of his thoughts towards the sugarcane industry.

Le Quartier de Castries

Most of the land had mediocre soils and ill-chosen plantation sites, except for Pais-Bouche, which boasted the best coffee and cocoa estates in Saint Lucia, and the valleys of the Rivière de La Brelotte and Grand Cul de Sac, both of which he states could support many more sugar factories than they did. He mentions that 2,000 slaves worked on the plantations but could easily hold 15,000 or 20,000.

Le Quartier du Joubert (Marigot and Roseau)

One of the least-developed areas on the island, despite its reputed excellent soils. There were only seven *sucréries* in the district, employing around 1,500 slaves, but a vision to hold 20 or 30 more with 10,000 slaves.

Le Quartier de L'ance-La-Raye

Despite the difficult terrain which made it nigh impossible for the cultivation of cocoa and coffee, it was perfect for sugarcane in which alongside he complimented the air and water of good quality. He noted four *sucréries* with a combined 1,000 slaves, and mentioned he thought the district could handle another twelve to fifteen more *sucréries*, meaning 6,000 or 7,000 slaves.

Le Quartier de la Souffrière

Saint Lucia's main economic district and second-largest town, the district had twelve *sucréries* and about 2,000 slaves. Again, he recommended the area could hold at least 30 estates in total with 10,000 to 12,000 slaves.

Le Quartier de Choiseul

The soil was said to be light, which made any crop production somewhat successful, which leant the seven sugar estates and 1,500 slaves a consistent, if by no means lucrative, rate of return. Lefort de Latour recommended that 20 estates could easily be sustained in the district with 6,000 or 7,000 slaves.

Le Quartier de l'Islet à Caret (Laborie)

A flatter region of Saint Lucia, especially compared to its northern neighbour of Choiseul. There were six *sucréries* with 1,600 or 1,700 slaves, but once again recommended the district could hold 15 or 18 *sucréries* and between 7,000 and 8,000 slaves.

Le Quartier de Vieux Fort

Surprising to Jean François Lefort de Latour that despite its merchant appeal, the district only consisted of six *sucréries* with 1,400 slaves. He estimated that Vieux Fort could easily sustain 15 or 16 plantations, with 7,000 or 8,000 slaves employed.

Le Quartier de Micoud

Despite having many rivers that could support several water mills (the most within any district of Saint Lucia), Micoud could only boast five *sucréries* with 1,200 slaves. With that, he estimated scope for at least 20 estates and 12,000 slaves.

Le Quartier du Praslin

Lefort de Latour thought the soil in Praslin was mediocre, but still able to produce cocoa, cotton and sugarcane, which included six *sucréries* with 600 or 700 slaves yet easily expanded to 12 estates and 6,000 slaves.

Quartier d'Ennery

He reported that despite the presence of cocoa and coffee estates, the lack of a decent port in the village hampered the export of the crops. It didn't stop the sugarcane though, as he recorded 1,100 slaves working on five estates, where he expected an expansion of 15 estates with 8,000 slaves.

Quartier du Dauphin

Again, despite the districts power of both the Lespérance and Marquis Rivers for waterwheels, Dauphin could only boast five *sucréries* and 1,200 workers, where 12 plantations and 7,000 or 8,000 slaves would bring the district back up to full power.

Quartier de Gros-Islet

Susceptible to droughts despite the light, sandy soil made Gros-Islet more suitable for military use than crops. With that though, it still managed to have five *sucréries* employing 1,600 or 1,700 slaves.

To summarise, Saint Lucia, in 1784, had 73 recorded sugar cane plantations, with an estimated workforce of 16,700 according to Lefort de Latour's report. His vision though, said that the island could easily reach 171 sugarcane plantations, and approximately 96,700 slaves (an increase of 98 estates and 80,000 workforce). In actuality, by the time of his death in April 1789, although Saint Lucia had boosted its economy, it did so with only the addition of 43 dedicated sugar estates once again in production across all districts barring Choiseul: Soufrière (9), Vieux Fort (8), Castries (6), Laborie (5), Anse la Raye (4), Gros Islet (4), Praslin (3), Dauphin (2), Micoud (1) and d'Ennery (1). For context, the island at this time had 180 coffee plantations, 57 cotton plantations and 88 cocoa plantations. These traditional crops were slowly declining though, whilst the sugar plantations continued to grow, reaching a record number of 102 in 1819. It took five years for Saint Lucia's plantation economy to be back on track following the report under Governor Baron de Laborie. The most startling fact though, is that despite the growth of sugarcane, until 1803 cotton remained Saint Lucia's primary export crop, and the dominance of sugarcane only really became a nineteenth century result.

Another element to consider is that in the three decades (1763 to 1794) since the introduction of sugar cane cultivation and production to Saint Lucia, it was predominantly under French rule (two periods; 1765 to 1778 under Governor Baron de Micoud and nephew Deputy-Governor de Micoud; and 1784 to 1793 under Governors de Gimat, de Ricard and Goyrand) where it flourished. The period between 1778 and 1784 under English rule saw a hampering of the agricultural practices on the island due to the mentioned military priorities. Couple this alongside the hurricane of 1780 that wiped out most of the plantations and crops, and you start to see why Jean François Lefort de Latour's report was vital to bring stability to Saint Lucia.

CHAPTER 4

The Brigand Wars

With the second French Revolution taking place in Paris, resulting in the arrest and imprisonment of King Louis XVI on 14th August 1792, the news travelled to Saint Lucia where law and order breaking down became the norm. After already hearing, then seeing, the horrors of the first French Revolution just three years prior, early 1793 saw the tipping point and the abandonment of all the plantations. Only a few women with children and the elderly and infirm were reported to have stayed behind, severely hampering the crops and ultimately grounding all trade to a halt. With the death of King Louis XVI in January of 1793, Britain severed all diplomatic ties that resulted in France declaring war in response. Republicans in British-held islands began to encourage slaves to rebel (named *Brigands*), with Saint Lucia no different with the formation of the St Lucia Jacobin Club. On the royalist's side, the white planters were fast descending into chaos and uncertainty, with the intention of retaining their crops and value fast sliding down the list of priorities. Wary of the mounting threat of an English invasion of Saint Lucia, Martinique and Guadeloupe - the National Convention in Paris abolished the enslavement of *'negro people'* on 4th February 1794 within all its colonies, resulting in all inhabitants becoming French citizens with full constitutional rights. Ironically though, as news eventually reached Saint Lucia, around September 1794, the English had already captured the island back with very little resistance on 1st April 1794. It didn't take long for the plantations to become deserted once again though, as planters and their families fled the villages or left the island altogether due to Victor Hugues; a protégé of the leader of the French Revolution, Robespierre, and who was appointed Commissaire of Guadeloupe when the island was re-taken back by the French in 1795. The Brigands rebelled in force against the British rule and were joined by Hugues and his insurgents, kick-starting the First Brigand War. With their help, by June 1795 Hugues had driven out not only the British, but most of the island's plantocracy too, with fear of reprisals due to the infamous use of the guillotine.

Governor Goyrand though moved Saint Lucia forward and tried to re-build the agricultural infrastructure since most of the crops and sugar factories had either been destroyed or abandoned. He tried to convince the ex-slaves-turned-soldiers that slavery would not be re-instated and although he was able to commandeer land and used compulsory paid labour and military labour to harvest crops, in the ten months of his governorship, little agricultural work was done. Despite the abolition of slavery in French colonies, most former slaves of the plantations preferred to remain in the mountains and grow their own provisions within their make-shift gardens rather than return to the towns and villages as paid labourers. This led to a lack of confidence from the planters and few risked returning to their estates between late 1795 and early 1796.

By May 1796, Saint Lucia was once again under British rule after the recapture of the island by Sir Ralph Abercrombie, appointing Brigadier-General John Moore as the Governor of Saint Lucia. Once again, he found himself struggling to convince the Brigands to return from the mountains as the insurgents were aiming to go for round two of the Brigand War. With the overwhelming majority of black and coloured people on their side and kickstarting the Second Brigand War, the pro-British and royalist French and Creole planters fled to town, leaving their estates unprotected and the few remaining slaves to do as they please. Under Governor Moore, his objective was to harass the Brigands, destroy their provision grounds and prevent them from receiving supplies from Guadeloupe or St. Vincent. He hoped this would force the Brigands back to their estates but soon realised that the Brigands hide-outs were difficult to find within the rugged terrain of Saint Lucia's mountains. With that, he turned to the abandoned estates and to establish military posts along the south-west coast from Vieux Fort to Soufrière. He mentioned that *"The houses all around are burned, but they have spared the sugar houses and mills alone, and these form both good barracks and posts for the troops"*. The end of the Second Brigand War came about in November 1797 after the surrender of the Brigands on the condition that "*. . . they should not be again reduced to slavery*". Most of the now ex-Brigands were inducted into the army of their former enemy and served under the British West India Regiment in West Africa, whilst others were allowed to leave Saint Lucia voluntarily, with both black and coloured persons ultimately ending up in Guadeloupe. Due to the two Brigands Wars, it was said that Saint Lucia's plantation slave population had diminished by more than 4,000: from 18,406 in 1790 to 13,391 in 1799. In 1807, England abolished the slave trade via the *Slave Trade Act 1807*, although slaves were still brought to the island from other Caribbean islands sometimes legally, other times not. By 1808, Englishmen were prohibited from engaging in such a trade, and in 1823, Britain proclaimed the Amelioration laws, which were enforced in Saint Lucia from 1826 onwards. Britain finally proclaimed full abolition of slavery in 1838.

The aftermath of the Brigand Wars

With the Brigand Wars in the rear-view by the 1790's, the planters of Saint Lucia were now in high debt of £500,000 (equivalent to a staggering £ 63,960,175.10 in 2025), mostly for the purchase of slaves. Over half of the island was now uncultivated, and creditors were demanding payment as the planters tried to re-establish their factories. The result came that the British General resorted to public auctions: offering slaves and abandoned estates for rent or sale. By the turn of the new century, the year 1800 saw a mix of owner origin throughout the plantocracy, with a combination of French and British, Creoles and Africans. Records show too that at this time, disenchanted people of colour returned to the estates: 3,100 men and 5,060 women. Due to the turmoil of the Brigand Wars, and the choice of marronage or re-submission to slavery, the latter option became the most appealing due to the regular rations of food, shelter and clothing, despite the harsh work required. As mentioned within the works of '*Morne Coubaril History*', they state that the "*annual crops exported from St Lucia in the 1780's was estimated to be about 9 million colonial livres or 6 million French livres tournois (equivalent to perhaps £250,000), in the last years of the 19th century it was well below £100,000*". The works also offers a glimpse of the value of estates and their fluctuation between the 1780's and the first half of the 19th century, mentioning that "*In 1785 a small sugar estate at Soufrière, belonging to the notary*

Clauzel, was sold for a sum equivalent to £6700. This estate was expected to yield an average net profit of more than £800 a year. After the death of Henry de Vaux de Bellefond in 1785, the gross value of his estate (Soufrière Estate, with four times as much land as Clauzel's) was fixed at the equivalent of about £25000. His nephew Philippe-Henry (who owned Morne Courbaril) also owned a coffee estate of nearly 60 hectares called Saint-Philippe. His widow and children sold it in 1815 to one Vittet for about £1500. This low price was partly accounted for by the fact that for years the estate had lain empty and abandoned, as Philippe-Henry had devoted his efforts to restoring, as far as he could, with little remaining capital and less than a hundred surviving slaves, the cultivation of the lands of Morne Coubaril. In 1833 Terre-Blanche was sold by court order; its remaining 37 or 40 hectares fetched £1000. Sold again ten years later, they made £500. Things continued in this pass for a long time. Thus, in 1900 the Pearl Estate at Soufrière was sold for £1500. In 1916, the value of Morne Coubaril was estimated to be £1400. In monetary terms, this was certainly less than a tenth of its value in the 1780's. In real terms, it was still less. It was only after the Second World War that St Lucian land values began to climb steep".

To carry on the Morne Coubaril story, the work also mentions its occupiers and its subsequent devolution from 1750. *"The occupiers of Morne Coubaril included Philippe de Vaux, who died in 1752; his youngest son Philippe-Henry, who died in 1807; the latter's youngest son Henry, who died after 1880; and Henry's youngest son Emile, who died in 1923. The sequence of ownership was more complicated. Philippe's other sons were planters elsewhere in St Lucia or, in the case of his eldest son, in Guadeloupe. His widow remained at Morne Coubaril, which was the home of their youngest son, who at some stage became sole owner. Something similar happened with the next generation. The third member of our list, Henry, was unable to pay off his brothers and sisters while also discharging the other debts of the estate. He turned to his relatively affluent brother-in-law from Barbados, John Goodman and, while Henry remained the occupier of the estate, it seems that John Goodman eventually acquired a lien on Morne Coubaril or even became the legal owner of the estate. Emile Devaux, who followed his father Henry at Morne Coubaril, was for much of the time not even a part owner of the lands he was managing. The ownership was in the hands of John Goodman's granddaughter,*

Irma de Gaillard de Laubenque. She married one of Emile's brothers. The latter died without children. In 1904 Irma (by then remarried to F. E. Bundy) sold Morne Coubaril to the three daughters (not the sons) of Emile Devaux. (After the sale Morne Coubaril remained charged with a mortgage of £430, which was not paid off until 1922.) In 1914 one of the three sisters died unmarried, and in accordance with St Lucian law half her share went to her parents while the other half was divided equally between her brothers and sisters. Thus did Emile and his wife acquire a sixth share in Morne Coubaril. After their deaths, their two surviving daughters continued to be the majority shareholders, the remainder of the shares being owned by Emile's sons or their heirs. For a time one son, Ferdinand, managed the estate. Later, local overseers were employed to do the job. The sugar cane was replaced, first by cocoa, then by coconuts, then by bananas. Among those who eventually inherited a fraction of the shares in Morne Coubaril was Ferdinand's son Reginald Devaux. He bought up the other shares until he had made himself sole owner of the estate. Some years later, in about 1959, he sold it to Mr Monplaisir, for a sum said to be about £18000. The rise in values had only just begun".

"In the course of time, the area of the estate had been somewhat reduced. In 1841 a small piece of land near the town of Soufrière was set apart for use by the Catholic Church as a Calvary to which processions went. This gave its name to a nearby house, Calvaire, near the boundary of the estate, to which Henry Devaux retired in the 1880's with an unmarried daughter. In 1844 some land adjacent to the town and fronting on the end of the Grand'Rue or High Street was donated, by Henry Devaux and his brother-in-law John Goodman, to the Anglican bishop of Barbados for the construction of a church. John Goodman was an Anglican, while Henry Devaux, in the words of a local newspaper, "although of the Romish Church, is desirous to have his Protestant labourers accommodated according to their conscience. Later some hectares in the south-western corner of the estate were detached to form a small estate for one of Henry Devaux's daughters and her husband; when the descendants of this marriage died out about the middle of the 20th century, this land was left to the children of one of Henry's grandsons, Gabriel Devaux, who sold it a few years later. (This little estate was called Stonefield, from the great number of

volcanic boulders scattered over it.) In 1916 Emile Devaux's eldest son, John; bought from the co-owners of Morne Coubaril, for £350, an area of about 16 hectares, being most of the estate south of the main road from Soufrière to Choiseul. He called it Jeanne d'Arc, and he had it run as a separate estate for more than thirty years. Then he sold it to his nephew, Reginald Devaux, who reunited it to Morne Coubaril before selling the whole as mentioned above."

It's also an interesting note that they mention that after a hurricane in 1831 that destroyed the Morne Coubaril House, a two-storey building was built a hundred yards from the old house. *"Saved from the wreck of the old buildings, and set up in the grounds, was a stone from the entrance to the old sugar mill. It bore a date. This date, according to the recollection of Edward Devaux, was 1777. This relic may well have been part of the very first sugar mill at Morne Coubaril, for it is known that the estate became a sugar estate between 1770 and 1785".*

Ceding to Britain for the last time

On 25th of March 1802, the *Treaty of Amiens* was signed, and Saint Lucia declared a French possession once again. Within the same year, after eight years of freedom and equality, Napoleon Bonaparte reinstated slavery across all French colonies. Alas, just fifteen months later, the British invaded once again, re-taking the island for the last time (the island was officially ceded to Britain in 1814) and bringing Saint Lucia under British rule until its Independence in 1979.

In 1815, the recording of slaves became more detailed, producing its first register where we can start to understand the name of the estate, estate owner or tenant, size of the plantation, crops and number of slaves employed. It even started to head into the names of the slaves (usually their first or nickname), age, any identifying marks and ethnic origin, if known. This was updated every three years until slavery abolishment in 1838.

Looking back, most of the estates changed hands at least once during the first three decades of the nineteenth century, with one telling example of the insecurity of the industry as the island re-established itself after decades of war: The Mamiku Estate in Praslin was sold ten times between 1818 and 1906. Internally, fraud and corruption became rife as plantations were cut up into smaller pieces, allowing aspiring landowners such as free coloured (and, after abolition, free slaves), an opportunity to enter the agriculture business, but with no flat rate of sale. With planters selling at uneven rates, Chief Justice John Jeremie, in the late 1820's, attached all slaves employed on estates to the soil, preventing their seizure by creditors and removing their option to be sold separately. By July 1829, he established an office for the registration of deeds and mortgages, offering transparency of who was indebted to whom. Upon completion of registration, it turned out that there were 1,918 mortgages, totalling a reported dept and liability of £59,498,249, severely hurting Saint Lucia's profitability and edged it towards the brink of bankruptcy. In response, Jeremie authorised the seizure and sale of the properties and within the decade of 1833 to 1844, 76 estates were sold by judicial sale (some more than once too). The added reasoning to this was that most of the planters had long since lost financial ownership of their estate, and the sales allowed a fresh class of capable planters to emerge, bringing money back into circulation on the island.

To highlight, Saint Lucia's plantation economy was never as strong as its neighbours of Barbados and Martinique. Despite the efforts of the French Governors de Micoud and de Laborie, and the early nineteenth century of British rule after the Anglo-French warfare, Saint Lucia ultimately paid the price for progressive tones towards sugarcane over cocoa and coffee, resulting in a greater need for reliable labour. With the abolition of the slave trade in 1807, and the introduction of the Amelioration laws in the 1820's with the prospect of full abolition, it put planters in an impossible position to generate consistent income. Back in London, Saint Lucia was becoming less of a focus for the cultivation of sugarcane, with more of a concern to retain the island as a strategic military post. Interestingly though, the white planters who just carried on the best they could, prospered when merging their role of planter and merchant, seeing sugar export rising (with the odd decline) between 1802 and 1831. By 1830, sugar export had risen, with a value of £105,128.7.0 (6,064 hogsheads), but it was not all positive though, as by 1836, it saw a significant drop to just a value of £45,875.5.0 (2,688 hogsheads), a common theme during the next 150 years.

Slave freedom and emancipation

The first five decades of the nineteenth century were seen in Saint Lucia with an uneasy apprehension as the sugar economy was debt-ridden and barely surviving, with the Castries fire of 1805, and again in 1813, the storms of 1817 and 1819, and several earthquakes all contributing as crops were destroyed or swept away, alongside three-quarters of all plantations seized for debts and sold at judicial sales between 1837 and 1849. By 1st August 1838, full freedom was granted to all slaves, with slavery replaced with the apprenticeship system that was widely adopted across the British colonies. This new system gave the ex-slaves (who now worked 40 hours of unpaid labour per week, but able to do how they please once finished) a taste of paid work. With the planters requiring workers during crop season and only having 40 hours of free labour available per person, the workers demanded increased wages that ate into the profits of the sugar production. With Emancipation came compensation from the United Kingdom and their Colonial Office. With £20 million eventually granted, the planters of Saint Lucia were divided, with some cashing in and bailing out of the industry, whilst others hoped to eliminate depts and start on a new footing. Compensation was calculated at £31 on average per slave for 8,725 field slaves, £30 per slave for 1,600 non-field slaves, £8 per slave for every child under the age of six (1,960 of such) and £8 for every aged and infirm slave of whom there were 1,000. This totalled £342,155 for 13,285 slaves (equivalent to £32,182,784.87 in 2025).

Until the 1890's, Saint Lucia was still perceived by colonial administrators and planters alike as a primary economy of agriculture, but with a now unbalanced approach to production. With workers now able to dictate their own lives, many chose to branch out on their own, resulting in the latter half of the nineteenth century having a contribution of about one-fifth of all sugarcane grown in Saint Lucia credited towards them. It was then seen that come the turn of the new century; the island's export economy had become dependent on the contributions from the locals. *'St. Lucia: Historical, Statistical, and Descriptive'*, authored by Englishman Henry Hegart Breen in 1844 (who was also mayor of Castries and went on to become administrator of Saint Lucia between 1857-61), showed a snapshot of Saint Lucia since the Brigand Wars, three further decades of slavery, and Emancipation. He wrote that he had a belief that sugar would continue to dominate the landscape soon, despite the problems facing the industry at that time. He noted that there were 42 sugar estates in 1789, compared to an improved 81 estates in 1843, with twenty of these located around Soufrière, ten in the quarter of Vieux Fort, and nine each within Castries and Gros Islet. The sugar estates of 1843 were larger too, facilitated by the report of improved mills. Breen was quoted as saying *"In 1789 the matériel of the sugar estates consisted of thirty-two water-mills, eighteen cattle-mills, and three windmills: now it comprises fifty-one water-mills, twenty-six cattle-mills, and six windmills, besides fourteen steam-engines, an improvement totally unknown at the period referred to"*.

The Sugar Duties Act 1846 and introduction of métayage

It wasn't all straight-forward though as England passed the *Sugar Duties Act 1846* which removed preferential treatment of sugar from British West Indian colonies in the British market. With sugar being produced at a lower price in Brazil, Cuba and Louisiana (and the former two still producing using slave labour), it became another hammer-blow to the sugarcane industry of Saint Lucia between 1846 and 1854. It caused a stir once these effects started to become clear back in London, with noise of the act to be repealed becoming louder. Instead, financial help was aimed alongside a concentration of the sugar industry across their colonies, and they favoured the territories of Barbados, St. Kitts, Antigua, Trinidad and British Guiana – no Saint Lucia to be named. It became worse for the island when the Navigation Acts were repealed from England, abolishing the protection in favour of free trade.

Following several bankruptcies and closures of West Indian sugar merchant houses in Britain, Saint Lucia planters were having their hands forced, cutting wages by 25 to 50 percent, with little or no capital forthcoming from the Colonial Bank or English merchant houses. It became so bad that it was reported there was only £10,000 in circulation on the island by 1851, and half of that in notes. Planters and merchants were often lacking the cash to pay their workers, resulting in a system of IOUs of scribbled notes of what was owed. Eventually, these IOUs became the currency of the day, being equal tender to the cash and notes that were unavailable.

Interestingly, a report by Lieutenant-Governor Charles Henry Darling in 1847 mentioned that out of six estates, only two showed a profit and both operating on *métayage* – one completely and the other partially. All others incurred losses (*métayage* is a type of land tenure where a cultivator, or *métayer*, pays rent to the owner in exchange for a share of the produce). It was seen as obvious that the planters and *métayers* had common interests and that during periods of crisis, *métayage* was the only respite from complete ruin for many estates both large and small. It wasn't all positive though, as some planters lamented the loss of control over their labour force, claiming that *métayers* often practiced slovenly and un-'planter-like' cultivation practices which reduced the sugar content of the canes. Planters also resented their dependence on the co-operation of *métayers* in the sugar manufacturing process at the factory, which they felt was unreliable and put the entire operation at risk. Yet it was thanks to the *métayers* that the amount of land under sugar cane increased even though the supply of waged labour steadily declined.

By the late 1850's, the global sugar price rose once again, and the planters started to look at immigration of indentured labourers (first from Europe, then from Barbados, Africa and East India) and mechanization. As predicted, as soon as the sugar prices rose, planters withdrew land from *métayage* agreements, sending the practice into decline.

CHAPTER 5

1874: Central Sugar Factories

By 1874, the sugar industry on the island was now relatively small but saw the building of four new central sugar factories as a group of local planters and businessmen bought it upon themselves to centralise and update the islands sugar production to improve efficiency. In 1874, the *St. Lucia Central Sugar Factory Company Ltd*, first managed by Emmanuel and Theophine DuBoulay, was started in Cul de Sac (*Cul de Sac Co. Ltd*), just south of Port Castries, with a £30,000 loan from the Government. In return for the loan the colony would take a quarter of the shares in the newly formed company offering holders of debentures (a loan agreement in writing between a borrower and a lender) a rate of interest of 6% per annum. All of this was achieved by the passing of *"Ordinance 6 of 18ᵗʰ April 1874"* (a law to *"promote the establishment of Central Sugar Factories and to authorise the raising of a loan for that purpose"*).

The result of the loan saw the Colony Records of 1876 reference a *'Central Sugar Factory'* fund within the government's local revenue section, with a value of £131.0.9 collected in 1875 when the fund was created. The revenue collected at the end of each year rose high in 1876 to £4,818.7.5 (stylised as £4,818 7 shillings and 5 pence), dipping a little to £4,120.6.3 in 1877, rose again to £5,017.15.4 in 1878 and £5,005.4.1 in 1880 but dipped considerably to £2,367.17.0 in 1881. It stabilised to £2,334.6.6 in 1882, £2,491.3.11 in 1883, £2,742.14.11 in 1884 and £2,692.5.2 in 1885, before rising slightly in 1886 to £3,436.3.4 in 1886. There was a huge jump to £118,995.13.1 in 1887, then back down to a final figure of £5,184.10.0 in 1888 before the records stopped in 1889.

In 1882, a second central factory was built in Vieux Fort (located on the Malgrétoute-Micoud Road, now Clarke Street), with Roseau and Dennery following soon after. It's not clear who owned these to start with, although it's generally understood that Dennery was owned by the Barnard family at some point after 1897. These four factories faced hardship from the beginning, with the unwillingness from the British Government to give protective sugar tariffs to the West Indies, Saint Lucia's small-scale, scattered and outdated sugar estates faced total ruin. To try and combat this, the four sugar factories introduced practices found in Martinique and Guadeloupe that resulted in an increase of scale of operations, abandoning marginal lands and bringing a modern approach to production – running 18 hours a day, 6 days a week from January until April/May. The four factories were able to weather the storm of the continuing low prices of sugarcane around the world and utilising the East Indian labour that had sailed to the island from 1859 onwards. It's important to mention though that *sucréries* were still very much in production of the cultivation of sugarcane, which were then sent to the central factories.

Jolien Harmsen tells some detail within '*Sugar, slavery and settlement: A social history of Vieux Fort St. Lucia, from the Amerindians to the present*' regarding Vieux Fort's approach to adaptation after the formation of the central sugar factory in the area. She mentions that by 1847 there were 19 estates that operated in the district, with most of them abandoned. The remainder were bought or leased back by the sugar company, mainly Black Bay, Anse Noir, Tourny, Retraite, two Beauséjours, Mon Repos, Pointe Sable and Canelles. Despite the abandonment of the other estates in the district, Harmsen mentioned that Bellevue continued to remain in private ownership, although did contribute all its canes to the central factory.

The estates had been chosen due to proximity to the central factory and linked up by a railroad system where during crop season, the canes could be put on the wagons and taken to the factory. Canelles however used to deliver their canes via two canoes that would land on the jetty and be taken up to the factory via the train.

One last note on the *St. Lucia Central Sugar Factory Company Ltd* – it was referenced within the Public Debt section of the Colonial Records from 1876 up to 1899, mentioning that the latter year saw only £16,300 repaid out of the initial £30,000 loan. It's also worth noting that in 1887, they borrowed another £10,000 from the Saint Lucian Government to a total of £40,000.

The Railways of Saint Lucia

An often-overlooked part of the attempted success of sugar cane cultivation in Saint Lucia is the railway tracks that now linked estate fields to the factories and nearest ports for the movement of canes and hogsheads, replacing cattle-drawn carts. Although the island lacks a level terrain for a full railway system, the latter decades of the sugar cane production did see Saint Lucia embrace the more modern techniques of the time and become more efficient in delivery. Although not on the scale of fellow islands such as Trinidad, Cuba and Barbados, the use of railways is an interesting footnote in the history of Saint Lucian sugar cane.

The following has been partly reproduced from David Rollinson and his *'Railways of the Caribbean'*. According to Rollinson, the Central Factory in Cul de Sac was reported to operate a 13-mile-long narrow-gauge railway, using 3 diesel locomotives and over 130 steel cane cars in the 1950's. Two Plymouth 4w PM were supplied to the factory in 1927-28, with the line apparently using wood-burning steam locomotives in the 1920's. Nothing remains of the lines presently.

The Roseau Factory had approximately 1,000 acres of sugar cane cultivation in the mid-1950's. The factory was reported to have had a narrow-gauge railway stretching 16 miles, with 3 diesel locomotives (two Motor Rail, one Ruston & Hornsby, and one Hibberd) and 145 cane cars. As the Central Factory, the use of wood-burning steam locomotives was the original fuel source, although it's not known when the change to diesel took place. The railway stayed intact once the cane fields were changed over to banana cultivation under *Geest Industries Ltd*, and was reported to have been used up to 1988. One of the Motor Rail locomotives is still on site at *St. Lucia Distillers Ltd* although no longer in use.

Dennery & Co. lacks any information on the length of track they installed, but did have a 3'9"-gauge Kerr, Stuart 0-4-2 tank locomotive in 1900, something Rollinson mentions would probably be their second locomotive after first being supplied by Fives-Lille of France. There's no remains though after the abandonment of the estate in around 1998.

Vieux Fort operated a 1929 Vulcan ironworks 4w DM and likely, earlier, a Hartley Armnoux & Fanning 0-4-0 tank built in 1891. These travelled non-stop twelve hours per day, from cane fields at Black Bay, La Tourney, La Retraite, Aupicon, St Urbain and Mankoté to the factory in Vieux Fort with over 18 miles of track. The track also ran down Clarke Street to the jetty for transportation to small ships, and then onto a bigger steamer moored further out in the bay. Wildly remembered are the two names of the locomotives used: John Bully and Baby.

1884: The sugar industry once again in crisis

Throughout the 1860's, 70's and early 80's, sugar prices were stable and reasonable, with labourers able to earn and make something from their savings. This changed though in 1884, when a sharp drop of price for muscovado sugar sent planters into debt and sugar estates went bankrupt across the island. Despite the launch of the *St. Lucia Central Sugar Factory Company Ltd* in 1874, by 1884 all four factories had failed and changed hands at least once. The value of exported sugar, rum and molasses had been £190,360 in 1883, but by 1886 this had been slashed to one-third: £64,000. It recovered slightly in 1893 (£95,000) but a further drop in value came in 1896 (£63,000). Of the 81 sugar estates operational in 1843, only 13 remained active by 1897.

A report and diary extracts from D.W.D. Comins written in 1891 mentions little on the sugar factories barring that both the Roseau Estate and Vieux Fort factory were owned by the *St Lucia Usines and Estates Company* and managed by the brothers Theophine and Emmanuel DuBoulay (the managers of *St. Lucia Central Sugar Factory Company Ltd* formed back in 1874*).* He reports upon his visit to Dennery that *"On the right is a sugar estate, the working of which is abandoned for want of money and owing to the low price of muscovado sugar".* He did though mention *". . . the harbour in which lie the sugar ships loading from the neighbouring usine (factory) in the Mabouya Valley".* Comins also reports that on his visit to the Roseau Estate, that the Peru, Bellairs and Mont d'Or estates all contributed canes to the Roseau Central Factory - and on the subject of the estates shop, *". . . as the licence for selling rum costs £30, a good deal of cooly*

(Indian labourer) pay must be expended before it can pay to take out a rum license." For context, a rum licence of £30 in 1891 would equate to £3,233.94 in 2025. Comins also mentions that in 1891, the Vieux Fort Central Factory and its surrounding estates had turned out 1,500 tons of sugar, operating day and night by electric, but ceased its production operations for the year by the time he had arrived only a few days after his visit to the Roseau Estate.

The Colony Record for 1891 also mentions in its report that muscovado and molasses had fallen hard in value compared to the proceeding ten years, the former bringing in on average £18,253 from a high of £64,830, and the latter £5,334 from £7,046. Only Usine was singled out as an improvement compared to the average of the last ten years, bringing a value of £60,870 to its usual £44,306. Molasses was once again singled out in the Colony Report of 1892, noting a considerable decrease in export value (£2,824). Also, there's a further mention in the same report of previous lands used for the cultivation of sugar have now been converted for the expected burgeoning of the cocoa industry. After 1884, abandoned fields were restored with cotton, coffee, cocoa, kola nut or pasture for cattle. It's noted that in 1885, the Desruisseaux Estate went out of the sugar business and immediately became the site of settlement of around 40 cottages. This growing trend of converting abandoned estates served the boom in villages, especially down the east coast of the island. It was also heard that within the districts of Gros Islet, Vieux Fort, Laborie and Dauphin, labourers grew their own provisions, amongst them sugarcane. There were said to be ten miniature *sucréries*, where small wooden hand mills, formed of a lever attached to a strong tree to squeeze out the juice of the canes, would be crafted. The resulting juice would be boiled down and ready for sale in the local markets. This saved them having to take their canes to a large estate for processing.

The *'A History of St Lucia'* publication lists a very handy outlook towards all major sugar estates operational in 1887-89 across the island, showing acreage under sugarcane, average sugar crop (quantities in hogsheads) and their status come 1896.

Estate	Mill Type	Average Crop of Muscovado Sugar in 1887-89	Status in 1896
Anse Canot	Steam	216	Abandoned
Anse Mahaut	Steam	70	Partly Abandoned
Anse Galet	Water	40	Abandoned
Anse Mamin	Steam	80	Abandoned
Anse la Raye	Water	40	Abandoned
Anse Noire Black Bay	Steam Water	}250	} Contributors to Vieux Fort Factory
Bonne Fortune	Cattle	40	Abandoned
Bois d'Orange	Steam	80	Abandoned
Bonne Terre	Steam	60	Abandoned
Beausejour (Massade)	Steam	60	Abandoned
Malgrétoute	Water	130	Partly Abandoned
Belle Plaine	Cattle	50	Abandoned
Beausejour	Steam	80	Abandoned
Beausejour & Au Repos	Water	100	Contributor to Vieux Fort Factory
Balembouche	Water	180	Almost Wholly Abandoned
Belle Vue	Wind	60	Contributor to Vieux Fort Factory
Beauchamp	Water	60	Almost Wholly Abandoned
Toc	Steam	130	Abandoned
Corinthe	Steam	80	Abandoned
Cap	Steam	180	Abandoned
C. Belair	Water	130	Almost Wholly Abandoned
Cannelles	Water	200	Partly Abandoned
Canaries	Steam	300	Partly Abandoned
Diamond	Water	140	Abandoned
Dauphin	Cattle	39	Abandoned
River Doree Desgatieres	Water Water	} 286	Almost Wholly Abandoned
Entrepot	Steam	60	Abandoned
Esperance	Water	40	Abandoned
Esperance	Water	50	Abandoned

Fond d'Or	Steam	150	Contributor to Dennery Factory
Fond Doux	Steam	80	Abandoned
Fond	Steam	250	Abandoned
Grandase	Steam	40	Abandoned
Hope	Water	123	Part-contributor to Vieux Fort Factory
Incommode	Steam	80	Contributor to Cul de Sac Factory
Jalouise	Steam	78	Abandoned
La Pointe	Steam	80	Part-contributor to Cul de Sac Factory
La Resource	Steam	60	Abandoned
Soucis	Steam	100	Contributor to Cul de Sac Factory
La Caye	Steam	130	Contributor to Dennery Factory
La Riche	Cattle	40	Abandoned
Le Parc	Water	100	Abandoned
Providence	Wind	40	Abandoned
L'Orangerie	Water	60	Abandoned
M. d'Or	Water	40	Abandoned
Marigot	Cattle	40	Abandoned
Marquis	Steam	140	Almost Wholly Abandoned
M. Plaisant	Steam	100	Abandoned
M. Courbaril	Water	120	Abandoned
Malgrétoute	Cattle	12	Abandoned
Malgrétoute	Water	150	Partly Abandoned
M. Lezard	Water	30	Almost Abandoned
Mondesir	Water	50	Abandoned
Perou	Steam	70	Contributor to Roseau Factory
Pearl	Water	250	Abandoned
Pt. Caraibe	Water	100	Abandoned
Pointe Sable	Steam	150	Contributor to Vieux Fort Factory
Palmiste	Water	140	Partly Abandoned
Roseau	Steam	250	Contributor to Roseau Factory

Richeford	Water	100	Contributor to Dennery Factory
Reduit	Steam	50	Abandoned
Ravine Claire	Water	30	Abandoned
Ruby	Water	100	Abandoned
Rabat	Water	50	Abandoned
Reunion	Water	200	Abandoned
Retraite	Water	120	Contributor to Vieux Fort Factory
Ressource	Steam	80	Contributor to Vieux Fort Factory
Ressource	Steam	60	Contributor to Vieux Fort Factory
Rayne	Steam	60	Abandoned
Soufriere	Water	120	Partly Abandoned
St Remy	Steam	80	Abandoned
Saphir	Steam	200	Almost Wholly Abandoned
St Urbain	Steam	80	Part-contributor to Vieux Fort Factory
Savannes	Steam	40	Abandoned
Sans Soucis	Steam	40	Abandoned
Soucis	Steam	100	Contributor to Cul de Sac Factory
Terre Blanche	Water	25	Abandoned
Tourney	Steam	100	Contributor to Vieux Fort Factory
Troumassée	Water	120	Partly Abandoned
Union	Water	200	Almost Wholly Abandoned
Union Vale	Water	140	Abandoned
Union Praslin	Water	40	Abandoned
Vide Bouteille	Water	25	Abandoned
Valet	Steam	86	Abandoned

Looking at the table, four-fifths of all large sugar plantations had been abandoned within one decade, with owners ruined or forced to find new ways of earning a living.

The local syndicate and the St. Lucia Usines and Estates Company

By 1895, the Central Sugar Factory at Cul de Sac was failing, namely due to short crops and low prices, and was provisionally taken over for a year by a local syndicate, which in 1896 had been purchased fully on the 19th September for £4,000. A judicial sale by the Colonial Treasurer, Mr. D.G. Garraway, against the *St. Lucia Central Sugar Factory Company Ltd*, the syndicate came to terms with the mortgagees who held claims of over £30,000. This meant that by 1897, the central factories of Cul de Sac, Roseau, Dennery and Vieux Fort belonged to two companies: the local syndicate as owners of Cul de Sac, and *St Lucia Usines and Estates Company Ltd*, who owned the factories at Roseau and Vieux Fort as well as the Dennery Company. The latter owners were headquartered in London at the offices of Drake & Co, a large company of sugar brokers. Interestingly, the London Manager, Henry Hales, had never visited the West Indies and was a dealer in sugar beet. He was mentioned in 1897 as saying *"We accidentally, so to speak, became West Indian proprietors by taking over an estate from a man who owed us money; that was it, practically"*. Further improvements were made to the Central Sugar Factory in Cul de Sac that helped the new syndicate put the factory on a profitable footing once again. It also saw the removal of an expensive diffusion plant (boiling canes rather than crushing them – a practice used in beetroot processing and hailed in the late 1800's as the latest innovation for sugar cane processing) that had proved useless.

At Cul de Sac, the local syndicate owned or leased 2,000 acres of land of which just one quarter (550 acres) were planted with sugar cane. In Roseau and Vieux Fort, the *St Lucia Usines and Estates Company Ltd* owned or leased thirteen estates with a total area of 5,925 acres, 2,086 of which were for sugar cane. The two factories also had a combined labour force of between 1,700 and 2,000. Vieux Fort drew its labour from the Vieux Fort and Laborie districts (7,572 persons in 1895), whilst the Roseau Factory drew 2,516 persons from the district of Anse la Raye. The Dennery Company owned or leased an area of 2,000 acres, of which 560 acres were in sugar cane and worked by 450 persons. With more than 10,000 people on their payroll, the *St Lucia Usines and Estates Company Ltd* were reported to provide nearly 22%

of Saint Lucia's population with an average wage of £1,100 per month out of crop time, and £2,000 per month during crop time (approximately £17,000 per year).

The sugar made in 1897 was chiefly of a high class but saw slight dips in its output between the four factories. An aggregate of 3,962 tons as against 3,698 tons in 1896, and of this amount 3,400 tons were exported in 1897 and 3,055 tons in 1896, with a value of £55,497 and £56,095 respectively. In addition to the main four factories, several small mills that were driven primarily by wind or horse power were being maintained for the purpose of producing muscovado sugar, the export of which in 1897 amounted to 457 tons and a value of £3,900, as against 493 tons, value £5,853, in 1896. Local consumption though was mainly of sugar syrup and produced primarily within the smaller mills. To combat the loss in revenue, the Central Factories attempted to switch to producing a low-class brown vacuum-pan centrifugal varietal of sugar that would give them a chance to compete on the world market. The manufacturing of rum saw a large increase in 1897, from 39,460 gallons (of which 37,360 were consumed locally) the year prior to 63,637 gallons in 1897, of which 37,344 went into local consumption. The large increase was attributed to the importation of 22,480 gallons of molasses from the British West Indies, with no such importation having occurred the previous year. In 1897 though, wages at the factories in Roseau, Dennery and Vieux Fort had been reduced from one-third to one-quarter (one shilling per day to a six pence), despite tasks being increased and working days going from 8.5 hours to 10.5 hours. The difficulty at times experienced by the proprietors of the central factories in getting a sufficient supply of labour, the population within easy distance from Castries being tempted away by the military works and the money to be made on the coaling wharves, while the more distant parts of the island a constant emigration to the gold fields of Cayenne (French Guiana) often hampered agricultural operations. In fact, the gold rush in Cayenne saw a forced reduction of area under cane at the Dennery factory, bringing sugar production down from 1,500 to 850 tons. The four factories turned to labourers from Antigua, St. Vincent, St. Martin and Barbados to fulfil the roles within the field and factories, enticing them and their families to the fertile valleys of Saint Lucia, as well as the latest machinery to produce sugar crystals for the English and American markets. It was reputed that Cul de Sac could make 2,500 tons in five months, working during the day; Roseau at the same time could produce 1,500 tons; Vieux Fort 2,000 tons; and Dennery 2,000 tons, but none produced at maximum capacity. It's also worth noting that in each case the bulk of the sugar was grown by the factory, but much was contributed by local proprietors.

In 1898, an attempt was made, which proved partially successful, to establish an export trade in rum between Saint Lucia and French Ports. The high productive duties, however, which were levied in France were seen as barriers to complete success in that direction. It did though see an increase in the export of molasses towards Martinique after the reduction of what was seen as a *"exorbitant duty"*. In the same year, the manufacturer of muscovado sugar continued its steady decline (680,900 pounds compared to 1,025,360 pounds in 1897 and 1,104,300 pounds in 1896), but the island did see an increase in Usine sugar exported (4,513 tons, up from 3,962 tons in 1897 and 3,055 tons in 1896). A remark in the 1899 Colony Record though mentions that a decrease in Usine sugar crop (4,176 tons) was attributed to the *"severe shaking which the canes received in the hurricane of September 1898"*. Sugar though was still seen as an important export trade for Saint Lucia come the turn of the century, with 24% of the yearly value in 1900 representing against the export leader of bunker coal (54%), with 71% of sugar and its products heading to the United States, 26% to the United Kingdom and 3% to other countries. With coal quickly becoming the dominant trade since the establishment of Castries as a coaling station, alongside the enlargement of the military works which enjoyed large employment opportunities, plus the largest on record for a cocoa crop to be exported with a good return of value, Commissioner of Saint Lucia, Sir Harry Langhorne Thompson, proclaimed the year 1900 as *"the most prosperous year in the history of the Colony since the time when sugar was supreme"*.

It's widely stated in previous print media regarding rum distilleries in Saint Lucia that at the turn of the 20th century, Marquis Estate (producing Marquis rum until the 1920's) was one of three rum distilleries (alongside Cul de Sac and Troumassee in Micoud) active. Unfortunately, it looks unlikely this was the case, as it has been recorded that the Marquis Estate was, by 1896, almost wholly abandoned. Considering Marquis is within the Gros Islet district, and with the Colony Reports recording only one rum distillery in the Castries, Dennery and Gros Islet districts, which was Cul de Sac. Marquis Estate of course may have had a distillery until 1896, as the Colony Records do state two rum distilleries being active in the aforementioned districts until 1896 and its abandonment.

By the turn of 1920, it was recorded that the *St Lucia Usines and Estates Company,* who had previously owned the Roseau Estate and Vieux Fort Estate, had sold all its estates by the same year. Its decline is summed up by the passage written within the Colony Record 1921 states that *"the year under review has proved, in so far as the local sugar industry is concerned, to be the most disastrous since the collapse of the sugar market some twenty-five years ago. This collapse, as so often happens, was proceeded by abnormally high prices and this led to much financial speculation locally. The result being that when the crash came, local speculators who had purchased sugar properties during the high prices found themselves saddled with obligation which proved very difficult to meet. This necessitated a considerable reduction in expenditure and led to the closing of some of the factories for long periods. Tempted by the high prices ruling the previous year, many of the smaller estate owners were encouraged to raise loans to enable them to import and erect mills and small factories. They have been hard hit by the general collapse of the sugar and syrup market and much sympathy is felt for them in their present difficulties".* By 1928, only 4,570 acres remained under cultivation, and primarily down to the wet weather and the sugar factories being in the process of reorganisation it did not make full crop. The output of sugar was low, being 4,042 tons, a decrease of 1,322 tons on the previous year.

Co-author Robert Devaux of *'Stories of Roseau Valley'* mentions that during the time of 1917 to 1922, the only variety of cane being planted in the Roseau Valley was known as *'Roseau Cane'*, which he described as a hybrid with the *'Bourbon Cane'* variety (one of the most common varieties found across the West Indies – also called *'Cana Blanca', 'Kenikeni', 'Kinikini', 'Otaheite', 'Louzier'* and *'Lāhainā'*). To increase production, over the next few years Roseau was converted to a higher yield variety of cane known as BH10(12).

By the mid 1920's, sugar prices dropped once again, and export earnings fell more than 40% between 1924 and 1931, resulting in a casualty of the Roseau Estate that went to auction in July 1927, with Harold Devaux purchasing both the Roseau and Cul de Sac estates and renovating and upgrading each with modern equipment and railway infrastructure. 1933 did though see some sugar innovations being introduced, including Caterpillar-Tractors for large scale ploughing, and the continued replacement of poor yielding canes by the standard variety BH10(12). 1934 even saw the successful introduction of Cuban parasitic fly, *Lixophaya*, and the Amazon fly, *Metagouistylum*, to afford a natural control of the cane moth-borer pest and increase in a higher proportion of sound canes and improved sucrose content. The Dennery Factory installed a 9-roller mill and improved their carrier equipment in 1936. Just a year later, progress was being made with not only the BH10(12) cane seedling, but the B. 2935 which worked in the drier areas of the cane estates compared to the former which preferred wetter areas. By 1939, the Colony Records even mention *"more promising commercial seedlings such as B. 3013, B. 3439 and B. 35187. Continued progress is to be recorded on the Barbados Land Settlement Scheme at Vieux Fort"*. Although hesitancy was surrounding these promising times as the records also mention the recent sale of part of the estate as an Air Base for the United States Government.

The number of rum distilleries active had dropped dramatically since a high of 9 in 1886 to just 1 in 1889, although in 1902 saw 2 distilleries recorded in the Colony Records and named as Cul de Sac and Troumassee (it was said that the Troumassee Estate produced 'Troumassee rum', and Cul de Sac Estate made cane juice rum). Troumassee ceased operations in September 1917, yet in 1921 it was recorded once again to be active alongside newcomers from Vieux Fort and Beauchamp, meaning four rum distillers were active alongside Cul de Sac until 1930. 1931 saw a slight change in the introduction of Dennery distillery, but the closure of Beauchamp and again of Troumassee (although this time due to a fire), leaving just Dennery, Cul de Sac and Vieux Fort until 1938. The introduction of a rum distillery at Dennery harks back to Walter Barnard, who from one of the three biggest family businesses exporting coal out of the harbour at Castries in the 19th century, started to move away from the coal industry and invest in sugar estates in the early 1900's. Unfortunately, Walter Barnard and his wife died young due to the Spanish Influenza in 1918, leaving orphan sons Denis (born 26th March 1909), Cyril and Bertie behind to be raised by relative Colonel Thorn (who was the Administrator of Saint Lucia) in the United Kingdom. Denis Barnard returned to Saint Lucia in 1930 at the age of 21 after he was educated at agricultural college in Trinidad and took over the Dennery Estate. In 1931 he took over the existing rum distillery on the estate and re-started the production of rum.

During this period, bananas were competing with cocoa as the island's third largest export crop, after sugar and limes. By the end of the 1930's, a quarter of the population of Saint Lucia were wage-employed, with twenty-five percent of them earning a wage in the sugar industry, whilst another twenty-five percent worked a wage on plantations that grew cocoa, limes, bananas, coconuts, vegetables or fruit. The other wage-employed were split between domestic servants, public roads, carpenters, fisherman, blacksmiths, bakers, coal carriers, messengers, porters amongst other roles.

Vieux Fort and Barbados

On 13th June 1936, co-director of the *Vieux Fort Sugar Company*, Joseph DuBoulay, offered the Saint Lucian Government 6,400 acres of land at £15,000 for use as a settlement scheme whilst retaining the factory, rolling stock and 600 acres of coconut fields. By November of that year, it had drawn up plans for a factory-owned sugar plantation, surrounded by peasant cultivators. With some to and fro due to the lack of capital by the Government, they turned to Barbados. Offering initially a joint purchase of the property, followed by a land settlement scheme involving a 50/50 share between Saint Lucias and Barbadians, Saint Lucia ultimately lacked the funds to invest and so on 28th May 1938, the Barbados Legislature passed a resolution for £43,000 to purchase the *Vieux Fort Sugar Company's* land and factory, headed up by the *Barbados Settlement Company's* General Manager L.A. Chase. However, with the *International Sugar Agreement* coming into effect in 1938 (meaning each West Indian Island was allocated an annual sugar export quota which it was not allowed to exceed) during the

Vieux Fort Sugar Company sale, and with Saint Lucia allowed for the 1938-39 season just 9,600 tons, with 2,000-3,000 tons for the Vieux Fort factory, it lacked the opportunity to produce a profit (with them needing to expand cultivation from 600 to 2,500 acres, and production to 5,000 tons of sugar, plus another 1,000 tons from canes grown by independent contributors). Despite the knowledge of the agreement coming in during their purchasing negotiations, the *Barbados Settlement Company* had hoped for a special concession from the Colonial Office, saving as many ratoon canes as it could for the 1939 season and planting another 300 acres for the 1940 season. Employing 700 persons by August 1938, with the factory, rum still and store house being repaired, by December this had grown to 1,200 persons. The 18 miles of railway track linking the cane fields to the factory were overhauled, as were the locomotives and factory equipment. A new caterpillar tractor, a large plough and a Ford V8 lorry were imported, and a laboratory installed in the factory.

With the outbreak of World War Two, the *Barbados Settlement Company* was instructed to curtail its sugar production to just 2,000 tons for its 1941 season and effectively sabotaging the schemes survival. Not long after, the United States were granted a lease on a large portion of the *Barbados Settlement Company's* acreage to build a military base (now the Hewanorra International airport), rendering the project nigh-on impossible. On 30th June 1942 after only four years of operation, the *Barbados Settlement Company* wound down its business, with a loss of £25,794. In 1943, co-author Robert Devaux of '*Stories of Roseau Valley*', mentions the Roseau Company purchased and transferred all the railway rolling stock and the machinery of the distillery from Vieux Fort, resulting in the new Roseau distillery producing rum for the first time in 1944.

CHAPTER 6

The Death of Sugar

In 1945, the sugar industry employed 2,000 to 3,000 persons during crop season, and 1,000 persons out of season. A year later, four stoppages and strikes occurred, one of which, at La Caye Estate in Dennery, lasted eight days due to the high levels of distrust between workers and employers. With the introduction of the *Factory Ordinance No.8* of 1943 (introduced to entice workers back to the sugar valleys), the laws made provisions for workers safety and welfare, resulting in a 16% increase in wages for labour and management before the 1946 crop season. The Colony Report 1948 mentions an interesting encouragement towards local sugar interests by the Ministry of Supply to rehabilitate the sugar factories. They provided a more liberal programme of manuring, involving the use of phosphatic fertilisers which laboratory analysis of local sugarcane soils had shown to be essential for increased yields. Another encouraging feature mentioned was the introduction of heavy equipment for mechanising the cultivation of sugar cane, although it does go on to state that it is also recognised that substantial increases in sugar can only be achieved by the introduction of new capital and additional factory equipment for the revival of sugarcane growing on other lands. By 1950, there had been a substantial increase in the tonnage of sugar manufactured over the previous 4 years, with the interest from some sugar producers shown in sugar cane varietal and manurial experiments being highlighted within the Colony Report 1949 and 1950. Some had even seen fit to increase the economic value of the existing sugar cane acreage by manufacturing by-products such as sugar cane wax.

A further strike though on 17th March 1952 saw 5,000 workers at Dennery, Roseau and Cul de Sac Estates down their tools for 13 days in the hope of gaining further wage increases – to no avail. The result of the strike saw the company that owned the Cul de Sac (*Cul-de-Sac Co. Ltd*) and Roseau Estates and Factories (*Roseau Co. Ltd*) go into voluntary liquidation in March 1953 but soon after, the Government threw its financial support behind a newly formed local company named *Sugar Manufacturers Ltd*, which in October 1953 bought up the assets in Roseau and Cul de Sac to continue operations. This newly formed company was headed up by Francis Carasco, Harold Devaux and Sir Garnet Gordon, with Abel Ghirawoo the General Manager of both sites. 1954 saw the introduction and establishment of a *Cane Farmers Association*, according to co-author Robert Devaux of '*Stories of Roseau Valley*', with branches formed on most of the estates of the three surviving sugar factories. Two experienced agriculturists were appointed by the Government sponsored programme to advise small cane producers. Nurseries were established for the multiplication of improved planting materials, alongside a credit scheme for the supply of fertilizers and assistance during the harvesting period, with the organisation of transportation of small producers' canes to one of the factories. A positive note was also mentioned for the years 1955 and 1956, with the *Sugar Labour Welfare Fund Committee* financing housing schemes at Ciceron and Dennery on lands donated by the various sugar companies. A housing scheme was also started at Bexon, on lands leased by *Sugar Manufacturers Ltd* and was proposed to ultimately build 46 houses for rental and hire purchase to sugar workers.

1957 though saw more strikes, with Denis Barnard and his sugar factory at Dennery (*Dennery Factory Co. Ltd*) going up against John Compton of the Saint Lucia Labour Party. The *St Lucia Workers Co-operative Union*, the bearers of the initial 1953 strike, had learned its lesson and once again attempted a ". . . *demand for increased wages for all workers employed by the day, task and in the factories*". They also wished to be recognised as the sugar workers' representative body, but Managing Director of the *Sugar Manufacturers Company Ltd* Francis Carasco stood by the rates and refused to entertain the motion. Instead, union leaders George Charles, Martin JnBaptiste, and J. Burke King went to Roseau and called workers off their jobs on 25th March 1957. They were later joined by Minister of Industry Karl LaCorbinière and independent district representative for Dennery-Micoud John Compton where they caused a similar stoppage at the Crown Lands Estate in Cul de Sac. By the time they reached Denis Barnard and his Dennery Estate and Factories, a vote was called for the decision to strike. With the assumption from Dennis that the workers would not obey the strike call, it was with apparent evident displeasure that they did choose to do so and saw the beginning of six weeks of action. On 29th April 1957, a settlement was reached which included "*an increase in wages for all hourly and daily paid workers in the fields and factories, increased rates for task workers, improved methods of transporting canes by the wagon to avoid spillage, constant inspection of scales, recognition for future bargaining with the St Lucia Workers Union and that there would be no victimisation*".

The rise of the green gold

With sugars gradual decline from 1884, and in effect strangling the economy for its dependency on the crop (and causing labour ripples when hundreds if not thousands of workers would struggle to adapt to working other means once sugar estates closed), wage dependency on small incomes, plus poverty and poor work ethics among agricultural workers, the sugar industry had hampered Saint Lucia's social and economic advancement despite being its main source of income. The strength of the banana industry came to the forefront of conversation once again, this time led by the entrepreneurship of a Dutch-born, British-based businessman John van Geest. In 1954, van Geest brought together banana producers from four of the Windward Islands (Saint Lucia, St. Vincent, Dominica and Grenada) to market their bananas through one agent and by signing 10-year leases with each, van Geest undertook the shipping and selling of all bananas of marketable quality that the four islands could produce. The future looked bright for Saint Lucia, and with the resurrection of the *St Lucia Banana Growers Association*, the Government predicted that bananas would replace sugar as the island's main export crop within a year. Several abandoned sugar estates were even planted with bananas, as well as within small rural communities of persons who had initially worked on the American military bases in Reduit and Vieux Fort (both opening in 1940 and closing in 1947 and 1949 respectively), returning migrants and those with other income such as shopkeepers and teachers. Initially, many farmers were afraid to invest time and effort into a crop that had yet to prove its worth, and banana shoots imported from the Department of Agriculture of Central America and Dominica were left to rot on the side of the roads. It was not to last long though as the banana cultivation success spread rapidly and between 1954 and 1958 banana production island-wide expanded three-fold (306,000 stems to 1,098,000 in 1958 according to the Colony Report 1957-58). Sugar though stagnated and in 1957, bananas, or what was to be nicknamed *"the green gold"*, outpaced sugar as the biggest exported crop in Saint Lucia.

By 1958, the *Dennery Factory Co. Ltd* ceased sugar production and changed over to bananas, with just an average of 2,500 tons per annum of sugar in its last season, and in April 1959, following the 1957 strike and barely avoiding more industrial action in 1958 and 1959, the Roseau and Cul de Sac Estates and Factories (owned by *Sugar Manufacturers Ltd*) sold 68% of its shares to *Geest Industries Ltd*. Upon their takeover, *Geest Industries Ltd* immediately converted the Cul de Sac estate from sugar to bananas and shut down the Cul de Sac Factory in 1961. It was reported that Geest had promised the Government that it would continue sugar production but backtracked none-the-less.

It's worth noting that it wasn't all a downturn in the late 1950's for the cane workers. Due to successful negotiations between the *United States Virgin Islands Sugar Corporation* and the Saint Lucian Government, it resulted in the recruitment of 190 Saint Lucian cane-cutters by the company in 1958. In 1959, the workers created a very favourable impression by their standard of output and a request was made in 1960 for 103 more. The *Antigua Syndicate Estate Ltd* also employed Saint Lucian labour to assist in reaping their sugar crop; and after a lapse of four years 60 cane-cutters were recruited for employment in Guadeloupe during the 1959 harvesting season.

With 1960 seeing only one sugar factory remain in operation (Roseau Estate), production was declining from 10,873 tons in 1956 to 5,498 tons in 1959-60. By the years 1961-62, this had dropped further to 3,880 tons. By 1963, and with 900 persons employed by the Roseau Estate, co-owners *Geest Industries Ltd* and *Sugar Manufacturers Ltd* put the estate lands of Roseau into banana cultivation. Saint Lucia ceased to produce sugar altogether: exactly two centuries after the crop was first introduced. According to '*Stories of Roseau Valley*', the Roseau refinery continued its rum operations using a raw imported molasses from Barbados, whilst the Cul de Sac refinery was transferred to Roseau too and placed within a separate building on the grounds.

Jolien Harmsen, Guy Ellis and Robert Devaux of '*A History of St Lucia*' probably wrote the position of sugar in Saint Lucia in the best way:

"*A cynic might say that in St Lucia, the sugar industry never really took off – and then took a mighty long time to die*".

CHAPTER 7

Formation of St. Lucia Distillers Ltd

In 1963 Denis Barnard's son Laurie Barnard (born 26th February 1945) started working for his father on the Dennery Estate. Although the estate had converted to banana production in 1958, Laurie's main area of responsibility was the rum distillery, and his efforts were focused on modernization. In 1972, Denis Barnard entered a joint venture with *Geest Industries Ltd*, who still produced rum at their Roseau Factory despite the focus on banana cultivation, and merged the two distilleries together to form *St. Lucia Distillers Ltd*. The Dennery distillery was mothballed in the same year and equipment moved to the Roseau Estate. By 1973, *St. Lucia Distillers Ltd* released their first own-label rum (previously only bulk rum was produced and sold) with the Denros Bounty Rum brand, whilst Denis stepped down from the board of directors, leaving Laurie Barnard as the only family member.

With only a Coffey Column Still available, the opportunity to produce an aged rum came in the form of the Admiral Rodney Rum brand which was trademarked and launched in 1981. By 1987, *East Caribbean Distillers Ltd*, a subsidiary of *St. Lucia Distillers Ltd*, was set up to focus on island produced spirits such as gin (Duncans), vodka (Krimshaya) and brandy (Lavelle) for the local market, as well as rum bottlings including Five Blondes, Buccaneer and Ron D'Oro. It was not to last long though as *East Caribbean Distillers Ltd* fizzled out by the end of the 1990's. Andrew Edward joined as Managing Director from *Geest Industries Ltd* but had left by 1988 which was also the year of Denis Barnard passing.

As the decade turned to the 1990's, the Barnard family bought the *Geest Industries Ltd* shares in 1992 and became sole owners of *St. Lucia Distillers Ltd*. In 1993, a joint venture with a Martinican company, G&P Dormoy, was formed to create the *West Indian Liqueur Company (WILCO)* that would produce rum creams and liqueurs, gaining technical knowledge and recipes for producing products such as the La Belle Creole range. The acquisition of a second-hand bottling line also meant the end of hand-bottling at *St. Lucia Distillers Ltd.* By 1994, *Barbay Limited*, a wholesale and supply company located in the north of the island and ran by the brother of Laurie, Craig Barnard, was acquired and moved down to the Roseau Estate, bringing the distribution and marketing of *St. Lucia Distillers Ltd* products in-house. Interestingly, by the 1980's, Mount Gay rum from Barbados was the biggest selling brand across the island of Saint Lucia, until *Barbay Limited* widened the island's availability of Bounty Rum, ultimately becoming number one and retaining its crown to this day.

The fire of St. Lucia Distillers and re-introduction of sugarcane to Saint Lucia

In 1998, 24.9% of the shares of *St. Lucia Distillers Ltd* were sold to Trinidad based *Angostura Ltd* which was seen as a strategic move to gain access to export distribution and quality standards. Alan Lang became Managing Director in the same year (leaving in 2001), overseeing the installation of a new bottling hall and relocation of the existing bottling line. He also completed and introduced what is now known as the Rhythm of Rum distillery tour. In 1999, Chairman's Reserve Rum was launched in Saint Lucia, with it then trademarked 2nd November 2001 ahead of international availability (at this time, you could sell in Saint Lucia without a registration, but not overseas). In 2002, Admiral Rodney Rum was re-launched with new packaging, and by 2005, *CLICO Holdings Barbados Limited (CHBL)*, a subsidiary of *CL Financial* which was the majority shareholder of *Angostura Ltd*, purchased the other 75.1% of the shares of *St. Lucia Distillers Ltd.* with Laurie staying on as Managing Director. Despite Bounty and Admiral Rodney rums being available, the production of bulk rum was still a key area for export, with rums being bought into the United Kingdom, for example, by Hayman's, who would then bottle and label for the regional supermarkets. This practice though started to be phased out around 2005. *CLICO Holdings Barbados Limited* bought the *Angostura Ltd* shares in 2006, now owning 100% of *St. Lucia Distillers Ltd.* However, on May 2nd, 2007, the administration building within the distillery grounds which housed offices, blending and the laboratory was destroyed by fire. Nearly two years to the day, on May 1st, 2009, the move into a new administration building was complete, led by Margaret Monplaisir, and by September of the same year, the commission of a new sugar cane mill was granted which kick-started the re-introduction of sugarcane to Saint Lucia for the first time since 1963.

Starting out with just 5 acres within the distillery grounds (eventually growing to 15 acres), the lands were resown to produce sugarcane, starting out originally with four varieties, albeit now only concentrating on only two (green cane and blue cane) which were sourced from the West Indies Breeding Station in Barbados. During the once-a-year cane harvest, all stalks are cut by hand instead of machine, then crushed on-site together using a 2-roller mill. Approximately 60% of the mix is green cane, whilst 40% is blue cane with the extracted cane juice put into small fermentation tanks. The fields yield 7-9% of juice overall, from 28 metric tons per acre. This produces a yield of 12,000 litres of cane juice, and 4,000 LPA (Litre of Pure Alcohol). It was recorded that sugarcane rum was put to age as early as March 2010, with its first commercial use within the limited edition bottling of 1931 4th Edition and which can now be found within the rum blends of Chairman's Reserve Legacy and Chairman's Reserve 1931.

In 2010, *CLICO Holdings Barbados Limited* were in financial trouble and under judicial management, which was followed on 25th October 2012 by the death of Laurie Barnard. Margaret Monplaisir became Managing Director in his absence, driving the use of the sugarcane juice rum to continue Laurie's legacy. In 2016, *Groupe Bernard Hayot* of Martinique purchased *St. Lucia Distillers Ltd* and installed Loic Leger as Managing Director from 2020 to 2024, with Monplaisir becoming CEO.

The distillery at *St. Lucia Distillers Ltd* has of course numerous people that not only produce the brands of rum available but help market globally, putting Saint Lucia on the map for quality, difference and impact in a growing market of rum around the world. From Distillery Manager Andre Winter, who joined in 1976 until leaving in 2022, to Cellar Master Cyril Mangal who joined *St. Lucia Distillers Ltd* in 1989 and can still be found to the present day around the warehouses. Master Blender Evanius Harris was there from the beginning in 1972 until 2017, overseeing the major rum brand launches that have come to define Saint Lucian rum, and who's role is now headed up by Deny Duplessis. Duplessis also heads up the Quality Assurance, taking over in 2018 from Roger Miller, who retired after joining in 1999. Ian John has been at *St. Lucia Distillers Ltd* since 1999, before being appointed Distillery Manager and Master Distiller in 2018, whilst overall production has been looked after by Lennox Wilson since 2009, making sure every bottle and batch hit the expected mark before being released. Of course, you need a team to shout about *St. Lucia Distillers Ltd,* with Bruce Perry acting as Sales and Marketing Director from 1995 to 1998 until the appointment of Michael Speakman, who is still making sure, alongside a team that includes Sergin David, Pontinus Clery and Mervin Charles, that everyone who visits Saint Lucia has access to a rum wherever they are on the island.

The future of Saint Lucian rum protected

On 18th April 2024 *St. Lucia Distillers Ltd* submitted their Geographical Indication (GI) application for '*Saint Lucian Rum*', which was subsequently granted on 13th November 2024 by the registrar of Companies and Intellectual Property in Saint Lucia. A GI is an IP right used on products that have qualities or characteristics attributable to a specific geographical origin, meaning for *St. Lucia Distillers Ltd* and the definition of Saint Lucian rum production, it is confirmed "*Saint Lucia Rum is a spirit drink obtained exclusively by alcohol fermentation of sugarcane-based raw materials, distillation, and ageing/maturation on the Caribbean Island of Saint Lucia*".

The relevant pieces of the GI submission are stated and reproduced in full below and offers an insight into the steps to be taken for the production and marketing of Saint Lucian rum.

2. DESCRIPTION OF THE SPIRIT DRINK INCLUDING PRINCIPAL PHYSICAL, CHEMICAL AND ORGANOLEPTIC CHARACTERISTICS OF THE PRODUCT:

2.1 Product Description

Saint Lucia Rum is a spirit drink obtained exclusively by alcohol fermentation of sugarcane-based raw materials, distillation, and ageing/maturation on the Caribbean Island of Saint Lucia.

The rum possesses distinct sensory values unmistakably reflective of the artisanal intertwining of the island's French and English cultures in its creation under strict processing conditions on the island.

All varieties of rum may be single distillate or maturate or a mixture of distillates or maturates, derived from substrate of sugarcane molasses, sugarcane juice or any other substrate from a sugarcane source, alone or in combination, and may be distilled on pot still or column still or in combination.

Saint Lucia Rum comes in the following varieties:

Premium Rum – distilled and blended in Saint Lucia and aged in Saint Lucia for a minimum of 1.5 years but less than 5 years.

Superpremium Rum – distilled and blended in Saint Lucia and aged in Saint Lucia for a minimum of 5 years but less than 10 years.

Ultra-premium Rum – distilled and blended in Saint Lucia and aged in Saint Lucia for a minimum of 10 years.

Flavoured Rum – distilled and blended in Saint Lucia; aged or unaged or a mixture of aged and unaged Saint Lucia Rums to which natural flavouring materials have been added with or without the addition of sugar. If the predominant flavouring material added is a known spice, the Flavoured Rum may be designated Spiced Rum.

Unaged Rum – distilled and blended in Saint Lucia; either unaged or aged in Saint Lucia for less than 1.0 year.

2.2 Chemical and Organoleptic Properties

The physical and chemical properties of Saint Lucia Rum must meet the following chemical and organoleptic requirements.

2.2.1 Chemical Requirements

The declared alcohol strength shall be not less than 37.5% alcohol by volume and the declared bottling alcohol strength shall be not greater than 80% alcohol by volume. Methanol (methyl alcohol) concentration shall be not greater than 400 mg/L of absolute alcohol. The concentration of total congeners shall be not less than 150 mg/L of absolute alcohol. The concentration of ethyl carbamate (urethane) shall be not greater than 0.15 mg/L.

2.2.2 Organoleptic Requirements

Saint Lucia Rum has a noteworthy complexity of aroma, taste, and a distinct flavour profile with balanced notes of sweetness, tropical fruitiness, and slightly salty notes reminiscent of the sea breeze in Saint Lucia.

2.2.2.1 Appearance

Transparent and clear appearance, with a liquid consistency.

2.2.2.2 Colour

Hues depend on age and type of cask used and range from colourless to straw, amber, gold, dark brown, mahogany or light burgundy.

2.2.2.3 Aroma (Nose)

Primarily a pleasant balance of sweetness derived from the substrate of sugarcane origin and spiciness initiated in fermentation, developed in distillation, and further enhanced during maturation. Permeating this base is an array of (tropical) fruity flavours ranging from honey, raisin and banana to ripe apple, coconut, and orange peel.

2.2.2.4 Flavour (Palate)

A distinct flavour profile with balanced notes of sweetness, and tropical fruitiness. Saint Lucia Rums characteristically present slightly spicy and salty notes with hints of vanilla and anise. The aged rums also present oakiness and other woody notes.

3. GEOGRAPHICAL AREA CONCERNED

Saint Lucia Rum is exclusively fermented, distilled, aged, matured and blended on the 238 square mile island of Saint Lucia located 14°N and 61°W, or about 24 miles (39 km) south of Martinique and 21 miles (34 km) north of St. Vincent. The Atlantic Ocean borders the island on its east coast and the Caribbean Sea borders on its west coast. Saint Lucia is situated in the Windward Islands of the Lesser Antilles within the archipelago island chain of the Caribbean.

Sugarcane juice is derived from sugarcane grown on the island of Saint Lucia.

4. METHOD FOR OBTAINING THE SPIRIT DRINK

The production of Saint Lucia Rum is a multi-stage process.

Saint Lucia's rum production process displays both the independent fermentation and distillation of sugarcane molasses and the independent fermentation and distillation of sugarcane juice. The former preserves the dominant traditional practices of English styles of rum production and the latter reflects the French rum production culture, reminiscent of rhum agricole. The distillates and maturates of these two rum styles are sometimes combined to deliver rum blends with delightful expressions of both English and French rum production cultures.

4.1 Planting the Sugarcane
For those rums that use sugarcane juice as the fermentation substrate, this must be obtained from sugarcane grown exclusively in Saint Lucia. The sugarcane is cultivated in alluvial soils that are mineral-rich, well-drained and have good nutrient retention capabilities. The sugar cane crop reaches physiological maturity within 12 months. The sugarcane is planted in the fertile valleys which stretch from the base of the hill ranges to meet with the sea/ocean. Under the influence of frequent rainfall, nutrients in the soil in the valleys are continually replenished by nutrients washed down from the hills.

4.2 Harvesting

The sugarcane crop is manually harvested between February and November and the stalks are loaded onto carts for transportation to the mill house. At the mill house, the sugarcane stalks are cut into smaller lengths and then fed into the mill to extract the sugarcane juice by pressing. Bagasse which is generated as a by-product is applied to the sugarcane fields as mulch.

4.3 Obtaining Sugarcane Molasses

The molasses only comes from sugarcane and is sourced from sugarcane-producing countries with the following quality requirements: Brix – min 80°; pH - min 4.95; Ash: - max 12.5% by weight.

4.4 Yeast Propagation

Strains of Saccharomyces cerevisiae yeast are propagated in sugarcane molasses diluted with filtered Saint Lucia surface and/or groundwater. Once a sufficient concentration of healthy and actively budding yeast cells is propagated, the yeast culture is transferred to the fermenter and the fermenter is filled with fresh diluted sugarcane molasses substrate.

4.5 Fermentation

The fermentation process is mediated by strains of Saccharomyces cerevisiae yeast through their addition to diluted sugarcane molasses, or to sugarcane juice from Saint Lucia (see section 6.1). For sugarcane molasses fermentation, the o Brix of the sugarcane molasses is reduced to 18-22 °Brix by the addition of Saint Lucia surface water and/or groundwater. Yeast is then added, and fermentation allowed to proceed to completion, achieving final alcohol concentrations of approximately 7.0% to 8.5% alcohol by volume. For sugarcane juice fermentation, the freshly pressed sugarcane juice is immediately transferred to fermenters, yeast is added, and fermentation is allowed to progress to completion, achieving final alcohol concentrations of approximately 7.0% to 9.0% alcohol by volume. A combination of wild yeast naturally found on sugarcane stalks and a yeast strain isolated from sugarcane is used in sugarcane juice fermentation. Sugarcane molasses fermentation is temperature-controlled and takes 36 – 45 hours to be completed while sugarcane juice fermentation is not temperature controlled and takes a longer period of 72 – 80 hours.

The use of a strain of yeast which was isolated from sugarcane serves to enhance favourable flavour development, in part, due to the yeast's natural familiarity with the substrate. Particularly in the case of sugarcane juice fermentation, the impact of inherent natural yeast and other microbes is also encouraged. For some batches of sugarcane juice fermentation, only natural yeast and other microbes naturally occurring on sugarcane are used.

4.6 Distillation
Distillation enables the concentration of alcohol and select congeners coming from the fermented sugarcane molasses or fermented sugarcane juice. It also serves to control or eliminate undesirable components in the fermentation media from entering the final distillate.

The distillation process takes place in pot and column stills fully or partially made of copper. Light to medium bodied rums are produced on the column still whereas the pot stills produce medium to heavy bodied rums with robust flavour notes. The distillation of column still rums, especially at suppressed alcohol strengths (circa 94% alcohol by volume), in a simple two-column Coffey column still design, results in the retention in the distillates of a significant proportion of the congeners generated during the fermentation process. This French-influenced practice allows for the production of column still distillates which are high in congeneric levels, approaching levels typically seen in traditional pot still English-style rum distillations. The lower column still distillation alcohol strengths strike a balance between the traditionally low distillation alcohol strengths of French-style rums and the traditionally high distillation alcohol strengths of English-style column still rums. This practice in Saint Lucia has allowed for the production of superpremium 100% column still sugarcane molasses rums which have high congeneric levels similar to many admired pot still rums.

The fermented sugarcane molasses or fermented sugarcane juice is heated by steam to the point of boiling, to allow the concentration of alcohol and the selective concentration of desirable congeners which were generated during fermentation. Though proper design, operation and control of the fermentation process forms the basis for rum flavour development, every effort is made to ensure that the results of distillation deliver flavour profiles that remain true to Saint Lucia Rum, and which afford further enhancement of these flavours during ageing/maturation. These factors determine the character of the rum in terms of the presence of flavour-active components, balance, and intensity.

4.7 Ageing/Maturation
The alcohol strength of the rum is reduced to 60% - 63% alcohol by volume, but may vary, by adding filtered rainwater, harvested in Saint Lucia, before being transferred to wooden casks for ageing and maturation.

Saint Lucia Rum must be aged and matured in sealed new or used American and/or European oak casks or other wooden casks as required, only on the island of Saint Lucia. Used casks previously storing other alcohol beverages such as brandy, sherry, port wine, whisk(e)y (including bourbon), wine, etc. are used.

The filled casks are kept in ageing warehouses in Saint Lucia situated at altitudes of approximately 3 metres above sea level, environmentally influenced only by the natural climatic conditions.

The climatic conditions are warm and humid with an average annual temperature of approximately 28°C. The position of the warehouses in warm, humid conditions at low altitudes accelerates the complex series of chemical reactions occurring in the ageing process, allowing the desired aromas and flavours described in Section 4 to develop quickly and with great intensity.

4.8 Blending
The blending of Saint Lucia Rum must take place on the island of Saint Lucia.

Blending with rums from outside Saint Lucia or with rums which do not satisfy the technical specifications of Saint Lucia Rum is not permitted. To support the reputation of the existing brands and the creation of new ones as tastes evolve, the art of blending in the production of rum in Saint Lucia is more important than ever.

All aged and unaged rums of the required marques undergo very thorough chemical and organoleptic evaluations before being harmoniously blended, as required, for the production of blended Saint Lucia Rum.

The marques in each blend are carefully selected to complement each other to produce a well-balanced and complex product that delivers a unique flavour profile and enjoyable experience to even the most discriminating consumer.

Plain caramel colour may be used to make slight colour adjustments to ensure colour consistency in the final blend.

The blends are diluted to attain the required alcohol concentration using demineralised water processed from harvested and filtered Saint Lucia rainwater. The complex blends are then allowed to rest in tanks to allow a minimum marination time of 48 to 72 hours to achieve the balance, smoothness and consistency required for every batch.

4.9 Bottling
Blended rums are placed in containers with sizes appropriate for the intended markets. Glass, plastic or other appropriate approved food-safe containers may be used, along with approved metal, plastic, or wooden closures. The filled and properly sealed containers are then packed into cartons. The cartons are then sealed, palletized, shrink wrapped and sent off to the warehouses where, on approval by the Quality Assurance Facility, are then ready to be fed into the distribution channels.

5. LINK WITH GEOGRAPHICAL ENVIRONMENT OR ORIGIN

The specificity of Saint Lucia Rum lies in the combination of many factors stemming from:

i. The agro-ecological conditions of the surrounding hills that support and replenish the rich minerals and nutrients found in the surface water, groundwater and the alluvial soil of the planting area and which are all intertwined, particularly affecting the fermentation and sugarcane cultivation aspects of the production processes for Saint Lucia Rum.

ii. The year-round micro-climatic conditions which are advantageous to the ageing/maturation of Saint Lucia Rum.

iii. The authentic character of the production process with a conscious effort to preserve the artisanal quality stemming from years of tradition.

iv. The thoughtful and careful introduction of elements of modern science into the traditional production process.

These aspects have served to merge nature, tradition, art and science into the operation, culminating in the delivery of a rum truly representative of the history and culture of Saint Lucia.

Saint Lucia is a tropical island with a tropical rainforest climate, moderated by northeast trade winds, with a dry season from 1 December to 31 May and a wet season from 1 June to 30 November. Average annual temperatures are an approximate low of 24o C and an approximate high of 29°C; average relative humidity of 76% and average annual rainfall of 1500 mm on the coast to 3000 mm in the mountain rainforests.

These climatic conditions produce sugarcane crops with high sugar levels which are essential for obtaining sugarcane juice highly concentrated in sugar. This is a good stimulant for fermentation and is therefore favourable for the production of rum.

Historically, sugarcane was predominantly grown within the island's northern alluvial plains and the coastal alluvial areas in the South. The alluvial soil is mineral-rich, well-drained and has the capacity for excellent water and nutrient retention, favouring sugarcane cultivation.

The historical practice of sugarcane production and rum distillation in the valleys with similar geographical and climatic conditions continues until today.

The ageing area is situated at an altitude of approximately 3 meters. The warm and humid conditions at low altitudes accelerate the natural chemical changes in the ageing process, which allows the aromas and flavours to develop quickly and with greater intensity.

5.1 Environmental Conditions
The volcanic island of Saint Lucia is more mountainous than most Caribbean islands, with the highest point being Mount Gimie, at 950 metres (3,120 feet) above sea level. Forests cover about 77% of the land area.

The island's volcanic igneous rock formations (andesite and basalt) with small areas of coral reef formations in the northern and southern parts of the island afford rich minerals and nutrients to continually descend to enrich the surface water, groundwater and the alluvial soil and further distinguishes it from other Caribbean territories.

St. Lucia Distillers is nestled in the Roseau Valley on the west coast of Saint Lucia, in the heavy rainfall region of the island and simultaneously near the surrounding hills and ridges, the Caribbean Sea and the Roseau River.

Roseau Valley is surrounded to the north by Barre St. Joseph and La Croix Maingot Hills, east by Sarrot and Barre de L'isle Ridges, south by Massacre and Bois d'Inde Hills and west by the Caribbean Sea.

This location affords a microclimate that creates the ideal conditions for influencing the rate of maturation and the development of the distinct flavour attributes of Saint Lucia Rum. The transformation of the rums as they age is comparatively superior, creating a smooth tasting and mellow spirit which varies in colour from straw to mahogany or light burgundy, giving the Master Blender the ideal foundation from which great rum blends can be created. The blending process utilizes 100% harvested Saint Lucian rainwater.

5.3 Human and Process Factors

The constant change in leadership between the French and the British resulted in a skill set and expertise in the methods of fermentation and distillation of rum influenced by both cultures. Honed over centuries and handed down through generations, the use of traditional techniques is still relied on in the production of Saint Lucia Rum.

Throughout the multi-stage process outlined in Section 6 above, skilled personnel maintain the ancestral approach with a keen knowledge of fermentation and distillation techniques to create complex and vibrant flavours that continue to this day and preserve the authentic character of Saint Lucia Rum.

5.4 Reputation

After the establishment of a small but thriving artisanal rum industry, Saint Lucian rums quickly established a reputation for quality. Bolstered by its reputation for complexity and taste, by 1890, Saint Lucian Rum grew to be the second highest revenue earner on the island. Production for many years was mainly for local consumption with many small stills being operated by private owners. Small quantities of rum continued to be exported to France throughout Saint Lucia's rum history. It wasn't until the late 1980s and 1990s that St. Lucia Distillers, the last remaining large distillery, began the process of establishing exports of rum to other parts of Europe and to North America. The success of this export thrust was centered on the excellence of the rum and its unique qualities. This success created a reputation for Saint Lucian rums that combines a distinct aromatic character from pot still distillation with an intense honeyed raisin fruit from the sugarcane molasses base. In addition, there is a distinct brine saltiness to the rums which distinguishes Saint Lucian rum from rums of other islands.

The reputation of St Lucia Rum is not only steeped in its rich history but is attested to by experts in the industry. See Appendix 1.

6. SPECIFIC LABELLING RULES

The words "Saint Lucia Rum" shall appear on the labelling and shall be accompanied by:

i) The words "Geographical Indication" or the initials "GI" in a font size that is comparable to other lettering on the label; or

ii) The Saint Lucia Rum GI logo (registered as a trademark) is owned by the GI applicant.

The following shall appear on the principal display panel of the label:

1) Brand name
2) Product name
3) Alcohol content
4) Net content
5) The name and address of the manufacturer
6) The country of origin

The labelling may eventually use a Saint Lucia National GI logo.

7. REQUIREMENTS OF THE NATIONAL LEGISLATION

Saint Lucia Rum is protected as a Geographical Indication in the Intellectual Property Registry of Saint Lucia and meets the requirements legally laid down in Saint Lucia Rum Technical Specifications, the Excise and Tax Act Chapter 15.07, and the St. Lucia National Standard SLNS 12: 2003 – Specification for Rum.

APPLICANT: St. Lucia Distillers Limited, a Limited Liability Company incorporated under the laws of Saint Lucia.

SUPERVISORY AUTHORITY:

Saint Lucia Rum must be produced in accordance with the technical specifications set out herein for the Geographical Indication. These technical specifications are the basis for which all Saint Lucia Rum producers must comply. The Technical Specifications demonstrate the geographical link with the country of origin and include details of the principal physical, chemical, organoleptic and specific characteristics, and labelling requirements of Saint Lucia Rum.

In order to maintain the authenticity of the Geographical Indication for Saint Lucia Rum, the Saint Lucia Bureau of Standards (SLBS) or an accredited Certification or Control body, which must be competent and impartial, will be responsible for verifying the Geographical Indication of Saint Lucia Rum in accordance with Saint Lucia's laws and international obligations.

CHAPTER 8

Sugar Production and Export:
An Overview

Saint Lucia's history with sugar was complicated, with external factors very much putting the island on a back footing ever since the first *sucrérie* back in 1763. With the lack of records from the late 18th century, it's difficult to determine exactly the sugar types being produced in this era, and indeed once the Colony Records for Saint Lucia begin in 1828, it still only lists 'sugar' in the books alongside a separate listing for molasses. Knowing though that a sugarloaf (where muscovado sugar was refined by a series of boiling and filtering processes, and poured into a large number of inverted conical molds) was the usual form in which refined sugar was produced and sold until the late 19th century (until granulated and cube sugars were introduced), it is natural to presume this was the form taken to ship muscovado (unrefined cane sugar that contains natural molasses), the sugar type of choice for Saint Lucia's *sucréries* up to the 1870's. Unfortunately, until the mid-19th century, the British government used a system of punitive taxes to make it impossible for its colonial producers in the Caribbean to refine their own sugar and supply Britain with finished sugarloaves. Instead, muscovado was shipped in hogsheads to Europe where it was then refined into white sugar. This would explain the consistent year to year export of muscovado from Saint Lucia, which looked to have started in 1822 until 1937 (*see page 236*). It would also have answered the 'sugar' aspect to the Colony Records recordings, presuming this would be muscovado production, but though between 1828 and 1859 the records of this unknown variety carried on, with the years between 1838 and 1859 mentioning export of 'both' varieties, which considering the detail these Colony Records looked to have gone into, seems likely that this unknown variety was not the favoured approach of muscovado production. Neither would it be molasses, as this was recorded separately from 1838 and every year onwards until 1937.

It's also difficult to work out what the mystery sugar type is from the countries exported to. Looking at the Bristol Import and Export Shipping Records from between 1770 and 1917[1], it offers up a recording of the ship '*Conway*' landing into Bristol on 18th October 1805 and bringing into the city "*J. Mc Cullom, 193 hhds, 38 bls sugar, 45 bales cotton, 21 bls coffee, 7 bags cocoa. T. Daniel & Sons 25 hhds sugar. J. Alexander, 25 ditto. P. Ingles & Co, 128 ditto. Total 371 hhds, 38 bls sugar, 45 bales cotton, 21 bls coffee, 75 bags cocoa*" – no further to explaining, even when looking into *T. Daniel & Sons* who were one of the biggest sugar merchants in the city, an insight into what this sugar type could be. It also doesn't offer us much of an insight when looking at the units of measure recorded. The unit '*hhd*' is the abbreviation for hogsheads, the 18th and 19th centuries choice for the measure of sugar's weight (equivalent to approximately 1,000 pounds, 225-250 litres, 59-66 US gallons or 49-54 imperial gallons), whilst '*bbl*' was the unit referring to barrel (142 litres or 37 US gal). Since the Colonial Records for Saint Lucian began, these were the two main units primarily used, for example, in 1830 Saint Lucia exported 6,064 hhd, and 1,401 bbl - it's obviously not showing a rate equivalent for its records but two separate sizes, and therefore weights of sugar containers, which is then presumed the weights of such were 'ordered' by the sugar merchants in the territories who required. The years 1849 to 1855 though do throw a spanner in the works on this theory, as 1849 records 4,548 hhd and 213 t exported of sugar. The unit '*t*' is the abbreviation for ton (equivalent to 2,240 pounds) but does not indicate what the ton is referring to in terms of container used, and again does not show a rate equivalent, further fuelling the mystery of the early sugar exports.

Refined sugar was exported though, presumably via sugarloaves, to the West Indies, Grenada, Trinidad & Tobago and 'Foreign States', although sporadically. For example, 1843 saw just 3 hogsheads exported to the West Indies, one of a handful of years in the 1840's to see such – although their units of measurements are scattered, from hogsheads to puncheons (a unit for volume instead of weight), packs and tons. The 1850's and 1860's offer no records for refined sugar, but it picked up again in 1873 and now under the unit of '*lbs*' (pounds, equivalent to 0.45359 kg). It then picks up again in 1885, and finally

1886, although still none the wiser on the mystery sugar type despite 2,900 lbs making its way over to Trinidad and Tobago.

¹ Bristol Shipping Records: Imports and Exports, 1805. Identifier:72948-C-06: October 18ᵗʰ, 1805, p74

Muscovado

Muscovado sugar export has, alongside molasses, a regular record of being the request of a variety of territories around the western world. Much like the unknown sugar variety previously mentioned, muscovado (unrefined cane sugar that contains natural molasses), was transported sporadically within hogsheads and barrels (raw form of muscovado was transported within the hogsheads, and liquid form via the barrels) from 1838 until 1848 when the first unit recording of ton was mentioned. Only a handful of years in the 1850's are recorded for export under these units, until the first recording from 1860 states the unit of pounds, a trend that would continue until 1905. This year also starts the more precise recording of the countries and territories exported to, whilst showing an overview of the trends of muscovado. The 1860's saw export to countries such as Great Britain (who incidentally imported every year from 1860 until 1937 and can likely be presumed to be active before then despite the lack of records mentioning so), Barbados and the United States alongside the odd year imports by countries such as Bahamas, St. Vincent, Newfoundland and the Danish West Indies. The records now state that the overall quantity exported is in *lbs,* with a then division between *hhd, t* and *bbl.* The total value of the muscovado export sales looked relatively stable, from £91,813 in 1860, a slight dip to £69,480 in 1863, but rising back to £95,700 (1864), £92,404 (1865) and £89,360 (1866). By the end of the 1860's, the value had hit the century mark, bringing in £103,937 (1868), £102,700 (1869) and £133,275 (1870), all of which were generated by Great Britain (purchasing at least 10,000,000 lbs of muscovado each year), with the odd top up for example by Dutch West Indies (40,300 lbs in 1868), Danish West Indies (6,400 lbs in 1869) and United States (1,300 lbs in 1870).

Moving into the 1870's, (and the introduction of the Central Sugar Factories to Saint Lucia) and the value increases further, reaching a high of £165,360 in 1872. Although fluctuations occur over the decade, the only noticeable dip is in 1876 where it decreases to £92,832, although rises a year later (£127,615), back down to £97,050 in 1878, then rises once again to round out the decade at £148,608. Again, Great Britain leads the way in being the biggest export market for muscovado sugar, however the French West Indies start to be become a regular, importing around the 100,000 lbs mark at the beginning of the 1870's, although dropping to only 6,400 lbs by 1879. The United States also start to become a regular near the latter end of the decade, starting with just 82 lbs (1874), to 691,800 lbs (1877). The 1880's though offers a downward spiral of the value being exported, from a high of £143,584 in 1880, to just £20,466 in 1890. Great Britain still leads the way in importing the most muscovado consistently, but the total weight of such has gone from 13,332,800 lbs in 1880, to just 3,273,900 lbs by 1890. It's a surprising result considering the second central factory was built in Vieux Fort in 1882, followed by Roseau and Dennery before the end of the decade, yet the value and total have dropped considerably despite these approaches to streamline the sugar industry in Saint Lucia. However, it's also worth remembering that sugar prices dropped sharply in 1884, specifically muscovado too, resulting in planters being plunged into debt and sugar estates across the island going bankrupt. The Colony Report in 1891 mentioned that muscovado production had fallen hard in value, and that estates were starting to be restyled towards cocoa, cotton, coffee and kola nut, further cementing exports to fluctuate between 3,272,900 lbs (£20,466) in 1890 to just 101,200 lbs (£474) by 1899.

Interestingly though, the United States are a regular importer of muscovado despite the hardships of production and pricing, with Canada also becoming a mainstay from 1893 onwards. It's also worth noting that the likes of Colon – presumed to be Colon of Panama (600 lbs in 1890), Halifax – again presumed to be Halifax of Nova Scotia (8,000 lbs in 1899) and Havre in Normandy, France (16,600 lbs in 1899) also come into the picture, albeit for one year only, alongside the occasional return of Trinidad & Tobago (1898), Dutch West Indies (1890 and 1896), Grenada (1892 and 1894) and St. Vincent (1894). It's worth noting too that 1898 saw the attempt to establish export trade between Saint Lucia and French ports, which would explain the 16,600 lbs of muscovado making its way to Havre in France in 1899.

The turn of the century also sees the records change from *lbs* to *t*, with 1 lb equivalent of 0.000453592 t. The United Kingdom still leads the way in export quantity in the first handful of years from 1900, followed by the United States and Canada, although it trends downwards in total quantity (387,600 lbs in 1900 to just 85,200 lbs in 1903), with the value plummeting from £1,903 to just £266 in the same stretch. By 1905, the United States were no longer recorded, with Canada becoming the second largest market to be exported to, bringing in more muscovado sugar than the United Kingdom in 1905 (630 t compared to 162 t), although quickly reversing itself in 1906 and 1907, and ultimately no export to Canada then until 1911. Montserrat, Dominica and France make an appearance as export markets in 1908, although with minimal quantities compared to the United Kingdom, contributing to the rising total value from a low of £403 in 1907 to £707 in 1908, finishing on a high of £1,139 in 1909.

The next decade saw muscovado rise and decline in its now usual fashion, from a low of £291 in 1913, rising to £4,851 in 1915 and peaking at £61,101 in 1919, before lowering to £5,190 in 1920. It also, once again, saw the unit of measure change from *t* to *cwt* (an abbreviation for "hundredweight," a unit of weight or mass, equal to 100 pounds in the United States and 112 pounds in the United Kingdom). The United Kingdom still lead the way in being the biggest export market during the decade (although it didn't bring in any muscovado in 1918), with a more scattered approach to further markets that included the return of St. Vincent (1912), Dominica (1911), Martinique (1914, 1916 and 1917), Grenada (1914), Antigua (1918), Montserrat (1918) and Barbados (1918). For the 1918 anomaly of the lack of United Kingdom import, Barbados lead the way for one year only with 590 cwt of muscovado, higher than the United Kingdom's previous year of 538.36 cwt too. It wasn't to be sustainable though as Barbados don't make an appearance for two more years, with only 2 cwt being recorded for 1920.

As muscovado export heads into the last full decade of export, the 1920's, it now becomes clear that the United Kingdom retains its lead of being the biggest importer of such, with the United States, Canada and Antigua propping up on the odd year. The total value once again fluctuates, from £5,190 in 1920, down to £782 in 1922 (recorded in the Colony Report as being due to *"abnormally high prices"*), rising to £9,508 in 1924, then finishing on £2,235 in 1927 (there were no records of muscovado export from 1928 to 1936). Surprisingly, the total quantity (which is now back to *t* for the recorded weight) rose from 267 t in 1921 to 497 t in 1924, with the high value of £9,508, yet just one year later, 430.7 t were exported, but now just a value of £4,774, meaning yet another crash in the market value of muscovado, which may explain the decision by most estates to stop producing this variety of sugar for export. Please refer to *Chapter 14.5 Muscovado Sugar Export* for more detailed records, page 236.

Usine

With the introduction of the Central Sugar Factories in 1874, the Colony Records start to mention the export of *usine* sugar from 1876 onwards. Unfortunately, it's not clear on the types of sugar produced at the factories, and the fact that there are separate records for molasses and muscovado for the same period, it's quite possible that the recordings show the overall quantity of sugar variations combined that are produced solely from the sugar factories. Although knowing the level of detail in the Colony Records, it strikes as odd that they wouldn't mention the variations of sugar being exported from the sugar factories, unless the individual sugar recordings within the same export pages of the Colony Records are as such and would have been 'obvious' to the Government reader at that time. It also highly unlikely if the sugar factories produced their own versions of sugar types to run alongside the separate records of molasses and muscovado as there were no other production facilities to do so on the island.

Comparing the history of the factories existence though does offer some insight into the values recorded. A relatively consistent overall quantity of sugar produced from 1876 (760 t, or tonnes) to 1881 (820 t), bringing in a value of £18,256 to £22,960 respectively, before it hits a tonnage high of 1,462 t in 1882 and a value of £47,892, although dipping slightly to 1,395 t (£27,900) by 1884 (coinciding with all four factories facing the dramatic fall in sugar prices). A change to pounds *(lbs)* as we head into the latter end of the 1880's sees a steady rise between 4,779,000 lbs in 1885 to 6,093,000 lbs by 1889, with the value rising much the same way from £40,223 to £63,922 respectively. 1890 though saw a rise in the total quantity to 7,888,900 lbs, but a lower value now of £63,111. A slight improvement though as the 1890's develops, with a high of 10,346,600 lbs (£76,213), but a slow decline to finish the decade off with a recording of 8,834,424 lbs (£56,319). The export countries are much the same as muscovado, with the United Kingdom leading the way, the United States a consistent second, with Grenada and St. Vincent a semi-consistent factor until the end of the century alongside the odd Dominica (1889), French West Indies (1896), Montserrat (1885) and France (1887).

The turn of the century records a low of £23,029 in 1902 (8,253,484 lbs), but upturns to hover around the £50,000 mark towards the end of the decade, with the United Kingdom and Canada offering dominance in the countries exported to. The last decade of records for usine though offer little, with 1910 breaking the £60,000 barrier for the last time, before there were no recordings at all until one last entry in 1919 for 34,514.53 cwt (hundredweight) and a value of £46,720. Interestingly, a wide variety of countries took advantage of Saint Lucian sugar in these latter years, with the United Kingdom and Canada being propped up by Montserrat, Dominica, St. Vincent, Grenada, Barbados and Bermuda – albeit it with sometimes as little as ¹⁄₁₀ of a ton (Grenada, 1909). By 1920, the *St Lucia Usines and Estates Company* had sold all its estates, ending the usine export opportunities. Please refer to *Chapter 14.6 Usine Sugar Export* for more detailed records, page 244.

Molasses

The export of molasses (principally obtained from the refining of sugarcane) from Saint Lucia has been a steady record since 1822 until 1959. Originally recorded as a quantity of *p* (puncheons, equivalent to 70-120 gallons), the total quantities exported hovered around the 1,000-p mark between 1828 and 1845, bringing in a value of between £3-6,000. There was the odd anomaly to mention, including a high of 2,631 p in 1828 (£12,249) to a low of 670 p (£5,119) in 1840, but relatively stable none-the-less, although lacking such record of which markets the molasses was chiefly exported to during this era. By 1857, the Colony Records started to present the molasses destinations, as well as separate recordings of not just puncheons, but also gallons (*gal*) depending on the country or region in question. For example, 1857 saw 803 puncheons and 85,695 gallons (£6,231) of molasses head to Great Britain, whilst 71 puncheons and 7,800 gallons (£578) went to the British West Indies Colonies, 227 puncheons and 24,970 gallons (£1,816) to United States, and finally 10 puncheons and 1,005 gallons (£120) to Danish Colonies. From 1858 onwards, gallons became the normal unit of measure for molasses with the 1860's offering a relatively stable export of around the early 100,000-gal mark (approximately £3,600 on average) and a wider list of countries bringing in Saint Lucian molasses, led by Great Britain and the British West Indies, with Barbados and the United States propping up the total. The odd flash of St. Vincent, British Guiana, St. Kitts and Dominica rounds off the 1860's.

The next decade starts off with a slight dip from the year prior, with 153,000 gal (£6,120), but rises to 234,800 gal (£9,392) by 1871 and hovers around this mark until 1875 with a high of 296,800 gal and £11,872. 1875 also saw the United States import the most molasses for the second year running, although not enough to keep the trend from seeing a considerable dip to just 111,100 gal (£4,444) a year later. However, it had doubled up by the end of the decade, with the French West Indies propping up where the United States were now lacking (119,160 gal compared to 43,230 gal respectively in 1878).

The 1880's saw a varied approach to the export market, with Great Britain only importing for six of the ten years and the United States contributing just twice. However, the French West Indies became the biggest importer of Saint Lucian molasses, generating the most consistency to bring the total quantities in the 1880's around the 200,000-gal mark (£10,000). The 1890's continued the trend with the French West Indies, although the total value of molasses would take a sharp turn, from £8,595 in 1890, to £3,722 in 1894, £1,443 in 1896 and finally just £859 by 1899. The decade was propped up by Martinique (245,160 gal in 1893) and Barbados (23,640 gal in 1895), with the odd purchase from the United Kingdom (1890, 1891, 1893 and 1897). The turn of the century saw even more wild fluctuations, with a rise to £1,086 in value come 1900, with the total yearly export of 57,960 gal going straight to the French West Indies (which unfortunately was its last purchase). Canada entered the market by 1901, and although having Grenada purchasing molasses in 1902, between the two of them Saint Lucia only recorded 5,640 gal (£94). A rise though the next year to 59,570 (£992) can be attributed to the return of the United Kingdom and France but ultimately could not turn the tide as by 1906, only Canada imported 11 casks, with a value of just £16. By the end of the decade though, fortunes had changed for the better as 1910 saw a high of £1,914 from 95,220 gallons, all of which went to Canada, a relatively consistent country until 1939 of importing molasses from Saint Lucia. The recorded figures though once again show the start of turmoil of the wider sugar export on the island, with a low of 6,135 gal (£155) in 1913, to a high of 68,324 gal (£4,974) in 1919, yet then a huge tumble to just 2,964 gal (£112) by 1921.

From 1921 onwards, the Colony Reports start to refer to molasses as 'fancy molasses', a lighter, sweeter, and milder-flavoured type of molasses which is extracted earlier in the sugar refining process. Whether this was down to the trends of the era (it was a popular choice for baking, cooking, and as a natural sweetener in beverages) or the ease of production, it's hard to know for sure. What can be ascertained though is that the difference in molasses saw an upheaval in fortune, as the 1920's saw a relatively steady quantity around the 150,000-gallon mark (£8,000), although it did start to decline as it headed into the 1930's with just 39,394 gallons (£2,272). Canada was still leading the way, followed closely by the United States in terms of export markets, with the odd one-off purchase by St. Martin (1922 and 1923), Barbados (1921 and 1926) and St. Vincent (1925).

The last decade of recorded countries of export, the 1930's, saw Canada retain its dominance of bringing in Saint Lucian molasses, with the United States dipping in consistency and Bermuda topping up a handful of times until the latter two years where Newfoundland came into the market. The 1930's saw a relatively consistent total quantity, hovering between 20,000 – 27,000 gallons (approximately £1,300), although an anomaly arose in 1936 where 24,602 gallons were exported, but for a value of just £522, where the year prior saw 28,264 gallons return a value of £1,380. The 1940's only saw four years of records for the export of molasses, with a high of 128,945 gallons in 1940 (£2,485), to a low of just 10 gallons a year later (£33). The 1950's, and the last decade of complete records, shows once again a fluctuation of volumes and market prices, from a high of 218,891 gallons (£46,460) in 1951, down to 81,167 gallons (£24,153) just one year later, but then back to 220,579 gallons (£27,108). The decade finished off with just 40,000 gallons and a total value of £4,800. Please refer to *Chapter 14.11 Molasses Sugar Export* for more detailed records, page 250.

Miscellaneous Varieties

On the odd occasion, the Colony Records record a small burst in a specific type of sugar being exported. *Sugar Syrup* was mentioned three times between 1895 and 1897, with the French West Indies and Grenada importing from Saint Lucia a high of 455 gallons for a value of £23.

Malhado (unrefined sugar that is high in molasses and offers a dark brown colour) also has a three year opportunity, where in 1903 the United Kingdom took 882 casks (£1,984), 803 casks (for a higher value of £2,049), and a considerably lower 313 casks just a year later (£939). In 1904, there was a separate entry for *Sugar Casks*, although the type of sugar within is up for debate. 1,233 casks went to the United Kingdom, resulting in a value of £3,699.

Around the same time, *Molascuit* (prepared from molasses and fine bagasse) saw some opportunity for export, with 1,517 bags (£379) sent to the United Kingdom in 1906, rising to 3,700 bags (£925) split between the United Kingdom, France, Barbados and Grenada a year later. 1908 saw a slight reduction to 2,594 bags (£648) between the United Kingdom and Grenada, finally finishing with just 7 tonnes (£21) to Grenada in 1909.

1912 saw the Colony Records mention the export of *Vacuum Pan* sugar (the crystallization of sugar carried out by boiling sugar syrup in a batch-type evaporative crystallizer called a vacuum-pan), which was recorded between the units of *cwt* (hundredweight) and *lbs* (pounds). The United Kingdom became the most consistent in importing Vacuum Pan sugar, from 1912 to 1939, although wasn't necessarily the biggest importer in terms of total volume depending on the year. Canada was the second largest importer, followed by the early onset by St. Vincent, Dominica and Martinique. It's difficult to review the figures due to the haphazard approach to the units used (it converts to tonnes by 1921) but the total values look to be relatively consistent (around the 80,000-cwt mark and £50,000 value), with a high in 1920 of 74,779 cwt and 109 lbs, with a total value of £141,125 (predominantly to the United Kingdom). The totals look to drop considerably and level out from here-onwards though, with 1922 recording a quantity of 5,829.2 tonnes (£66,741) and the decade rounding out with 4,536 tonnes (£51,237) by 1929. The 1930's saw relative consistency again, focusing exclusively on the United Kingdom and Canada as export markets, starting around the 3,973-tonne mark (£35,554) and improving to 7,182 tonnes (£64,237) by the end of the decade. There were no records between 1940 and 1946, but Vacuum Pan sugar was picked up in 1947 and grew steadily from 4,615 tonnes (£477,305) to a high of 9,125 tonnes (£1,598,687) by 1956. The records show though that this wasn't sustainable, as by just 1960, the total quantity had dropped to 78,825 lbs, with a value of only £690. The last record offered the lowest to finish on, with 4,057 lbs exported with a value of just £366. Please refer to *Chapter 14.12 Vacuum Pan Sugar Export* for more detailed records, page 258.

CHAPTER 9

Sucrérie and Slave Conditions

'Mamiku: The Tale of an 18th Century Sugar Plantation in St. Lucia' by Louise Shingleton-Smith highlights some of the conditions of the *sucrérie* in Saint Lucia, specifically in this case the Mamiku Estate in Mon Repos. The estate came to be during the mid-eighteenth-century courtesy of Claude Anne Guy de Micoud (future Baron de Micoud) who in 1767 purchased a 1,200-acre estate in the district of Praslin. Its current name is derived from Micoud's wife, Madame de Micoud (*"Ma Micoud"* in the local dialect). With the land cultivated as a sugar estate, and becoming one of the largest in Praslin (of eight at the time that were classed as sugar out of a total of thirty-seven estates), the Micoud's represented the typical wealthy land-owning class on the island. The late eighteen century was a time of prosperity across the West Indies, despite Saint Lucia's late arrival to the growth of sugarcane and topography of the island hampering wide scale cultivation. Shingleton-Smith also mentions that in the late 18th century *"It was also stated in French correspondence of the time that the high morality of the slaves on the plantations was also a factor in the inertia of the island's agricultural prosperity"*. Despite these setbacks, the Micoud's would manage to set a reasonable standard of living for themselves, taking advantage of the new roads being built, land being developed and high levels of property value.

Around this time, *"a small, wealthy minority of plantation owners lived abroad. Their estates were run by relatively poor white, salaried managers. Planter families, like the Micoud's, lived and worked on their own estates, creating an upper middle-class sector"*. Alongside Government officials, businessmen, clergymen, lawyers, military personnel, various drifters and indentured servants, the Micoud's contributed and influenced Saint Lucia's cultural flavour. Slavery, unfortunately, became an overwhelming majority of the island's population, led by black Africans from the continents west coast.

Shingleton-Smith states though that *"amongst the slaves, those born and raised in slavery on the island were designated as 'Creoles' in slave registers and manuscripts of the period. These persons were afforded relatively more advantages and opportunities on the plantation than their African-born counterparts. Creoles were allowed to serve as slaves drivers, housemaids, and skilled craftsmen. Those brought directly from Africa were relegated to the bottom of the pecking order on the estates"* . . . *"Upon arrival in the colonies, they would be sold to plantation owners for a price based upon their age, sex and fitness level. After several months of on-site acclimatization called 'seasoning', during which time as many as a third would perish, the surviving slaves could often be bought and sold through local markets. Planters whose estates went bankrupt advertised their slaves for sale in the local newspaper, pronouncing the 'desirable traits' of the slaves such as obedience and good health".*

As mentioned in *Chapter 3: The Growth of Labour*, a small mixed-race population also lived on Saint Lucia, referred to as 'free people of colour' and the offspring of white men (sometimes the estate owners or managers) and slave women. Adding to this situation, most European immigrants into the colonies were males and many therefore turned to black/mulatto women for companionship. Free coloureds owned and farmed land and sometimes achieved sufficient affluence to afford slaves of their own to work on their properties, with small populations of free blacks also developing on the islands who had purchased their freedom by finding ways to earn and save money during their periods of enslavement. Despite these stories of reward, Shingleton-Smith states that *"Whatever money could be generated, the free mulattos and blacks across St. Lucia were generally quite poor".*

In 1778, an inventory of the Mamiku Estate revealed that it comprised of *"390 carrés of land* (approximately 1,200 acres), *buildings for the manufacture of sugar, dwelling houses of the white and the blacks, the plantations of provisions and canes, the canal, the lime kiln, the canoes, the pottery . . . 30 oxen, 27 mules, all goats and sheep and 100 slaves of all ages . . . "*

The overall layout of the estate was said to be typical of other sugar estates of the time. Essentially such would see a river running through the property that provided fresh drinking and cooking water (and possibly used to turn the water wheel at the mill if the chosen source of power. Refer to *Chapter 13.5 Sugar Mills and Type* for more detailed records, page 189). The various sugar buildings were large and the centre of the estate's activities, which included a boiling house, curing house and sugar mill itself. Surrounding the sugar fields would be pastureland for grazing animals, with the hillsides used for growing provisions for the workers of the estate. Most of the land on the larger plantations was in the form of woodlands and tropical forest, providing fuel for the boiling house and timber for the buildings – almost half of the Micoud Estate was woodland, with the rest cleared for cane fields, pastures and various buildings. The Micoud's home was located on a hill above the cane field and working buildings, where the family would be removed from the noise and odours of the sugar processing, as well as the slaves and other workers of the estate. The houses for the workers were located near the sugar buildings, as were the kitchen, stables, tradesmen's shops, the hospital and the *cachot* (dungeon). Slave huts on the estate were usually grouped in straight rows near the sugar buildings and would be no larger than about twelve by twenty feet in size. On the Micoud Estate, each thatched-roof hut housed an average of three slaves.

By 1790, the deed of the Mamiku Estate had been transferred to Madame de Micoud after the Barons' attempt to mitigate any personal damage after the British occupation after 1778 and becoming the scapegoat for the French reversal of fortune. The estate though eventually made a full recovery and started to grow cotton like much of the estates across the island due to the higher prices on the world market than sugar. The estate could now count 460 *carrés* (approximately 1,472 acres), and included a rum factory, dungeon, mill house, three megass houses (more commonly known as bagasse, a fibrous by-product of sugarcane), a pottery, a yaw's (an infectious disease hospital), bakery, boat house, manager's house and fifty-four Negro huts, of which one was a kitchen and another a hospital.

In terms of the workers conditions, the role changed little across the estates of Saint Lucia. Slaves lived under the harshest of conditions, in very isolated parts of the island. Performing virtually all the tasks inherent of the daily operation of a working plantation, they could be segregated into one of two broad categories: field work and domestic service. There also existed a separate group of slaves who occupied highly trained positions and demonstrated high levels of skill and intelligence. Field workers performed the most arduous demanding work and were usually divided into three working gangs. The first was comprised of strong men and women who were assigned the gruelling tasks of preparing the soil for planting, harvesting and carrying the weight of the cut cane to the mill. The second gang contained the weaker slaves, pregnant or nursing mothers, and new African arrivals. Although less strenuous than the members of the first gang, they were still responsible for weeding and cultivation of food crops. The third and last gang would be made up of children between the ages of eight and thirteen years. The young children would remove trash from the sugar mills and performed other light duties around the estate. All the gangs had slave drivers at the helm – usually male and used whips to maintain the working pace of the gangs.

Although men and women were treated equally within the field gangs, with Shingleton-Smith even mentioning that *"evidence suggests that most of these groups of workers had more women than men in their ranks"*, men could occupy various and specialised skilled positions on the plantation from which women were selectively excluded. Roles included masons, coopers, carpenters or blacksmiths. As each estate assumed the nature of a self-contained village, the slave population filled the various needs including construction and repair of buildings, roads and bridges. The most coveted assignments for slaves on a plantation, especially for women, were those involving domestic service in the estate household. Such roles included cleaners, washerwomen, seamstress, servants and cooks, in which the latter was only available for the most trusted slaves due to fear of a slave poisoning their master. It's also worth noting that the cooks in the estate-owners' homes were male, whilst female cooks were positioned to cook for the slave population only.

Mamiku Estate also manufactured rum during its time, that sometimes counted for as much as one-third of the plantation's revenue. Women often ran the distilleries as they were believed to be more resistant than men to the temptations of drinking or stealing the rum, especially when 'strong rum' (also named 'tafia') was the local choice of many. The workers in the distilleries were often given rum rations as benefits of their positions.

Slaves were given one reprieve in their weekly routine and in keeping with the Christan traditions, Sundays were reserved as official days of rest. This day was also an opportunity for the slaves to earn small amounts of income for themselves, for example female slaves would take their home-grown fruit and vegetables from the estate to sell at the local markets.

Slavery punishment was also feared upon across the estates, where slaves lived by rules and under restrictions that were very strongly enforced. According to Shingleton-Smith *"slaves were not allowed to strike or speak rudely to members of the white community. The playing of loud drums, which could be used to send signals to runaways or rebels, was also forbidden. Keeping weapons was absolutely prohibited, as was the theft or destruction of horses, cattle and other livestock. Thrashings, shackling in iron, or being confined for days in small dungeons were such commonly applied modes of punishment for slave infractions that a position of Protector of Slaves was created in Saint Luicia"*. The duties of the Protector of Slaves involved keeping records of slave-related crimes and punishments meted out. There were laws in place, which forbade owners from torturing or killing their slaves, but unfortunately not always enforced with regularity. However, on the other side of the coin, slaves who were tried and disciplined by the island's judicial system could receive more cruel and severe punishment, including being burnt alive, broken on a wheel, or be crippled by the severing of hamstring tendons.

CHAPTER 10

The Sucrérie Today

With only *St. Lucia Distillers Ltd* within the Roseau Estate the last remaining working historical estate of sugar cane and rum production left on the island, it does bring into question of what has happened to the remnants of Saint Lucia's sugar past. The below offers a small guide.

Cul de Sac Sugar Factory *(Castries)*

There are no remnants left of the sugar factory, all but demolished and hard to find even an idea of where the buildings could have been.

Vieux Fort Sugar Factory

The foundations of the Vieux Fort Sugar Factory can be found on the west side of current day upper Clarke Street (originally the Malgrétoute-Micoud Road).

Dennery Sugar Factory

There are no remnants left of the sugar factory, and much like Cul de Sac, it's hard to work out where the buildings could have been.

Balenbouche Estate *(Laborie)*

From the late 1700's to the 1930's Balenbouche Estate was established as a sugar estate, and in 1964 Erik and Jennie Lawaetz purchased Balenbouche Estate from the Floissac family, along with other surrounding farms. Jennie Lawaetz refurbished the largely empty 180-year-old plantation house with antiques, but the couple did not live in Saint Lucia permanently and in their absence the properties were mismanaged. In 1984, Eric Lawaetz's daughter-in-law, Uta Lawaetz, visited Balenbouche Estate and realized that the property was in critical financial and legal condition. Uta and her husband, Caribbean artist Roy Lawaetz, decided to stay and face the tremendous challenges, including the government acquisition of most of the family land in the late 1980's. Yet they persevered and were able to save the Balenbouche plantation house and surrounding acreage. Roy and Uta began repairing and renovating the old buildings and establishing new crops, such as Carambolas, passion fruit, ginger lilies, vegetables and tobacco. The estate has been owned and managed by the Lawaetz family ever since and over the years, Uta and daughters Verena and Anitanja Lawaetz gradually converted the property into an eco-friendly guesthouse, organic farm and retreat centre. The grounds include the old water wheel, two pot stills, molasses pots and a handful of derelict buildings that offer an insight into the layout of the distillery and mill.

Riviere Doree Sugar Mill *(Choiseul)*

Ruins of the old sugar mill can still be accessed, with guided tours by the Riviere Doree Revival Group offering the opportunity to visit up-close.

Mamiku Estate *(Micoud)*

The Mamiku Estate was originally acquired in 1766 by the Baron de Micoud, but was eventually a British military post, set up by General Sir John Moore in 1796. The post endured much action, culminating in a famous battle with the 'Brigands' that left 15 soldiers dead, 20 wounded and the de Micoud home a burnt-out ruin. The captain of the post committed suicide after the battle so as not to live out his life in disgrace and for two hundred years, the de Micoud estate ruins were left virtually undisturbed. This was not, however, the end of Mamiku Estate. It eventually returned to its former glory as a profitable sugar estate and today, Mamiku Estate is a hardworking plantation producing bananas, cocoa, tropical flowers and fruits, with the botanical gardens added in 1997 as part of Agro - Tourism. The entire estate has been owned and operated by the Shingleton-Smith family since 1906, when Henry Martin Shingleton-Smith bought the estate for £500.

La Sikwi Sugar Mill *(Anse la Raye)*

One of the oldest sugar mills still visible in Saint Lucia, La Sikwi was built in 1860 within the Invergoil Estate and restored in 1990. It eventually housed a museum and tropical gardens surrounding, but by 2025 it had fallen into disrepair.

Morne Coubaril Estate *(Soufrière)*

Tours are available for the Morne Coubaril Estate, offering the opportunity to see the mule-driven sugar cane mill and the taste of fresh cane juice alongside replica stick huts, similar to those used two centuries ago by local villagers, and gardens around that offer close-up views of the more popular local flora. The plantation has been resown to produce cocoa, coffee and copra.

Soufrière Estate

Soufrière Estate has been transformed from a working plantation that once produced, sugar, limes, copra, and cocoa, into one of the major heritage sites in the region, as well as a tourist attraction that includes the Diamond Botanical Gardens (also known as the St. Lucia Botanical Gardens), waterfall, mineral baths, nature trail, Old Mill Restaurant, and the historic Soufrière Estate with tour guides available to explore. The watermill was constructed in 1765 and was originally built to crush sugar cane, but more recently it was used to provide hydroelectric power for Soufrière. In 1983, Mrs. Joan Devaux, daughter of Mr. André du Boulay took over the management of the Estate.

Fond d'Or Estate *(Dennery)*

Now the Fond d'Or Nature Historic Park, it is home to remnants of sugar plantations (including three different sugar processing technologies: the cattle mill, the waterwheel, and the steam engine) positioned in the Mabouya Valley in the heart of the Dennery Basin.

Jalousie Plantation *(Soufrière)*

The Jalousie Plantation has had a history of owners including Lord Glenconner, famously known for his friendship with Princess Margaret. It was Glenconner who first transformed the land into a resort which was then called 'Jalousie Plantation Resort' and it welcomed many Royals and celebrities through its doors. From then the ownership has changed a handful of times before becoming Sugar Beach, A Viceroy Resort in 2012. Remnants of the old water wheel and sugar cane rollers are still visible within the grounds.

Mon Repos Sugar Mill *(Micoud)*

The Old Sugar Mill within the village of Mon Repos hosts guided tours of the mill as well as a café and gift shop.

Anse Mamin Plantation *(Soufrière)*

This 600-acre, 18th century French Colonial plantation property is a part of the Anse Chastanet and Jade Mountain resort properties. The slaves that lived here worked to produce molasses, but now the ruins can be toured, including inside the building where the production of molasses and cocoa took place.

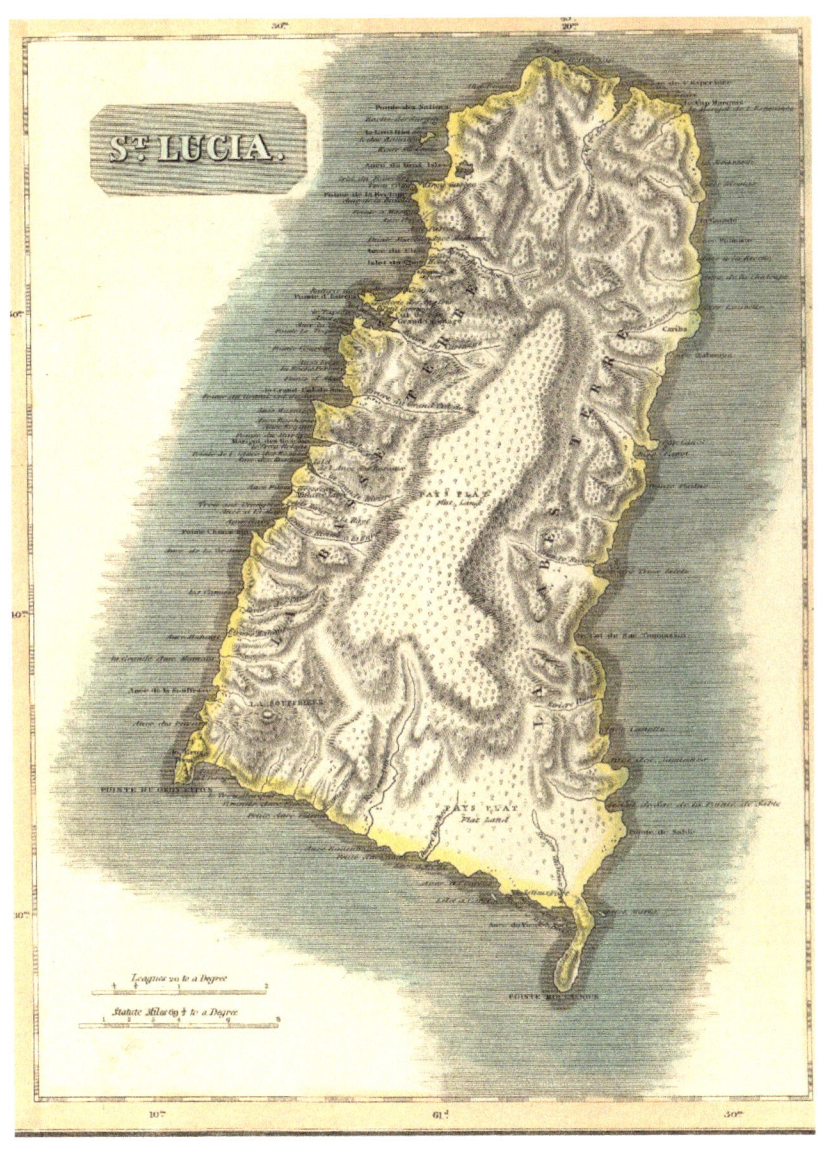

1817 Map of Saint Lucia under British rule.
(Image courtesy of BritishEmpire)

St. Lucia Central Sugar Factory Company Shares Certificate.
(Image courtesy of Mike Veissid and Scripoworld.com)

St. Lucia Central Sugar Factory Company Token.
(Images courtesy of Numista)

Cul de Sac Sugar Factory circa 1905.
(Postcard courtesy of Sasu Postcardman)

Vieux Fort with the sugar factory to the left, circa 1920.
(Postcard courtesy of WorthPoint)

The ruins of the Troumassée Estate sugarcane mill in Micoud.
(Image courtesy of Tony Joseph)

The ruins of a sugar mill within Mon Repos, Micoud.
(Image courtesy of TortoisePath)

Copper pot still within the grounds of the Balenbouche Estate, Laborie.
(Image courtesy of Dave Marsland collection)

A copper vessel for the boiling of cane juice within the grounds of the
Balenbouche Estate, Laborie.
(Image courtesy of Dave Marsland collection)

The ruins of the boiling house at Balenbouche Estate, Laborie.
(Image courtesy of Dave Marsland collection)

A copper pot still within the ruins of the Balenbouche Estate, Laborie.
(Image courtesy of Dave Marsland collection)

The ruins of the sugarcane mill at Balenbouche Estate, Laborie.
(Image courtesy of Dave Marsland collection)

The ruins of the sugarcane mill at Jalousie Plantation, Soufrière.
(Image courtesy of Dave Marsland collection)

The cane rollers of the sugarcane mill at Jalousie Plantation, Soufrière.
(Image courtesy of Dave Marsland collection)

The donkey powered cane rollers at Morne Coubaril Estate, Soufrière.
(Image courtesy of Dave Marsland collection)

The Roseau Valley and St. Lucia Distillers, circa 2010's.
(Image courtesy of St. Lucia Distillers Ltd)

A motor rail locomotive at the Roseau Estate, Anse la Raye.
(Image courtesy of Dave Marsland collection)

The cane fields and cane crushing building at St. Lucia Distillers, 2022.
(Image courtesy of Belle Portwe Studio)

The manufacturers plate on the Vendôme Pot Still at St. Lucia Distillers, 2022.
(Image courtesy of Belle Portwe Studio)

Bounty Rum bottle and label, circa 1985.
(Image courtesy of Dave Marsland collection)

Admiral Rodney Extra Old Rum,
(Image courtesy of TuesdayPints)

Crystal White, Kwèyòl Spice and Chairman's Reserve Original, circa 1999.
(Images courtesy of St. Lucia Distillers)

Chairman's Reserve and Admiral Rodney, circa 2016.
(Image courtesy of St. Lucia Distillers)

1979 Ruby Reserve and Javalatté
(Images courtesy of St. Lucia Distillers)

Nutz' n Rum and the label for Koko-nut Rum
(Images courtesy of St. Lucia Distillers)

Buccaneer Rum label and Old Fort Reserve Rum
(Images courtesy of St. Lucia Distillers)

TØZ Rum range.
(Image courtesy of St. Lucia Distillers)

1931 Rum range, including Chairman's Reserve 1931.
(Image courtesy of St. Lucia Distillers)

Berry Bros. & Rudd 16-year-old, Plantation 2003 and Elements 8 Gold.
(Images courtesy of Berry Bros. & Rudd, Planteray and Elements 8)

Label for Ron D'Oro, Hamilton 2005 and La Belle Creole Orange Bliss.
(Images courtesy St. Lucia Distillers and Ed Hamilton)

CHAPTER 11

Saint Lucian Rum

Since the first recorded rum distillery of Saint Lucia in 1763, rum production has been a tie into the larger scale of sugar cultivation, although perhaps a more primitive form as the standard seen around the world today. From harvesting the cane, to grinding the juice out, boiling the cane juice to thicken, skimming of the scum and mixing with molasses, distilling it twice and making a high strength rum at the end (See *Chapter 2: The Arrival of the Sucrérie* for more detail of the early practice), the palates of the 1800's were no doubt rough and ready. Despite this, there was no shortage of requests for rum from Saint Lucia, with plenty of countries and territories across the world importing the island's rum for over 200 years from this small part of the Caribbean. It hasn't though, all been the huge success that other colonies surrounding Saint Lucia revelled in.

Although there is no record of the number of rum distilleries actively producing from the late 1700's and first half of the 1800's, the Colony Reports that started in 1828 start to offer a glimpse of the volume of rums exported to the likes of Great Britain, West Indies, North American British Colonies, United States and other 'Foreign States'. In the early records, the liquid unit of puncheon was the common sight, with one puncheon equalling 70-120 gallons. The numbers show in 1828 that 304 puncheons were exported, dipping slightly a year later to 274 puncheons before rising again in 1831 to 421 puncheons. It dips dramatically to just 57 puncheons in 1834, before rising and steadying to around 120 puncheons from 1839 to 1841. Yet again though, another dramatic dip to 67 puncheons in 1842, and further still to 21 puncheons just a year later. By 1844 though, a considerable rise to 1,121 puncheons was recorded as we then headed into the more common use of British imperial gallons as the unit of choice (equivalent to 4.54609 litres). From a high of 43,418 gallons in 1847 to a low of 840 gallons in 1850, the inconsistency of rum exports was a telling sign of the competition Saint Lucia faced against fellow colonies such as Jamaica and Barbados, as well as the wider islands economy and political affairs.

In 1851, despite their being 10 rum distilleries recorded, only 958 gallons of rum were exported (several of the working distilleries were not mentioned in the years surrounding 1851 within the Colony Records, perhaps showing what little importance it was given in these yearly reports). Rum exports grew to 38,848 gallons by 1855, although dropped by half to 16,148 gallons by 1859. Come 1860, the records start to show the individual countries that Saint Lucia exported rum to, including the Swedish West Indies (Saint Barthélemy) in 1860 (465 gallons), Danish West Indies (islands of Saint Thomas, Saint John and Saint Croix) in 1861 and 1873 (480 gallons and 126 gallons respectively) and Barbados in 1873 (400 gallons – which was just under half of the total export volume of 881 gallons for that year). A consistent presence from 1823 to 1880 was the export of rum to Great Britain, regularly sourced as the country bringing in the highest quantities of rum from Saint Lucia.

By 1885, rum distilleries were mentioned once again, recording 8 active rum stills and exporting 22,166 gallons, rising to 9 just a year later (despite only exporting 2,426 gallons) but declining to 7 by 1889 (with a huge drop to just 355 gallons exported despite 62,351 gallons being produced). Around this time, France became the biggest market for Saint Lucian rum, taking considerably higher quantities than most other territories from 1885 to 1914. With the available figures from 1896 to 1938, the quantities of rum made at the distilleries across Saint Lucia can now paint a picture of the inconsistency that export levels have faced as the years roll towards through to the early 1900's. The number of rum distilleries rose to 8 in 1890, but then a steady decline to just 1 rum distillery by 1901 (within the Cul de Sac Estate) that saw export figures hover around the 13,000-gallon mark, despite production levels of 85,712 gallons (1901) and 89,362 gallons (1902). The lone Cul de Sac distillery showed its impact in the export numbers though as it declined from 22,838 gallons in 1901 to just 3,623 gallons by 1907 (with the United Kingdom taking only 8 gallons that year despite a total rum production of 57,213 gallons).

Although a steady rise from 1,280½ gallons produced in 1896 to a peak of 71,419 gallons in 1909 (alongside an improvement in export figures to 27,883 gallons in the same year), it lowers itself to 46,131 gallons just one year later. Despite a rise in 1911 to 62,471 gallons, it decreases over the next three years to 48,259 gallons in 1915, despite the large export growth to 39,054 gallons of rum in 1912. During World War One in 1917, rum production had hit a level of 63,213 gallons, which considering there were only two rum distilleries between 1902 and 1916 (Troumassee alongside Cul de Sac), is a relatively small return as the sugarcane estates turned to other agricultural practices. The level of export dropped during the war too, from 18,014 gallons in 1916 to just 477 gallons a year later (the full amount only going to Dominica). Troumassee Distillery closed in September 1917 but re-opened in 1921, joining Vieux Fort and Beauchamp in bringing the number of distilleries to 4 as it settled around the 50-55,000-gallon mark from 1920 to 1924. By 1927, there was a dramatic drop in production from 34,161 gallons the year prior to just 1,700 gallons, with it holding steady until a rise to 29,918 gallons in 1930. On the export side though, lows of 361 gallons (1922), 63 gallons (1925) and 37 gallons (1926) – with the latter two years only going to Ships' Stores (named as such to describe the supplies and equipment required for the operation and upkeep of a ship), saw the market in disarray for rum, until a rise to 2,013 gallons in 1929 thanks to the United Kingdom and its re-interest in importing Saint Lucian rum regaining ground since 1927.

The introduction of Dennery and their rum distillery did not seem to see a rise in production as it steadied around the 30,0000 gallons mark until the records stopped by 1933. Unfortunately, the Colony Records also lack any export numbers for rum between 1931 and 1935, which during the same time frame, Beauchamp distillery had vanished (1931). Although it's worth mentioning that within the Colony Report 1935, it states that there was difficulty in disposing of the factory molasses, with only a proportion being used for the manufacture of rum for local use. It looks that it wasn't worth recording compared to the grander crops being produced at that time. It's worth noting also that between 1931 and 1935, although no records of export were made, re-export of rum from other colonies were mentioned (although of little value) via the Ships' Stores. Export records came back in 1936 with

4,091 gallons recorded, rising to 10,251 gallons by 1938. Unfortunately, the Colony Reports were discontinued at the end the year until its re-introduction in 1948. In the meantime, Vieux Fort distillery closed its doors by 1944, although a year later the Roseau Estate started producing rum and continues to do so under *St. Lucia Distillers Ltd*, despite the closure of distilleries at Cul de Sac in 1960 and Dennery in 1972. The Colony Report of 1947 recorded an export quantity of 13,431 gallons, although with no record of the country it went to. Unfortunately, once again there were no export opportunities for rum between 1948 and 1960, although it did have one last run with 22,709 gallons in 1961 and 15,578 gallons in 1962.

Despite the cease in sugar production by 1963 across Saint Lucia, the Roseau Estate continued to produce rum using molasses imported from Barbados, and with the formation of *St. Lucia Distillers Ltd* in 1972, rum production is still very much a focus. With only a Column Still to hand and a small warehouse to age within, the Roseau Estate was a far cry from the historic production methods and output and acreage of the lands from the 1700's. But as we move into the 21st century, and with technological advances seeing much improvement of rum quality, embracement of further stills, the re-introduction of sugarcane to Saint Lucia and a wider use of barrel types amongst other integral cogs in the rum making wheel, Saint Lucia re-positioned itself as one of the world's most respected rum producers.

The methods and equipment of a rum distillery

The following offers an insight into the equipment and methods used to produce rum from sugarcane at *St. Lucia Distillers Ltd*, with much of the basic core practices and methods you'll notice to have been unchanged over the last 200 years.

Water Source:

St. Lucia Distillers Ltd uses two water sources. The first is the nearby Roseau River, and the second of harvested rainwater that's collected in various places around the distillery grounds, such as the roofs of the facility buildings. A backup option is available - a reserve pond owned by the Ministry of Agriculture if rainfall is insufficient. The water sourced from the Roseau River is used primarily for fermentation and equipment cooling and is pumped from the Beru pond that has the collected Roseau River water (which can hold approximately 50 million gallons), just 1.5 miles east of the distillery. The harvested rainwater is stored in tanks that can hold 75,000 imperial gallons, with an approximate annual collection of 3.5 million gallons. The rainwater is treated in the RO plant (the water is filtered and undergoes a reverse osmosis) and is used primarily for blending the rums. The water in Saint Lucia is known to be very soft due to the basalt and lack of limestone within the rock structure of the island.

Sugarcane and Molasses:

The Roseau Valley is predominantly agriculturally driven towards bananas; however, Laurie Barnard oversaw the re-introduction of sugarcane to Saint Lucia in 2009, starting with cultivating just 5 acres of land within the distillery grounds. Since then, a high of 15 acres of land have been resown to produce sugarcane, starting out originally with four varieties of such, but now concentrating on only two (green cane and blue cane) which were sourced from the West Indies Breeding Station in Barbados. During the once-a-year cane harvest, all stalks are cut by hand instead of machine, then crushed on-site together using a 2-roller mill. Approximately 60% of the mix is green cane, whilst 40% is blue cane with the extracted cane juice put into small fermentation tanks. The fields yield 7-9% of juice overall, from 28 metric tons per acre. This produces a yield of 12,000 litres of cane juice, and 4,000 LPA (Litre of Pure Alcohol).

Imported molasses has been the primary raw material used to produce rum since the merger in 1972, sourced originally and predominantly from Guyana in South America. Since 2018 though, high grade molasses is now imported from Dominican Republic and Central America (primarily Panama) via a tanker that can hold 2,000-2,500 metric tonnes. This tanker pumps offshore from the Roseau Bay via an underwater 8-inch marine hose that's connected to a 12-inch, one-mile-long pipeline. The pipe runs parallel to the Roseau River to the distillery, straight into the 6 molasses tanks. Originally there were four tanks able to hold 600 metric tons each, but with an additional two in recent times, the total now hits 5,300 metric tons, creating enough molasses supply to last one year. The brix level of the molasses is around 85, which is brought down to around 20 via dilution prior to fermentation.

Energy:

Steam requirements are met via three boilers, powered by recycled ship oil, resulting in a substantial saving from the usual purchase of diesel.

Fermentation:

Two cultured yeast strains are used; a commercial strain (Yeast A) creates the purist spirit possible and is used for Coffey Column Still rums that are generally not for ageing. The other strain (Yeast B) is a Caribbean yeast cultured from the natural yeast found near the base of the sugarcane. This creates a high-level of congeners, making rums full of flavour for ageing. It's worth noting that only one yeast strain is used per run of rum, as Yeast B would overpower Yeast A if they were ever combined. *St. Lucia Distillers Ltd* use a semi-continuous batch fermentation process, with the yeast propagated within a 500 imperial gallon tank, although it is filled to 300 imperial gallons with wash (a molasses/water mix) and Yeast A is added. Once the propagator has sufficient yeast cells, it is transferred into a larger vessel (named the Mother Vessel). There are two of such, each holding 50,000 litres. Once one of the Mother Vessels reaches 80% capacity, a continual feed of the wash heads to the eight open air concrete fermenters. The discharge of the wash goes into the fermenters with the yeast that has grown into it (a cell count of 250 million per ml), which is sufficient to start the fermentation and ferment the sugars within the molasses. All of this happens within the first 24 hours of production, whilst the next stage of fermentation can take 24-36 hours overall. The 8 open fermentation tanks have a capacity each of 15,000 litres and are kept at a temperature of 32°C (90°F) courtesy of a heat exchanger. Once fermentation is complete, the mildly alcoholic wash (around 7% abv) is rested so further natural flavours can develop (for example natural bacteria and ester formation), with lighter rums rested for shorter periods than aged rums.

If the fermentation process involves sugar cane juice, it involves a combination of ambient, wild yeast and commercial yeast.

Stills:

Before the commissioning of the John Dore 1 Pot Still, there was a pot still in use by *Geest Industries Ltd* at the Roseau Estate, but by 1972 it had been given away with the concentration focused on the Coffey Column Still. It wasn't until Mount Gay Rum from Barbados and their use of the pot still produced a popular flavour style that Laurie Barnard saw the opportunity to bring a Saint Lucian stamp to such an offering.

John Dore 1 Pot Still: A 450-litre double-retort pot still made by the John Dore company in 1998. With a capacity of 100 imperial gallons (454 litres), it can produce 25,457 LAA (Litres of Absolute Alcohol) per year, at around 85 to 87% abv. The two connecting retorts result in a middle cut (heart) of just 30-40 litres of 88% abv high-ester rum.

The fermented wash enters the pot and is heated up to 80°C. The resulting vapours enter the swan's neck and into the first retort, mixing with pre-charged liquid from previous batches. The resulting increase (approximately 40-60% abv) in alcohol concentration moves into the second retort. Once it leaves the second retort, with an abv between 85-87%, it is transferred to the spirit safe, and the distiller will release the foreshots (heads) of the run. The distilled spirit has a lot of oils and esters within, so the heads are sent to the low-wines tank. Once finished, the middle cut (or heart) is collected. Once the distiller reaches 85% abv, the run switches to the high-wine tank. Anything below 60% abv will go into the low-wine tank. Once complete, the pot is re-charged with fresh wash, whilst the low-wine tank is used to re-charge the first retort, and the high-wine tank the second retort. Overall, one run of the John Dore 1 Pot Still produces around 30-40 litres, from around 4.5-5 hours distillation whilst a typical day can see 6 to 7 batches created. The John Dore 1 Pot Still is primarily used for aged products, and for the distillation of sugar cane and molasses, with each offering a different profile during its run.

Molasses Distillate: Sweet, coconut, brown sugar, green apples, grapefruit, lime, spice.

Sugar Cane Distillate: Sweet, grassy, green apples, brown sugar, honeycomb, marshmallow, blackcurrant.

John Dore 2 Pot Still: Another double-retort pot still, although larger than the John Dore 1 Pot Still at 6,000 litres. Commissioned in 2005, the John Dore 2 Pot Still produces 168,000 LAA annually, and performs the same task as the John Dore 1 Pot Still but can produce 13 times the capacity. Its primary use is for aged rum and the distillation of molasses, resulting in an abv between 85-87%.

Molasses Distillate: Sweet, coconut, brown sugar, ripe apple, orange, banana.

Vendôme Pot Still: A hybrid still of a pot still with an attached nine-plate rectifying column neck at the top; it began operation in February of 2003 after being purchased from *Trinidad Distillers Ltd* (a shareholder of *St. Lucia Distillers Ltd* at the time). It has a capacity of 1,364 litres and produces 20,360 LAA annually. Due to its short rectifying column, it can recycle condensed rum back around, producing a slightly lighter rum than the two John Dore Pot Stills. However, a distillate run takes longer due to the vapours leaving the neck and condenser, heading back to the top and falling onto the top plate. The more volatile congeners will rise and go back into the condenser, with the heavy congeners sinking back to the pot. It can take 6 hours to produce one batch of 60-70 litres. Much like the John Dore 1 Pot Still, the Vendôme Pot Still can be used to produce both molasses and sugar cane distillates, both at 85-87% abv.

Distillate: Sweet, brown sugar, green apple, orange, lime, papaya.

McMillan Ltd Coffey Column Still: A twin column still, commissioned in 1985 and made in Prestonpans, Scotland. It has a 45-plate rectification column and has an annual capacity of 1 million LAA, with a daily output of 4,500 LAA. Three distillates are extracted at between 93-95% abv from different plates of the rectifier column, with lighter spirits (designated as RS 201, or Roseau Spirit 201) taken from a high plate (number 40) that are used for blending lighter rums such as 'Bounty' and 'Denros'. The medium style rum is collected from plate 32 (designated as RS 203), while the heavy rum style is collected

117

from plate 30 (designated as RS 204). Both plates are used for aged rums such as 'Admiral Rodney' and 'Chairman's Reserve'. The McMillan Ltd Coffey Column Still replaced the previous Column Still used from (approximately) 1972 to 1985.

Aging:

Originally, the primary aging warehouse was housed within the main distillery building, able to hold a few hundred barrels, but in June 2021, two new warehouses were opened to increase production, each able to hold 3,500 barrels over 8 levels. The distilled rums typically enter the cask at around 63% abv, with an evaporation rate, or angels share, of 7% for the first year and then down to 5 to 6% per year thereafter. *St. Lucia Distillers Ltd* top up the barrels every two to three years to battle the angels where appropriate. It's also worth noting that certain bottlings of 'Chairman's Reserve' re-enter casks at 60% abv for a second ageing period. At the time of print, the oldest rums maturing in the warehouses are from 1999, from the John Dore 1 Pot Still, and in ex-bourbon casks. The primary use of ex-bourbon barrels (American white oak) is key at *St. Lucia Distillers Ltd* to produce all the rum brands associated with them, however experiments with European oak (Port), Red and White Wine casks and Brandy can be found.

Blending:

St. Lucia Distillers Ltd is known as a blending company, moving away from stating single maturation ages on the front of their rum bottles as seen with other rum and aged spirit producers. The blending hall within the distillery grounds holds tanks up to 10,000 gallons in capacity and can contain a variety of matured rums depending on the endgame of rums required to be produced. The widely accepted use of caramel colouring is also added if required to offer consistency between batches (this by no means affects the flavour of the rum in question).

Quality Assurance:

A range of tools are used to control and improve the quality of all products produced at *St. Lucia Distillers Ltd.* Tests include pH levels, alcohol concentration and chemistry of liquid levels (levels of congeners for example) amongst other tests.

CHAPTER 12

The Rums Brands of Saint Lucia

With the formation of *St. Lucia Distillers Ltd* at the Roseau Estate in 1972, rum production moved from bulk to own brand, with the Denros Bounty Rum becoming the first to be released in 1973. This Chapter looks at the brands in more detail, with much of the information gained from first-hand interviews with both current and past members of production and management staff at *St. Lucia Distillers Ltd.* Below lists a comprehensive look into the releases under the name of *St. Lucia Distillers Ltd* - a note though that some blends of bottlings have adapted over the years (and mentioned where possible), as well as the loss of records due to the fire in 2007 and may be incomplete. With that, the information is correct at time of going to print.

Denros Bounty Rum:

The year 1973 saw Denros Bounty Rum hit the shelves of the local stores in Saint Lucia with two expressions: Denros Bounty White Rum and Denros Bounty Gold Rum. A molasses driven, unaged rum from the distilleries Coffey Column Still, with the Denros Bounty Gold Rum being presented with added caramel colouring. Over the proceeding years, the brand evolved into an aged product whilst also reducing the name 'Denros' from the label. With that, the Denros Bounty White Rum became known as Crystal White Rum, whilst Denros Bounty Gold Rum became Bounty Gold Rum.

Denros as a name, is an amalgamation of *'Dennery'* and *'Roseau'*, and the act of bringing the last two rum estates on the island together.

Denros Strong Rum:

Denros Strong Rum is an unaged rum produced from the Coffey Column Still and delivered at a mighty 80% abv. A staunch favourite among rum drinkers in Saint Lucia, its primary use is within punches or drunk straight by the more adventurous. A surprisingly versatile rum with delicate flavours, Denros Strong Rum is seen as one of the best for high proof rums available on the market.

Bounty Rum:

After its move towards being named Bounty Gold Rum, the brand focused itself as the 'Spirit of Saint Lucia', presenting the brand alongside key dates in the Saint Lucia calendar such as the Saint Lucia Carnival. It captures and conveys the island's most dynamic and festive qualities, which stem from the island's traditional and cultural roots. Bounty Rum is the island's number one selling rum, and is presented as such upon billboards, posters and murals on many of Saint Lucia's bars and highways.

In 2018, Bounty Gold Rum was joined as part of a revamp of the Bounty Rum brand with several single named brands, produced by *St. Lucia Distillers Ltd* since 1972, that transitioned themselves under the 'Bounty Rum' banner. These included.

- **Crystal White Rum**, a 100% Coffey Column Still, aged for 2 years in ex-American oak barrels and carbon filtered. Presented at 40% abv, although now labelled as Bounty White Rum.

- **Crystal Lime Rum Liqueur**, a natural citrus flavoured 100% Coffey Column Still rum and launched in 2005 to offer an alternative to the growing trend towards BACARDÍ Limón. Now re-labelled as Bounty Lime Rum Liqueur with a new lower abv (25%) to its original 35% abv. It's also worth noting that the recipe changed to facilitate the growth of Bounty Lime Rum Liqueur into new territories, going from 70g of sugar per litre to just over 100g (In the EU and the

UK, to be classed as a liqueur, it requires a minimum of 100g of sugar per litre).

- **Kwèyòl Spice Rum**, produced as part of the islands Creole heritage and aimed mainly for the export market, it combined local spices including nutmeg, cinnamon and vanilla to a 100% Coffey Column Still, two-year aged rum, presented at 35% abv. The bottle also contained a vanilla pod. Now re-labelled as Bounty Spice Rum, minus the vanilla pod within the bottle.

The re-brand also brought a newly produced rum of Bounty Dark Rum into the mix. With the new approach and identity, 'Bounty Rum' launched internationally for the first time in 2018, hitting the UK at Notting Hill Carnival alongside 15 states of the United States. Following this, Bounty Sorrel Rum Liqueur was released for the festive period of 2019 (and annually since), alongside Bounty Strong 151 in late 2022.

- **Bounty White Rum**, a 100% Coffey Column Still, molasses-based rum, aged 2 to 3 years in ex-bourbon casks and presented at 40% abv. The wood colours are filtered after blending.
Tasting notes include zesty, clean aromas with fresh tropical citrus on the nose. The opening on the palate offers some sweetness, which gives way to a mellow citrus character on the finish.

- **Bounty Gold Rum**, a 100% Coffey Column Still, molasses-based rum, aged 2 to 3 years in ex-bourbon casks and presented at 40% abv. This is a different blend to the Bounty White Rum.
The palate offers a soft, rich raisin fruit, with a hint of honey and vanilla spice. A medium-bodied palate, with ripe sultana fruit, vanilla from the oak, and a hint of spice. The finish brings a good balance, clean, with an enjoyable finish.

- **Bounty Dark Rum,** a blend of Coffey Column Still, molasses-based rum, aged 2-5 years in ex-bourbon casks, with Vendôme Pot Still, molasses-based rum, aged 3-4 years in ex-bourbon casks. Once blended, Bounty Dark Rum is presented at 43% abv.
Offering a round and complex nose, with a taste of caramel, clove and chocolate alongside cinnamon and tobacco. The addition of the pot still rum brings a rich, spicy finish with subtle coconut and caramel notes.

- **Bounty Spiced Rum**, a 100% Coffey Column Still, molasses-based rum, aged 2 to 3 years in ex-bourbon casks and presented at 40% abv. Involves a fresh infusion of vanilla and cinnamon, with macerated *Richeria Grandis* bark, locally known as '*Bois Bandé*'.
Sweet spice on the nose with vanilla, nutmeg and cinnamon. Ripe honeyed raising fruit with an explosion of vanilla and nutmeg on the palate.

- **Bounty Coconut Rum Liqueur**, a 100% Coffey Column Still, unaged molasses-based rum with macerated coconut extracts and cane syrup included with dilution using distilled water. Presented at 25% abv.
Offers a refreshing smooth mouth feel with warm luscious coconut and fresh tropical fruit flavours.

- **Bounty Sorrel Rum Liqueur**, a 100% Coffey Column Still, unaged molasses-based rum with macerated local flowers of the Roselle Shrubs, commonly known as Sorrel, as well as fresh cinnamon, nutmeg and clove before dilution with distilled water and sugar and presented at 25% abv.

- **Bounty Lime Rum Liqueur,** a 100% Coffey Column Still, unaged molasses-based rum with macerated citrus extracts and cane syrup included with dilution using distilled water. Presented at 25% abv.
Offers a refreshing smooth mouth feel with explosions of zesty lime citrus and tropical floral aromas.

- **Bounty Strong 151 Rum**, a 100% Coffey Column Still blend of molasses-based rums. The blend consists of fresh Coffey Column Still rum of 93.5% abv, proofed down with a 65% abv, 3-year-old aged Coffey Column Still rum.
  Waves of toasted marshmallow on the nose, alongside warm vanilla bean and prune. A palate of dry and savoury yellow fruit, saffron, fresh cinnamon bark and burnt citrus, leading to a touch of honeysuckle sweetness on the finish.

Admiral Rodney Rum:

Coffey Stills are a more modern and efficient approach to rum production. These tall, continuous distillation towers enable a higher volume of rum to be produced consistently but perhaps lack the 'impact' that the traditional Pot Still would offer, especially from neighbouring countries to Saint Lucia such as Jamaica, Guyana and Barbados. With *St. Lucia Distillers Ltd* starting life out with a Coffey Column Still, Admiral Rodney Rum was trademarked and launched in 1981 to show off that despite using a Coffey Column Still, it can produce a rum that can extract the impactful flavours of the ex-bourbon barrels available to them whilst retaining the body of concentration delivered by the Coffey Column Still. The brand was relaunched in 2002 with new packaging.

- **Admiral Rodney Extra Old Rum**, a 100% Coffey Column Still blend of molasses-based rums. Aged separately in ex-American oak casks, then blended and bottled at 40% abv, offering an average blend age of 10 to 12 years.
  An incredibly attractive nose packed with complexity. Rich honeyed fruit with prunes, sweet raisins and well-integrated oak toast. On the palate concentrated, complex with velvety caramel crème brûlée and hints of vanilla, spice and chocolate from long ageing. Well balanced and harmonious with an exceptionally long finish.
  In 2009, it won Gold at the International Wine & Spirits Competition in London, Gold at the World Spirits Competition in Germany and the Rum Trophy at the International Spirits Challenge.

With a 2009 launch into the UK, Admiral Rodney Rum became the known in the rum community as a great example of aged column still rums, and was no surprise when in 2018, the introduction of two new expressions expanded the Admiral Rodney Rum range ahead of a further international launch. Alongside a subtle label revamp to the existing Admiral Rodney Extra Old Rum bottle, *St. Lucia Distillers Ltd* also started the release of a line of limited-edition bottlings, named the *Officer's Releases*, as well as producing a bottling for the Danish market.

- **Admiral Rodney HMS Princessa Rum,** two 100% Coffey Column Still, molasses-based rums pulled off the middle and lower sections of the still which results in a robust and complex flavour profile. Aged separately from 5 to 7 years in ex-bourbon casks, then aged separately in ex-Ruby Port casks before being blended and presented at 40% abv.
  Honeyed raisins on the nose, vanilla and tobacco. Sweet with intense brown sugar, crème brûlée and balanced by dry toasty oak. Complex finish with caramel, and tropical spice.

- **Admiral Rodney HMS Royal Oak Rum**, a 100% Coffey Column Still, molasses-based rum pulled off the middle section of the still, offering a 6 to 12-year-old rum that has been aged in ex-bourbon casks, blended and presented at 40% abv.
  A nose of prunes, raisin fruit, toasty oak and tropical spices. Intense mouthfeel of sweet sultana fruit, tobacco and chocolate, with vanilla from the oak that leads to a complex finish with sweet fruit, caramel and spice.

- **Admiral Rodney HMS Formidable Rum**, a 100% Coffey Column Still, molasses-based rum that contains rums pulled from the lowest portion of the still, resulting in a much heavier and more flavourful rum. These rums are then aged from 10 to 15 years in ex-bourbon casks, blended and presented at 40% abv.
  A honeyed aroma with raisin fruit, spices and vanilla. Complex palate of luscious, sweet sultana fruit and balancing toasty oak, leading to a long finish.

-   **Admiral Rodney HMS Monarch Rum**, two 100% Coffey Column Still, molasses-based rums pulled off the middle and lower sections of the still which results in a robust and complex flavour profile. Aged separately from 5 to 7 years in ex-bourbon casks, then aged separately in ex-Ruby Port casks before being blended and presented at 40% abv. Made originally for the Danish market, the rum also includes just under 20g of sugar per litre.
    Notes of raisins and vanilla and small touches of red berries. Soft and sweet with pleasant brownie, confectionery and candied fruit before a long aftertaste steals the show with hints of oak and tropical spices.

-   **Admiral Rodney Officer's Release No.1 Rum,** a 100% Coffey Column Still, molasses-based rum that contains rums pulled from the lowest plate that results in a balance of aromas, which intensify and become more complex during aging. The rum was placed into ex-bourbon casks in 2006 and rested for 13 years, followed by a finishing period in ex-Ruby Port barrels (themselves a 13-year-old version) for 9 months and presented at 45% abv.
    The rum displays a nose of an exotic combination of rich honeyed raisins, sultanas, spicy vanilla and toasted oak. The palate is intense with initial sweet, honeyed fruit, chocolate, liquorice and tobacco. The well-integrated oak gives definition and balance to a dry complex finish of candied fruit and spices.
    Only 4,200 bottles were produced.

-   **Admiral Rodney Officer's Release No.2 Rum,** a 100% Coffey Column Still, molasses-based rum that contains rums pulled from the bottom plates. These distillates have the balance of flavours which enable a long maturation period to provide intensity and complexity. The rum was placed into ex-bourbon casks in 2009 and rested for 12 years, followed by a finishing period in ex-Irish Whiskey barrels (in partnership with *Walsh Whiskey*) for 9 months and presented at 45% abv.
    The rum displays an intense nose of honeyed raisin, candied

fruits and toasty liquorice oak with a hint of toffee. On the palate, sweet tropical fruits give way to spicy vanilla-tobacco intensity and a definite hint of peaty earthiness from the Irish whiskey cask. Wonderfully balanced and complex. Only 5,000 bottles were produced.

Admiral Rodney Rum was named after Admiral George Brydges Rodney, 1st Baron Rodney (13th February 1718 – 24th May 1792), who famously 'broke the line' and vanquished the French fleet at the Battle of the Saints in 1782 (see *Chapter 3: The Growth of Labour*).

Chairman's Reserve Rum:

Following the commissioning of the John Dore Pot Still (now named John Dore 1) in 1998, the vision of Laurie Barnard to introduce *St. Lucia Distillers Ltd* first foray into pot still rums came to fruition with the launch of Chairman's Reserve Rum in 1999 into Saint Lucia (with credit to Barry Hart who worked in the sales and marketing department at the time and came up with the name). By 2nd November 2001, Chairman's Reserve Rum was trademarked and able to be presented internationally (at this time, you could sell in Saint Lucia without a registration), hitting the shores of the UK on 10th July 2008 for example.

Multiple bottlings have been released since 1999, starting with Chairman's Reserve Original Rum and leading to a range that has brought eyes from around the world towards *St. Lucia Distillers Ltd* and their craftmanship, winning multiple awards along the way.

- **Chairman's Reserve White Label Rum**, a blend of molasses-based rums that contains an unaged rum from the Coffey Column Still, a rum aged 2 to 3 years in ex-bourbon casks from the Coffey Column Still, and a rum aged 2 to 3 years in ex-bourbon casks from the John Dore 2 Pot Still. All three components are blended (bringing 8 to 9% of the final blend as aged rum) and charcoal filtered to remove colour before being presented at 40% abv.
  Offers a clean, refreshing citrus nose, with hints of raisings and confectionary sugar. Opens dry on the palate, but

finished with notes of cream, zesty citrus and fresh lime towards a structured finish.

Previously, the original launch of Chairman's Reserve White Label Rum (entering the local market around 2008) saw 5 different Coffey Column Still rums in the blend, all from different plates that added to the complexity of the finished blend. An aged rum of 3 years from within ex-bourbon casks, the colour it picked up as part of the ageing process was very gently filtered out to leave behind as much aged rum character as possible. This bottling was also presented at 40% abv.

An interesting note to this is that Chairman's Reserve White Label was originally a request from the US market to have a bottling from Chairman's Reserve that could compete on the market against brands such as Bacardí. This was named Chairman's Reserve Silver, until further markets requested a name change to its current iteration.

The second iteration of the Chairman's Reserve White Label Rum saw it become a blend of 3 to 4-year-old rums from both the Coffey Column Still as well as the John Dore 2 Pot Still, once again aged in ex-bourbon casks but this time presented at 43% abv. This version became discontinued in 2023.

- **Chairman's Reserve Original Rum,** a blend of molasses-based rums that contains a rum aged 3 to 4 years in ex-bourbon casks from the Coffey Column Still and its middle plate, a rum aged 3 to 4 years in ex-bourbon casks from the Coffey Column Still and its lower plate, and a rum aged 3 to 4 years in ex-bourbon casks from the John Dore 2 Pot Still. All three components are blended and re-introduced to casks for a further 6 months before being presented at 40% abv as an average of 4 to 5 years old.

Offers cooked banana, caramelised fruits and spicy oak derived vanilla on the nose, with a well-balanced mid-palate of chocolate, golden raisin, tobacco and clove, which dissipates over a long creamy finish.

There have also been 3 label changes over the 15 years until 2024. The Chairman's Reserve Original Rum has also seen two limited edition bottle wraps released, highlighting Saint Lucia's art and conservation efforts. The first was created by Saint Lucian artist Llewellyn Xavier and released in 2018 under the theme of 'Celebrating our Caribbean Passions'. The second was released as Eco Series No.1, presented with art by Daniel Jean-Baptiste that highlights the rare Saint Lucian Parrot (*Amazona versicolor*). To help the conservation, EC$5.00 of every bottle of this edition is donated to the study and protection of the species.

- **Chairman's Reserve Spiced Rum**, a blend of molasses-based rums that contains a rum aged 2 to 3 years in ex-bourbon casks from the Coffey Column Still, and an unaged rum from the Coffey Column Still that has been blended with syrup, local spices and fruits for 3 to 5 weeks in tanks. Both components are then blended before being presented at 40% abv as an average of 2 to 3 years old. The spices include cinnamon, nutmeg, vanilla and cloves, alongside *Bois Bandé* bark and the fruits of orange, lemon, almond, raisin and coconut.
Offers an expressive aroma of bitter orange, nutmeg, cinnamon and sweet raisin. A rich mouthfeel bursting with exotic spices and balanced with a crisp citrus character.

- **Chairman's Reserve Legacy Rum**, a blend of molasses-based and sugar cane juice rums that contains a molasses rum aged 5-6 years in ex-bourbon casks from the lower plate of the Coffey Column Still, a molasses rum aged 5 years in ex-bourbon casks from the middle plate of the Coffey Column Still, a sugar cane juice rum aged 5 years in ex-bourbon casks from the John Dore 1 Pot Still, a molasses rum aged 6 years in ex-bourbon casks from the John Dore 2 Pot Still, and a molasses rum aged 6 years in ex-bourbon casks from the Vendôme Pot Still. All 5 of the rums are then blended before being presented at 43% abv as an average of 5 to 6 years old.

Offers an intense nose of sweet raisins, cigar tobacco, amber honey and vanilla, alongside a warm palate of grilled tropical fruit and candied walnut.

- **Chairman's Reserve The Forgotten Casks Rum,** a blend of molasses-based rums that contains a rum aged 3 to 4 years in ex-bourbon casks from the middle plate of the Coffey Column Still, a rum aged 3 to 4 years in ex-bourbon casks from the lower plate of the Coffey Column Still, and a 3 to 4 years in ex-bourbon casks from the John Dore 2 Pot Still. All 3 of the rums are then blended and re-introduced to cask for 4 to 5 years before being presented at 40% abv as an average of 7 to 9 years old.
Offers an expressive aroma of bitter orange, nutmeg, cinnamon, and sweet raisin. A rich mouthfeel bursting with exotic spices and balanced with crisp citrus character.

This expression was crafted to mimic rum found in the original forgotten casks of Chairman's Reserve, which were preserved from the horrific fire on May 2, 2007, at the Roseau Estate. The cellar master at the time, Andre Winter, was forced to find unusual storage space for his rum barrels during the rehabilitation of the distillery, and these casks were misplaced during this time of confusion. These 'forgotten casks' resulted in a rum which was too old to be released as Chairman's Reserve Original Rum, so it was decided that this rum would be released on its own as a limited-edition run of 2,000 bottles.

- **Chairman's Reserve 1931 Rum,** a blend of molasses-based and sugar cane juice rums that includes a molasses rum aged 6 to 11 years in ex-bourbon casks from the middle plate of the Coffey Column Still, a molasses rum aged 6 to 11 years in ex-bourbon casks from the lower plate of the Coffey Column Still, a molasses rum aged 7 to 8 years in ex-Ruby Port casks from the lower plate of the Coffey Column Still, a sugar cane juice rum aged 7 to 8 years in ex-bourbon casks from the John Dore 1 Pot Still, a molasses rum aged 10 to 11 years in ex-bourbon casks from the John Dore 1 Pot Still, a

molasses rum aged 8 to 9 years in ex-bourbon casks from the John Dore 1 Pot Still, a molasses rum aged 9 to 10 years in ex-bourbon casks from the John Dore 2 Pot Still, and finally a molasses rum aged 6 to 8 years in ex-bourbon casks from the Vendôme Pot Still. All 8 of the rums are then blended before being presented at 46% abv as an average of 6 to 11 years old. 92% of the blend is made up of the molasses-based rums, whilst 8% of the blend is made up of the sugar cane juice rum.
Offers sweet raisins and toasty oak notes on the nose, alongside leather, spice and tobacco. Rich sultana fruit with hints of crème caramel and buttery oak on the long, complex finish.

- **Chairman's Reserve 2005 Vintage Rum**, a blend of molasses-based rums from the John Dore 2 Pot Still and Coffey Column Still. An initial maturation period of 4 years, distillates are aged separately in different casks then blended for an additional 10 years of maturation. Presented at 46% abv with only 3,400 bottles released.
Pleasantly balanced on the nose, oaky and complex with notes of honey, orange, raisin, vanilla, toffee, brown sugar and mild green apple. An initial slight sweetness which quickly dissipates and gives way to oaky raisin notes with hints of vanilla, caramel and toffee, leading towards a mildly tannic centre with a pleasant spicy finish.

- **Chairman's Reserve 2009 Vintage Rum**, a blend of molasses-based rums that contains a rum aged 11 years in ex-bourbon casks from the middle plate of the Coffey Column Still, a rum aged 11 years in ex-bourbon casks from the lower plate of the Coffey Column Still, a rum aged 11 years in ex-bourbon casks from the John Dore 2 Pot Still, a rum aged 11 years in ex-bourbon casks from the Vendôme Pot Still and finally a 50/50 blend of rums from the John Dore 2 Pot Still and Vendôme Pot Still that have been aged for 11 years in ex-bourbon casks. All the rums are then blended and re-introduced to cask for 5 months before being presented at 46% abv as an 11-year-old blend.

Intense honeyed raisin nose with flambeed toffee, banana, vanilla and tobacco tones. A palate that is concentrated and powerful, offering sweet candied tropical, fruits, tobacco and spices. Buttery toasty oak gives structure and depth as well as a smooth and complex finish of smoky leather and dark chocolate.

- **Chairman's Reserve 2011 Vintage Rum,** a blend of molasses-based rums that contains two separate rums aged 11 years in ex-bourbon casks, one from lower plate and one from the middle plate of the Coffey Column Still. It also involves rums aged 11 years in individual ex-brandy casks, again one each from lower plate middle plate of the Coffey Column Still, John Dore 1 Pot Still, John Dore 2 Pot Still and Vendôme Pot Still, rums aged 11 years in individual ex-red wine casks from each of the Coffey Column Still, John Dore 1 Pot Still and Vendôme Pot Still, rums aged 11 years in individual ex-white wine casks from each of the Coffey Column Still and Vendome Pot Still. All rums are then blended to marry for 10 months. Presented at 46.8% abv.

In April 2020, the inaugural Chairman's Reserve Spice Lab competition was launched worldwide, offering bartenders the opportunity to create what they thought could be a worthy partner bottling to Chairman's Reserve Spiced Rum. Using an existing kit of six spices to add to a Chairman's Reserve White Label or Original rum base, they could add up to three additional flavours of their choice, all whilst sharing their journey through a digital marketing plan. Each competitor created their own launch plan, including signature serves, promotional events and activations, while also creating a sample version of their spiced rum idea. Despite the restrictions due to the Covid-19 pandemic, five global finalists were secured and invited to the final in December 2020, hosted online. The jury to determine the winner comprised of Margaret Monplaisir and Deny Duplesis of *St. Lucia Distillers Ltd*, Sly Augustin (bar owner of *Trailer Happiness* in London), François Badel (winner of the Chairman's Reserve Mai Tai International Competition in 2019) and Simon Difford (Editor of *Difford's Guide*). Each judge experienced the five finalists submitted spiced rum and were able to ask one-on-one questions highlighting their ideas, plans and understanding of spiced rum culture in Saint Lucia.

Completing his journey, Zachos Kyritsis from Greece was announced the winner, with the opportunity to head to Saint Lucia and work with Master Blender Deny Duplessis and Saint Lucian bartender and local Spice Lab winner Silas Celestin to create the first edition of the Chairman's Reserve Spice Lab bottling.

- **Chairman's Reserve Spice Lab No.1 Rum,** a blend of molasses-based rums from the Coffey Column Still, one of which is an unaged rum from the higher plate, and one which is from the middle plate and aged for two years in ex-bourbon casks. Presented at 40% abv at an average of 2 years old, the spices include ginger, cinnamon, turmeric, nutmeg and almond.

  The nose offers an expressive hit of candied ginger and almonds, followed by a palette of balanced tropical fruits that lead to a dominating note of nutmeg.

In 2023, the second edition of the Chairman's Reserve Spice Lab competition was launched, utilising the same concept as the first edition, but for this version guaranteeing three winners from the global final. With a judging panel including Margaret Monplaisir and Deny Duplesis once again, previous winners Zachos Kyritsis and Silas Celestin, and author Jeff 'Beachbum' Berry, and once again hosted live online, the three individuals to impress were announced as Dylan John from Saint Lucia, Johnny Morrison of the United Kingdom, and Leonardo Tamayo of Georgia, USA.

- **Chairman's Reserve Spice Lab No.2 Rum,** a blend of molasses-based rums from the Coffey Column Still, one of which is an unaged rum from the higher plate, and one which is from the lower plate and aged for two years in ex-bourbon casks. Presented at 40% abv, the spices and fruits in the final blend chosen include ginger, cinnamon, nutmeg, vanilla, bay leaf, prune and key lime.

  On the nose, bay leaf, honey, and rich brown sugar unfold alongside warm spices like cinnamon, nutmeg, and ginger.

The palate echoes these notes with added brightness from key lime and a smooth touch of toffee. The finish lingers on bay leaf, nutmeg, and a zesty hint of lime.

In 2018, and two years after the acquisition of *St. Lucia Distillers Ltd* by *Groupe Bernard Hayot*, the first official release to a third-party customer of a Chairman's Reserve Rum became a reality, with Martin Cate of Smugglers Cove in San Francisco, USA working in collaboration. This project became the precursor for what is now known as the Chairman's Reserve Master's Selection programme.

- **Chairman's Reserve Single Batch Rum**, made exclusively from the John Dore 1 pot still distillate that has been matured 6 years in a single ex-bourbon cask before bottling at cask strength of 57.4% abv.

In 2019, the Chairman's Reserve Master's Selection programme was officially launched, resulting in the opportunity for bars and liquor stores around the world to pick from a pre-determined list of available barrels from the *St. Lucia Distillers Ltd* warehouses, with each offering a variable in stills used, maturing age and final bottling strength. Although there are many releases under the programme each year, it's hard to bring them all to feature within this book, with names such as *Trailer Happiness* and *Berry Bros. & Rudd*, both in London, *Florida Rum Society*, *Salon du Rhum* of Belgium, Slovakia's *Svet Nápojov* and *Renbjer Fine Spirits* of Sweden taking advantage of the rum programme. To offer a rough guide though the breadth and depth of *St. Lucia Distillers Ltd* inventory of rum, below are some highlights of releases:

- **The Whisky Exchange 2006 13-Year-Old**, a molasses rum offering a 50/50 blend of John Dore 1 Pot Still and Coffey Column Still, aged in an ex-bourbon barrel and presented at 56.3% abv.

- **Master of Malt 2011 9-Year-Old**, a sugar cane juice rum offering a Vendôme Pot Still, aged in an ex-bourbon barrel and presented at 58.8% abv.

- **Harvey Nichols 2003 20-Year-Old**, a molasses rum offering a Vendôme Pot Still, aged for three years in an ex-bourbon barrel and the remaining 17 years laying in a Port Cask, and presented at 55.8% abv.

To celebrate the *Caribbean Community (CARICOM)* 50th anniversary (1973-2023), a limited bottle was presented by Prime Minister of Saint Lucia, Philip J. Pierre, to Mohamed Irfaan Alli, President of Guyana and Chairman of the CARICOM, in February of 2024.

- **Chairman's Reserve CARICOM 50th Anniversary Rum**, a blend of molasses-based rums that contains two separate rums aged 11 years in ex-bourbon casks, one from lower plate and one from the middle plate of the Coffey Column Still. It also involves rums aged 11 years in individual ex-brandy casks, again one each from lower plate middle plate of the Coffey Column Still, John Dore 1 Pot Still, John Dore 2 Pot Still and Vendôme Pot Still, rums aged 11 years in individual ex-red wine casks from each of the Coffey Column Still, John Dore 1 Pot Still and Vendôme Pot Still, rums aged 11 years in individual ex-white wine casks from each of the Coffey Column Still and Vendome Pot Still. All rums are then blended to marry for 6 months. Presented at 50% abv.

Marigot Bay Rum Cream Liqueur:

The range of Marigot Bay Rum Cream Liqueurs have been a staple of Saint Lucia since its launch in November 2009 and were designed to showcase local island flavours. In 2020, the brand became a focus for possible international launch with a new packaging look and repositioning of previously released single-label rum creams. This was the second repositioning of such, after the original Marigot Bay Cream Liqueurs range transitioned away from other rum cream brand names such as Koko-nut Rum and Tropical Lady.
Made using unaged Coffey Column Still rum, real cream and natural flavours, the Marigot Bay Cream Liqueur bottlings have become a staple on many of the bars across the island of Saint Lucia, especially within its namesake of Marigot Bay, the next bay north of the Roseau

Bay and location of *St. Lucia Distillers Ltd.*

The range of Marigot Bay Cream Liqueurs includes:

- **Marigot Bay Spiced Rum Cream**, a blend of unaged Coffey Column Still rum and real cream, with Caribbean spices of nutmeg, cinnamon, vanilla and clove, and presented at 12.5% abv.

- **Marigot Bay Peanut Rum Cream**, a blend of unaged Coffey Column Still rum, roasted peanuts, real cream and Caribbean spices, and presented at 12.5% abv.

- **Marigot Bay Coconut Rum Cream**, a blend of unaged Coffey Column Still rum, coconut cream and real cream, and presented at 12.5% abv.
  The original strength before the re-positioning was 20% abv.

- **Marigot Bay Chocolate Coffee Rum Cream**, a blend of unaged Coffey Column Still rum, dark chocolate, espresso coffee and real cream, and presented at 12.5% abv.

- **Marigot Bay Banana Rum Cream**, a blend of unaged Coffey Column Still rum, ripe banana flavour and real cream, and presented at 12.5% abv.
  The original strength before the re-positioning was 14% abv.

- **Marigot Bay Coconut and Rum**, an unaged Coffey Column Still rum with macerated coconut extracts and cane syrup included with dilution using distilled water. Presented at 25% abv, that offers a clear transparent appearance. Mainly available for the regional Caribbean export markets.

Before 2020, *St. Lucia Distillers Ltd* produced a handful of rum creams for the local market, resulting from the formation *West Indian Liqueur Company (WILCO)* back in 1993, that which are now either adapted into the current Marigot Bay Rum Cream brand as listed above, discontinued flavours of the Marigot Bay brand, or discontinued to make way and streamline the offering of available rum cream liqueurs. These included:

- **Javalatté**, an unaged Coffey Column Still rum launched in November 2005 that blended roasted coffee, cream and milk together, presented at 15% abv and an export bottling of 14% abv. Repackaged as Marigot Bay Chocolate Coffee Rum Cream.

- **Crème La Caye**, a 'home recipe' unaged Coffey Column Still rum cream (traditionally offered during Christmas in Saint Lucia), launched approximately 2009 to 2010. The product had a custard, crème brûlée character with nutmeg and a hint of vanilla. Originally created to rival Ponche Kuba Cream Liqueur (from Barbados) and Ponche Caribe Cream (from Curaçao), but also as an answer to the distillery fire in 2007 that saw the cease of production of cream liqueurs during the re-build. Presented at 11.5% abv, with an export bottling of 15% abv. Repackaged as Marigot Bay Spiced Rum Cream but with a different blend.

- **Nutz' n Rum**, the unaged Coffey Column Still rum cream liqueur brand launched, a unique and award-winning peanut rum cream that was presented at 14% abv, with an export bottling of 15% abv. It blended peanut butter with spices and fresh peanuts. Now labelled as Marigot Bay Peanut Rum Cream with a slight reduction of abv and recipe change.

- **Marigot Bay Chocolate Mint Rum Cream**, an unaged Coffey Column Still rum cream blended with flavours of chocolate and mint, presented at 14% abv.

- **Marigot Bay Chocolate Orange Rum Cream**, an unaged Coffey Column Still rum cream blended with flavours of chocolate and orange, presented at 14% abv.

- **Koko-nut Rum**, an unaged Coffey Column Still rum with macerated coconut extracts and cane syrup included with dilution using distilled water. Transformed into Marigot Bay

Coconut and Rum, then the recipe was used for Bounty Coconut Rum Liqueur, albeit with less sugar used.

- **La Belle Creole Tropical Lady**, an unaged Coffey Column Still rum used to produce a coconut rum cream liqueur, presented at 20% abv. This was also a template towards Marigot Bay Coconut Rum Cream. Discontinued in 2007 after the fire at the distillery.

- **La Belle Creole Orange Bliss**, an unaged Coffey Column Still rum, blended with Caribbean sour orange, sweetened with sugar syrup and presented at 35% abv. Discontinued in 2007 after the fire at the distillery.

- **La Belle Creole Cacao Creole**, an unaged Coffey Column Still rum blended with natural cocoa flavours and presented at 25% abv. Discontinued in 2007 after the fire at the distillery.

- **La Belle Creole Seventh Heaven Ginger and Bois Bandé,** an unaged Coffey Column Still rum used to produce blended with ginger and *Bois Bandé*, presented at 20% abv. Discontinued in 2007 after the fire at the distillery.

- **Ti Tasse Coffee Liqueur**, an unaged Coffey Column Still rum non-cream liqueur, blended with natural coffee flavours and sugar syrup. Presented at 22% abv and phased out approximately in 1998 after the purchase by *Angostura Limited*.

Discontinued Rum Brands:

Since 1972, there have been a handful of brands and bottlings that have been released by *St. Lucia Distillers Ltd*, or under licence to third parties across the world, but now discontinued. By no means is the below a full and comprehensive list but with the thanks of the staff, both current and former, of *St. Lucia Distillers Ltd*, this offers an insight into some recognisable bottlings, and in some cases became milestones in the achievement of *St. Lucia Distillers Ltd* being recognised as one of the rum world's most respected distilleries.

Released by *St. Lucia Distillers Ltd*:

TØZ:

Launched in December 2007, TØZ was designed to appeal to a younger consumer market with the release of two bottlings to UK, France and Italy. TØZ was named after the Troy ounce, the traditional method of measuring precious metals and gems. The brand was phased out around 2010 and 2011.

- **TØZ White Gold Rum**, a molasses rum blend of 85% Coffey Column Still (in which 5% of this was a port cask finish) and 15% combination of pot stills. The latter blend included a John Dore 1 Pot Still aged in ex-bourbon cask that made up 6% and the remainder (9%) was a John Dore 1/ Vendôme Pot Still blended 50/50. This pot still blend was aged in ex-bourbon casks separately for 7 years, then blended and transferred to port casks for final polishing of 6 months. It then underwent a gentle carbon filtration to remove colour and presented at 40% abv.

- **TØZ Gold Rum** was the same rum blend and abv as the TØZ White Gold Rum, minus the carbon filtration.

1931:

In 2011, to celebrate 80 years since Denis Barnard took over the rum distillery at Dennery Estate, the first bottle of '1931' was released that would honour the history of rum making in Saint Lucia. Six bottlings were released overall, each edition offering a different label colour, as well as the blend of rum within. Each bottle is individually numbered and became a collectors' item for connoisseurs of rum, the first such scenario of *St. Lucia Distillers Ltd*. The range has been coined 'Laurie's Playground', due to Laurie Barnard's approach to bringing different ideas together for each release, such as differing bottle strength to the core brands released at that time, blends of the stills available, maturation finishes and use of sugar cane juice. The last release, 1931 6th Edition, in November 2016 signalled the end of the brand (albeit not the end of the legacy as Chairman's Reserve 1931 was released in tribute to this era of creativity), with the use of the more rare and exclusive casks being used towards the Chairman's Reserve Master's Selection programme.

- **1931 1st Edition**, a molasses rum blend of 9 casks containing distillates from the John Dore 1 Pot Still, John Dore 2 Pot Still, Vendôme Pot Still and Coffey Column still, laid down between 1999 and 2004. Of the 9 casks, 7 were ex-bourbon casks and 2 were ex-port casks. The blend was assembled and placed back into ex-bourbon casks for a period of 3 months. A non-chill filtered rum; the final liquid resulted in a blend of rums ranging from seven to twelve years in age. Only 6,000 bottles were bottled on 17th May 2011 and presented at 43% abv.

- **1931 2nd Edition**, a molasses rum blend, the casks selected were put down in 2004, 2005 and 2006. These include casks containing 100% Coffey Column Still distillates matured in a combination of 7 ex-bourbon casks and 2 ex-port casks. In addition, blend also used selected casks that contained 100% Pot Still and 50/50 blends of Pot/Coffey Column Still aged in ex-bourbon casks. The blend was assembled and then placed back into ex-bourbon casks for a period of three months for a final marriage before being chill filtered. Only 6,000 bottles were bottled on 23rd July 2012 and presented at 43% abv.

- **1931 3rd Edition**, a molasses rum blend, involving Coffey Column Still distillates matured for 6 and 11 years and John Dore Pot Still distillates matured for 14 and 15 years. A blend of Vendôme and John Dore Pot Still distillates aged for 10 years, plus a 7-year-old Port Cask Coffey Still distillate and a 7-year-old Port Cask John Dore Pot Still Distillate are used. The distillates were blended and then placed back into ex-bourbon casks for 3 months, then chill filtered. For the first time in the range,12g of sugar per litre was present in this rum. Only 6,000 bottles were bottled on 28th July 2014 and presented at 43% abv.

- **1931 4th Edition**, starting with a molasses rum blend with the Coffey Column Still that contained a rum aged in ex-bourbon casks between 7 and 11 years, and a rum aged within ex-port casks at 9 years old. From the Pot Stills, a 15-year-old rum from John Dore 1 Pot Still, 9-year-old rum from John Dore 2 Pot Still, 10-year-old rum from Vendôme Pot Still and a 9-year-old rum John Dore 1/Vendôme Pot Still blend (50/50 split), all aged in ex-bourbon casks. To finish, a first press sugar cane juice, aged for 6 years in ex-bourbon casks from the John Dore 1 Pot Still. Presented at 43% abv and bottled on 8th December 2014.

- **1931 5th Edition**, first, a blend of Pot Still rums made up from 10-year-old John Dore 2 rum, 10-year-old Vendome rum, a blend of John Dore/Vendôme aged for 10 years, and a John Dore 1 sugar cane juice rum aged for 7 years, all aged in ex-bourbon casks. A Coffey Column Still blend of rums aged for 10 years in ex-bourbon cask, a 9-year-old in ex-bourbon cask, and a 9-year-old rum aged in ex-port casks. Bottled on 7th December 2015 and presented at 46% abv.

- **1931 6th Edition**, a blend of Coffey Column Still rums made up from rums aged for 11 years, 7 years and 10 years, plus a Caroni Trinidad aged for 9 years, all aged in ex-bourbon casks. Part of the blend from the Pot Stills is made up from John Dore 2 (aged for 11 years) and John Dore 1 (aged for 9 years), plus a John Dore 1 sugar cane juice rum aged for 8 years, all aged in ex-bourbon casks. The final part of the overall mix is a Pot/Coffey Column Still Blend, made up of a 7-year-old John Dore/Coffey Column Still blend aged in ex-bourbon casks. Bottled on 14th November 2016 and presented at 46% abv.

Other Bottle Releases by *St. Lucia Distillers Ltd*:

- **1979 Ruby Reserve Rum**, released to celebrate 40 years of Saint Lucia Independence in 2019. The blend of rums involves Coffey Column Still molasses rums that originate first from the middle plate and aged between 7 and 10 years within ex-bourbon casks, as well as the lower plate and aged for between 8 and 9 years in ex-bourbon casks. The Pot Still elements are John Dore 1 molasses rum aged individually for 8 years in ex-bourbon casks and 8 years in Spanish Brandy casks. It also involves John Dore 1 Sugarcane rums aged for 6 & 9 years in ex-bourbon casks. Vendôme Pot Still sugarcane rum aged for 7 years in ex-bourbon casks, a 50/50 blend of molasses-based John Dore 1 Pot Still and Vendôme Pot Still rums and aged for 10 years in ex-bourbon casks, a 50/50 blend of molasses-based John Dore 1 Pot Still rum and middle plate rum from the Coffey Column Still and aged for 12 years in ex-bourbon casks. Overall, the ages of the molasses-based pot still distillates range from 8 to 12 years while the age of the sugar cane rums are 6 to 9 years, with a 49.5% / 50.5% split between Coffey Column Still and John Dore 1 / Vendôme Pot Stills

Only 1,979 bottles were released and presented at 46% abv.

- **Victory '24 Rum**, a blend of molasses-based rums that contains a rum aged 3 to 4 years in ex-bourbon casks from the Coffey Column Still and its middle plate, a rum aged 3 to 4 years in ex-bourbon casks from the Coffey Column Still and its lower plate, and a rum aged 3 to 4 years in ex-bourbon casks from the John Dore 2 Pot Still. All three components are blended and re-introduced to casks for a further 6 months before being presented at 40% abv as an average of 4 to 5 years old.
Originally laid down in mid-2005, the rum was then transferred to an ex-Tawny Port cask in January 2006 and rested for 19 years. Presented at 49.72% abv and released in February 2025 to celebrate Saint Lucia's international

victories in 2024 – including Julien Alfred and her Gold Medal victory at the 2024 Summer Olympics in the 100 metres event.
Only 500 bottles were released.

- **Smuggler's Rum Punch**, an unaged Coffey Column Still rum blended with Caribbean fruit, presented at 15% abv, with an export strength of 20% abv. This was phased out in approximately 1998 after the purchase by *Angostura Limited.*

- **Old Fort Reserve Rum**, a 100% Coffey Column Still blended rum of 6-8 years old, matured in ex-bourbon casks and presented at 40% abv. Launched in 1997, this was discontinued in 2003.

- **Ron D'Oro Rum**, a 100% Coffey Column Still rum introduced in 1993 by *East Caribbean Distillers Ltd* as a result of an agreement with *Duncan, Gilbey & Matheson International Limited* (a London based company). Presented at 43% abv but discontinued since 2002.

- **Buccaneer Rum**, a Coffey Column Still rum presented at 40% abv under the *East Caribbean Distillers Ltd* banner from 1987 and discontinued in 2002.

- **Treasure Bay Caribbean Rum Punch** – unknown recipe and information.

- **Five Blondes**, a Coffey Column Still rum released in the late 1980's and presented at 43% abv under the *East Caribbean Distillers Ltd* banner. Discontinued in the early 1990's.

Bottlings released under 3rd party brand names, with rum produced at *St. Lucia Distillers Ltd*:

A note to consider when reading the following descriptions. Due to the rarity of information, only verified details are stated where possible, predominantly from the brand themselves if they are still active, or from trusted rum sources such as *The Lone Caner*, *The Fat Rum Pirate* and *Rum Diaries*. With that, some details have been left out that would normally be described (such as barrels for maturation). A fickle point of contention is the naming of the correct Pot Still used for the brand and/or bottling. Where possible, a process of elimination was used depending on the year of distillation to the available Pot Stills at *St. Lucia Distillers Ltd* at that time. On occasion, the term 'John Dore Pot Still' or 'Pot Still' has been used if the brand stated as such, but this may not reflect whether this means the use of John Dore 1 Pot Still, John Dore 2 Pot Still, or Vendôme Pot Still.

Elements 8 Rum:

Produced for the *Elements 8 Rum Company* based in the United Kingdom, Elements 8 was positioned by owners Carl Stephenson and Andreas Redlefsen as a premium rum and is the result of eight individual elements - terroir, cane, water, fermentation, distillation, tropical ageing, blending and filtration, and launched in July 2006. The range became discontinued in 2016 after *Groupe Bernard Hayot* made the decision to stop making their bulk rums available for purchase by 3rd parties (although the Elements 8 brand carried on by sourcing rum from other countries). The rums were fermented in three separate batches, using 3 different yeasts, and all were molasses based. According to *Difford's Guide* and their feature on the Elements 8 brand, the three yeast strains were each individually bath fermented to allow it to impart its own flavour to the 'wash', and ultimately the rum. 'Hybrid Distillers Yeast' offered a lightly flavoured rum with sweet and buttery aromas, 'Killer Yeast' made heavier rums with high levels of esters and alcohols, giving fruity and floral aromas, whilst the last strain was cultivated by *St. Lucia Distillers Ltd* and remained a secret towards its attributes.

-   **Elements 8 Platinum Rum,** eight rums aged for 4 years in ex-bourbon casks before blending, carbon filtered and presented at 40% abv.

- **Elements 8 Gold Rum**, later titled **Elements 8 Fine Aged Vendôme**, was a blend of eight Vendôme Pot Still and Coffey Column still rums, aged in ex-bourbon casks for up to 6 years and presented at 40% abv

- **Elements 8 Spiced Rum**, a blend of Vendôme Pot Still and Coffey Column Still rums, aged for 3 years in ex-bourbon casks with cinnamon, ginger, clove, star anise, vanilla, honey, nutmeg, orange, lemon and coconut infused during this period.

- **Elements 8 Barrel Infused Criollo Cacao Rum** was launched in 2013. It infused Saint Lucian Criollo cacao beans into the blend of Vendôme Pot Still and Coffey Column Still distilled molasses rums that were then aged for 3 to 6 years in ex-bourbon casks. The beans were infused in the blend of rums for 3 to 4 weeks before being presented at 40% abv.

Hamilton:

A range of rums, picked by Ed Hamilton of the *Ministry of Rum* in the USA from 2013 until 2016. Each of the Vendôme Pot Still rums in the Ministry of Rum Collection were distilled and aged at *St. Lucia Distillers Ltd*, then shipped to the USA in the barrels in which they were originally matured by Caribbean Spirits Inc.

- **Saint Lucia Pot Still 10-Year-Old Cask Strength Rum 2004**, presented at 65.5% abv. Contained five ex-bourbon casks, blended and all containing Vendôme Pot Still molasses rum.

- **Saint Lucia Pot Still 5-Year-Old Cask Strength Rum**, a single-cask molasses Vendôme Pot Still molasses rum, presented at 59.3% abv.

- **Saint Lucia Pot Still 5-Year-Old Cask Strength Rum 2009,** presented at 59.2% abv. Contained three ex-bourbon casks, blended and all containing Vendôme Pot Still molasses rum.

- **Saint Lucia Pot Still 5-Year-Old Rum 93 proof 2008**, presented at 46.5% abv. Contained four ex-bourbon casks, blended and all containing Vendôme Pot Still molasses rum.

- **Saint Lucia Pot Still 7-Year-Old Cask Strength Rum 2006**, a single-cask Vendome Pot Still molasses rum, presented at 63.8% abv.

- **Saint Lucia Pot Still 7-Year-Old Cask Strength Rum 2007**, presented at 59% abv. Contained five ex-bourbon casks, blended and all containing Vendôme Pot Still molasses rum.

- **Saint Lucia Pot Still 7-Year-Old Cask Strength Rum barrel #565**, a single-cask Vendôme Pot Still molasses rum, presented at 58% abv.

- **Saint Lucia Pot Still 7-Year-Old Cask Strength Rum cask #550**, a single-cask Vendôme Pot Still molasses rum, presented at 60.4% abv.

- **Saint Lucia Pot Still 7-Year-Old Rum 93 proof 2006**, presented at 46.5% abv. Contained five ex-bourbon casks, blended and all containing Vendôme Pot Still molasses rum.

- **Saint Lucia Pot Still 8-Year-Old Cask Strength Rum #278 2006**, a single-cask Vendôme Pot Still molasses rum, presented at 62% abv.

- **Saint Lucia Pot Still 8-Year-Old Cask Strength Rum 2005,** a single-cask Vendôme Pot Still molasses rum, presented at 65.8% abv.

- **Saint Lucia Pot Still 8-Year-Old Cask Strength Rum 2006**, presented at 62.1% abv. Contained six ex-bourbon casks, blended and all containing Vendôme Pot Still molasses rum.

- **Saint Lucia Pot Still 8-Year-Old Cask Strength Rum cask #592 2006**, a single-cask Vendôme Pot Still molasses rum, presented at 62.3% abv.

- **Saint Lucia Pot Still 8-Year-Old Rum 93 proof 2005**, a single-cask Vendôme Pot Still molasses rum, presented at 46.5% abv.

- **Saint Lucia Pot Still 9-Year-Old Cask Strength Rum 2004**, a single-cask Vendôme Pot Still molasses rum, presented at 61.3% abv.

- **Saint Lucia Pot Still 9-Year-Old Cask Strength Rum 2005,** presented at 67.4% abv. Contained seven ex-bourbon casks, blended and all containing Vendôme Pot Still molasses rum.

- **Saint Lucia Pot Still 9-Year-Old Cask Strength Rum cask #40**, a single-cask Vendôme Pot Still molasses rum, presented at 65.7% abv.

- **Saint Lucia Pot Still 9-Year-Old Cask Strength Rum cask #420**, a single-cask Vendôme Pot Still molasses rum, presented at 65% abv.

- **Saint Lucia Pot Still 9-Year-Old Rum 93 proof 2004**, presented at 46.5% abv. Contained three ex-bourbon casks, blended and all containing Vendôme Pot Still molasses rum.

Plantaray:

Plantaray (originally named Plantation) released several bottlings of Saint Lucian rum under their own label, including:

- **2005 Saint Lucia Extreme No.1,** a molasses pot still rum, aged for 11 years (9 years in ex-bourbon casks in Saint Lucia,

2 years Maison Ferrand's ex-cognac casks in Charente, France), and presented at 53.8% abv with only 200 bottles released.

- **2004 St. Lucia Grand Cru**, a molasses rum presented at 43% abv.

- **2005 St. Lucia Grand Terroir**, a molasses blend of Pot and Coffey Column Still rums, presented at 43% abv.

- **2003 St. Lucia Old Reserve**, a molasses blend of Pot and Coffey Column Still rums, aged for 10 years and presented at 43% abv.

- **2001 St. Lucia Old Reserve**, a molasses rum presented at 45% abv.

- **2010 Saint Lucia**, a molasses rum, aged for 9 years and presented at 53.6% abv.

- **2007 St. Lucia Extreme No.4**, a molasses rum from the Coffey Column Still and aged for 13 years (11 years in ex-bourbon casks in Saint Lucia, 2 years Maison Ferrand's ex-cognac casks) and presented at 58.9% abv with only 544 bottles released.

- **2010 Saint Lucia LMDW Single Cask**, a molasses rum aged for 11 years (7 years in ex-bourbon casks in Saint Lucia, 3 years Maison Ferrand's ex-cognac casks, and 1 year in amber Ferrand cognac casks), and presented at 53.2% abv.

- **2010 Saint Lucia**, a molasses rum from the John Dore Pot Still, aged for 7.5 years in ex-bourbon casks, 1 year in Ferrand casks, then finished for 6 months in Renegade Barrel No.2 (chestnut) casks. Presented at 53.6% abv.

- **2007 Saint Lucia For 15th The Nectar Anniversary Single Cask**, a molasses rum aged for 13 years and presented at 60.2% abv.

Berry Bros. & Rudd:

Berry Bros. & Rudd of London released several bottlings of Saint Lucian rum under their own label, including:

- A **16-year-old** pot still molasses rum, aged in ex-bourbon cask and presented at 46% abv.

- A **14-year-old** molasses rum, presented at 52.5% abv and bottled for 'The Nectar'.

- A **11-year-old** pot still molasses rum, distilled in 1999 and presented at 46% abv.

- A **14-year-old** molasses rum, presented at 46% abv.

La Maison du Rhum:

La Maison du Rhum released several bottlings of Saint Lucian rum under their own label, including:

- **2011 Sainte Lucie Batch #2**, a molasses rum from the Coffey Column Still, aged in ex-bourbon casks and presented at 45% abv, with only 4,114 bottles released.

- **2015 Sainte Lucie Batch #2**, a molasses rum with no stated age, however it does mention a distillation year of 2015 and bottling year of 2018. Presented at 45% abv, with only 2000 bottles released.

- **2012 Saint Lucie Batch #3,** a molasses rum from the Coffey Column Still, aged in ex-bourbon casks for 8 years and presented at 45% abv.

- **2013 Sainte Lucie Batch #4**, a molasses rum from a pot still, aged for 8 years in ex-bourbon casks and presented at 45% abv.

- **2013 Sainte Lucie Batch #4,** a molasses rum from the Coffey Column Still, aged for 9 years in ex-bourbon casks and presented at 45% abv.

- **2013 Sainte Lucie Batch #5,** a molasses rum from the Coffey Column Still, aged for 9 years in ex-bourbon casks, and both ex-Cognac casks and French barrels. Presented at 43% abv with only 4,618 bottles released.

- **2010 Sainte Lucie,** a molasses rum from the Coffey Column Still, aged for 7 years in ex-bourbon casks and presented at 45% abv. Only 2,885 bottles were released.

- **English Tradition XO,** a blend of rums from Saint Lucia, Jamaica and Trinidad, presented at 45% abv.

Other Independent Bottle Releases:

- **Blackadder 1999 Raw Cask Saint Lucia,** a molasses rum aged for 12 years and presented at 68.2% abv. Only 244 bottles were released.

- **Bonpland Saint Lucia Distillers,** a molasses rum aged for 14 years initially in Saint Lucia, then shipped over to Germany and finished in wine casks from Weingut Bernard Huber in Baden and Weingut Friedrich Becker in the Palatinate. Presented at 45% abv.

- **Cadenhead's 1999 SLJD,** a molasses rum from the John Dore 1 Pot Still, aged for 9 years and presented at 70.8% abv.

- **Castries Crème,** produced for Team Spirits Imports based in the USA. Castries Crème was a smooth peanut cream that blended roasted peanuts with rum, presented at 16% abv. Voted by the Beverage Tasting Institute as the Best Cream Liqueur in 2004, 2005 and 2006, with the product achieving a rating of 94 points.

- **Compagnie des Indes 2002**, a molasses rum, distilled in April 2002 and aged for 13 years in an ex-bourbon cask. This was bottled in October 2015 and presented at 43% abv and only 304 released for the European market.

- **Compagnie des Indes 2002**, a molasses rum, distilled in April 2002 and aged for 13 years in an ex-bourbon cask. This was bottled in October 2015, presented at 56.3% abv and only 226 released for the Danish market.

- **Duncan Taylor Single Cask Rum, Cask 5, 2002**, a molasses rum from the John Dore 1 Pot Still, aged for 11 years in an ex-bourbon cask and presented at 52.6% abv. Only 242 bottles were released by this Scottish based bottler.

- **Duncan Taylor Single Cask Rum, Cask 6, 2002**, a molasses rum, aged for 11 years in an ex-bourbon cask and presented at 54% abv. Only 226 bottles were released.

- **Famille Ricci 2000 Saint Lucia 22yo**, a molasses rum from the John Dore 1 Pot Still and aged for 22 years in ex-bourbon casks. Presented at 44% abv.

- **Famille Ricci Ovni 4**, a blended rum that uses a 22-year-old Saint Lucian rum (35%) alongside a 33-year-old Uitvlugt rum (35%) and 22-year-old Nicaraguan rum (30%). Presented at 49.6% abv.

- **Famille Ricci Ovni 5**, a blended rum that uses a 22-year-old Saint Lucian rum (25%) alongside a Trinidadian 31-year-old rum (35%) and 27-year-old Panamanian rum (40%). Presented at 57.3% abv.

- **Mezan Rum**, bottled in 1999/2000, presented as both a 37.5% abv bottling, as well as a separate 75.5% abv release. Now discontinued. Not to be confused with the current available brand and range of Mezan Rum that has been available since 2006.

- **Moon Import 1999 St. Lucia Rum Pot Still**, a molasses rum from the John Dore 1 Pot Still, presented at 46% abv.

- **Moon Import 2000 St. Lucia Rum Pot Still,** a molasses rum from the John Dore 1 Pot Still, aged for 14 years, and presented at 45% abv. Only 270 bottles were released.

- **Nobilis Rum 1999 St. Lucia No.17**, a molasses rum aged for 22 years and presented at 65.1% abv. Only 215 bottles were released.

- **Renegade 1999 Saint Lucia**, a molasses rum aged for 10 years in ex-bourbon casks, enhanced in Château lafite Casks, and presented at 46% abv. Bottled by Murray McDavid at Bruichaddich Distillery, Islay in Scotland with only 1,550 released.

- **RomDeLuxe 2000 St. Lucia Wild Series No.21 Barrel No.5 SLRP**, a molasses rum aged for 21 years and presented at 47.7% abv. Only 19 bottles were released by this Danish wine and spirit merchant.

- **RomDeLuxe 2000 Saint Lucia SLRP Wild Series No.21 Cask No.6**, a molasses rum aged for 21 years and presented at 49.1% abv. Only 21 bottles were released by this Danish wine and spirit merchant.

- **Rhum Ste. Lucie 1944**. An interesting bottling, said to be a 1944 vintage rum produced in Saint Lucia by one or even several of the distilleries that existed at this time.

- **S.B.S Jamaica / St. Lucia 2015**, a molasses single cask blend of rums, bringing together a pot still Jamaican rum with the WPL mark with a Coffey Column Still rum of St. Lucia Distillers. Matured in an ex-bourbon cask for 9 years and presented at 55% abv, with only 241 bottles released.

- **Silver Seal 1991 Devaux Saint Lucia Special Reserve**, a molasses rum presented at 43% abv.

- **Silver Seal Dennery Superior Lucian**, a molasses rum presented at 43% abv.

- **Silver Seal Saint Lucian Sestante Collection**, a molasses rum presented at 43% with only 300 bottles released by this Italian independent bottler in 2017.

- **The Royal Cane Cask Company 2000 Saint Lucia**, a molasses rum distilled from the John Dore 1 Pot Still and aged for 22 years. Presented at 49.6% abv with 227 bottles released.

- **The Secret Treasures 2005 Saint Lucia,** a molasses rum from the Vendôme Pot Still and aged for 6 years. Presented at 52% abv.

- **The Secret Treasures 2005 Saint Lucia**, a molasses rum from the John Dore Pot Still and aged for 9 years. Presented at 55% abv.

- **The Secret Treasures 2005 Saint Lucia**, a molasses rum from the Vendôme Pot Still and aged for 9 years. Presented at 53% abv.

- **The Secret Treasures 2010 Saint Lucia**, a molasses blend of rum from both the Vendôme Pot Still and John Dore Pot Still, aged for 9 years and presented at 55% abv.

- **Velier St. Lucia 2010 70th Anniversary,** a molasses rum celebrating Italian bottler Velier 70th Anniversary and selected by Global Rum Ambassador Ian Burrell. Distilled in 2010 from the John Dore 2 Pot Still and aged for 7 years. Presented at 58.6% abv and featuring a unique label designed by Singaporean artist Warren Khong.

Miscellaneous Rum Releases:

St. Lucia Distillers Ltd have worked with external companies to supply rum for projects to further highlight their flavours and versatility. Although not an exhaustive list, the below offer some highlights:

-   **Piton Rum Vibe**, two RTD (ready-to-drink) bottling's produced by Saint Lucian beer brand Piton (itself owned by Heineken), using Coffey Column Still rum and blended with fruit flavours. Both Cranberry and Pineapple & Coconut (both presented at 7.5% abv) were released in October 2024.

-   **Hotel Chocolat Dark Chocolate Rum Truffles**, produced in the United Kingdom and using Chairman's Reserve Original Rum. As per their own description, *"our dark chocolate truffle is whipped with a touch of cream to temper the richness and give it a smooth, creamy texture. The rum adds a depth of flavour of flavour and a boozy kick to the decadent truffle, and we seal the whole thing in a perfect 70% dark chocolate sphere".*

-   **Harvey Nichols Chairman's Reserve Mai Tai**, an RTD created in collaboration with Chairman's Reserve and luxury United Kingdom retailer Harvey Nichols. One 135ml can contains a single-serving mixture of Chairman's Reserve Original Rum with aged Rhum Agricole from Martinique, orange liqueur, pressed lime and orgeat syrup. Presented at 19% abv and released in November 2023.

CHAPTER 13

Saint Lucia Production Figures

The following tables of records have been adapted from numerous Saint Lucia Colony Reports (also known as Colonial Blue Books), courtesy of the *British Online Archives* in West Yorkshire and *The National Archives* in London. These Colony Reports were a yearly record of a colony's taxes, duties and other sources of revenue, military expenditure, legislation, laws, and proclamations, and import and export statistics amongst many others.

As a colony, Saint Lucia has had a record of such dating back from 1821 to 1963, and adapting where possible, as well as deciphering from the handwritten inputs, you can find an insight into the manufacturing and export figures of sugar and its different varietals, plus rum, as well as the agricultural figures from the sugar cane estates and appropriate connections to such. Please note, there is a lack of consistency of certain weights and measures as the years go on, so each record has been adapted as seen. Any missing years are either mentioned and noted, or the records of such were no longer present due to the format of the Colony Reports at that time. For example, the first year of 1821 has no records at all regarding exports, production or acreage of cane. Please refer to each table key for guidance where required.

Currency values stated as £sd and written as *Pound. Shilling. Pence (for example, £97,046, 11 shilling and 0 pence is formatted as 97,046.11.0)* until 1947 when the local currency changed to US$ on the Colony Reports.

CHAPTER 13.1

Quantity of Rum Produced at Local Distilleries

Key:

NR: No Record Available
gal: Gallon

Year	Parish Name and District Number	Rum Produced (gal)	Price per Gallon (£sd)
1828	Castries (1)	*18,000*	*1s*
	Gros Islet (1)	*11,800*	
	Anse la Raye (1)	*25,200*	
	Soufrière & Choiseul (2)	*28,112*	
	Laborie (2)	*9,000*	
	Vieux Fort (3)	*7,000*	
	Micoud & Praslin (3)	*28,803*	
	Dennery (3)	*12,000*	
	Dauphin (3)	*18,900*	
Total		**158,815**	
1829	*No Record*		

1830	Castries (1)	18,000	£1
	Gros Islet (1)	3,500	
	Anse la Raye (1)	25,200	
	Soufrière & Choiseul (2)	28,112	
	Laborie (2)	10,000	
	Vieux Fort (3)	7,000	
	Micoud & Praslin (3)	31,100	
	Dennery (3)	12,000	
	Dauphin (3)	1,190	
Total		136,102	
1831	Castries (1)	14,312	1s
	Gros Islet (1)	1,000	
	Anse la Raye (1)	6,300	
	Soufrière (2)	17,290	
	Choiseul (2)	2,800	
	Laborie (2)	2,335	
	Vieux Fort (3)	5,000	
	Micoud & Praslin (3)	22,400	
	Dennery (3)	9,253	
	Dauphin (3)	10,000	
Total		90,690	
1832	Castries (1)	8,000	1s 2d
	Gros Islet (1)	3,500	
	Anse la Raye (1)	1,000	
	Soufrière (2)	11,027	
	Choiseul (2)	2,000	
	Laborie (2)	-	
	Vieux Fort (3)	4,650	
	Micoud & Praslin (3)	16,375	
	Dennery (3)	8,000	
	Dauphin (3)	12,650	
Total		67,202	

1833	Castries (1)	10,000	10½d
	Gros Islet (1)	4,000	
	Anse la Raye (1)	2,600	
	Soufrière (2)	11,400	
	Choiseul (2)	1,900	
	Laborie (2)	6,200	
	Vieux Fort (3)	6,300	
	Micoud & Praslin (3)	18,300	
	Dennery (3)	3,559	
	Dauphin (3)	13,500	
Total		**77,759**	
1834	Castries (1)	15,000	NR
	Gros Islet (1)	3,000	
	Anse la Raye (1)	4,300	
	Soufrière (2)	15,450	
	Choiseul (2)	8,360	
	Laborie (2)	9,650	
	Vieux Fort (3)	7,450	
	Micoud & Praslin (3)	20,000	
	Dennery (3)	6,500	
	Dauphin (3)	20,000	
Total		**109,710**	
1835	Castries (1)	14,200	NR
	Gros Islet (1)	2,500	
	Anse la Raye (1)	4,800	
	Soufrière (2)	12,208	
	Choiseul (2)	4,500	
	Laborie (2)	15,650	
	Vieux Fort (3)	5,300	
	Micoud & Praslin (3)	17,000	
	Dennery (3)	4,870	
	Dauphin (3)	20,000	
Total		**101,028**	

1836	Castries (1)	12,600	NR
	Gros Islet (1)	4,200	
	Anse la Raye (1)	6,000	
	Soufrière (2)	1,587	
	Choiseul (2)	15,000	
	Laborie (2)	7,400	
	Vieux Fort (3)	2,100	
	Micoud & Praslin (3)	4,900	
	Dennery (3)	-	
	Dauphin (3)	14,400	
Total		68,187	
1837	Castries & Anse la Raye (1)	-	3s
	Gros Islet & Dauphin (2)	24,300	
	Soufrière & Choiseul (3)	9,000	
	Vieux Fort & Laborie (4)	5,000	
	Micoud, Praslin & Dennery (5)	14,710	
Total		53,010	
1838	Castries & Anse la Raye (1)	2,256	1s 8d
	Gros Islet & Dauphin (2)	13,600	2s
	Soufrière & Choiseul (3)	15,400	1s 8d
	Vieux Fort & Laborie (4)	NR	NR
	Micoud, Praslin & Dennery (5)	30,500	2s 6d
Total		61,756	
1839	Castries & Anse la Raye (1)	8,500	NR
	Gros Islet & Dauphin (2)	18,270	NR
	Soufrière & Choiseul (3)	21,000	NR
	Vieux Fort & Laborie (4)	10,340	NR
	Micoud, Praslin & Dennery (5)	14,400	NR
Total		72,150	

1840	Castries & Anse la Raye (1)	13,900	£0.25 to £3.2
	Gros Islet & Dauphin (2)	21,450	2s 6d
	Soufrière & Choiseul (3)	1,280	2s 6d
	Vieux Fort & Laborie (4)	3,490	NR
	Micoud, Praslin & Dennery (5)	117,000	NR
Total		157,120	
1841	Castries & Anse la Raye (1)	14,800	2s to 2s 5d
	Gros Islet & Dauphin (2)	21,425	2s
	Soufrière & Choiseul (3)	4,900	2s to 3s
	Vieux Fort & Laborie (4)	25,900	NR
	Micoud, Praslin & Dennery (5)	14,900	NR
Total		81,925	
1842	Castries & Anse la Raye (1)	41,700	1s 3d
	Gros Islet & Dauphin (2)	17,946	1s 3d
	Soufrière & Choiseul (3)	20,000	1s 3d
	Vieux Fort & Laborie (4)	17,400	1s 3d
	Micoud, Praslin & Dennery (5)	16,100	1s 3d
Total		113,146	
1843	Castries & Anse la Raye (1)	19,700	1s 6d
	Gros Islet & Dauphin (2)	13,900	1s 6d
	Soufrière & Choiseul (3)	16,908	1s 8d
	Vieux Fort & Laborie (4)	8,760	1s 8d
	Micoud, Praslin & Dennery (5)	11,687	1s 8d
Total		70,955	
1844	Castries & Anse la Raye (1)	24,000	1s 4d to 1s 8d
	Gros Islet & Dauphin (2)	22,000	1s 7d
	Soufrière & Choiseul (3)	17,670	1s 7d
	Vieux Fort & Laborie (4)	12,940	2s
	Micoud, Praslin & Dennery (5)	33,000	2s
Total		109,610	

1845	Castries & Anse la Raye (1)	23,328	1s 4d to 1s 8d
	Gros Islet & Dauphin (2)	21,191	1s 6d
	Soufrière, Canaries & Choiseul (3)	27,735	2s
	Vieux Fort, Laborie & part of Choiseul (4)	13,683	2s 6d
	Micoud, Praslin & Dennery (5)	24,600	2s 6d
Total		110,537	
1846	Castries & Anse la Raye (1)	24,614	1s 4d to 1s 8d
	Gros Islet & Dauphin (2)	17,388	2s 7d
	Soufrière, Canaries & Choiseul (3)	10,230	2s 10d
	Vieux Fort, Laborie & part of Choiseul (4)	8,926	2s 6d
	Micoud, Praslin & Dennery (5)	22,366	2s 6d
Total		83,524	
1847	Castries & Anse la Raye (1)	32,721	1s 4d to 1s 8d
	Gros Islet & Dauphin (2)	23,890	2s 6d
	Soufrière, Canaries & Choiseul (3)	8,460	2s 5d
	Vieux Fort, Laborie & part of Choiseul (4)	12,604	2s 6d
	Micoud, Praslin & Dennery (5)	28,373	2s
Total		106,048	
1848	Castries & Anse la Raye (1)	17,213	1s
	Gros Islet & Dauphin (2)	10,971	1s
	Soufrière, Canaries & Choiseul (3)	4,000	10d to 1s
	Vieux Fort, Laborie & part of Choiseul (4)	7,553	NR
	Micoud, Praslin & Dennery (5)	18,367	3s
Total		58,104	
1849	Castries & Anse la Raye (1)	12,513	2s 4d
	Gros Islet & Dauphin (2)	3,148	1s
	Soufrière, Canaries & Choiseul (3)	6,200	10d
	Vieux Fort, Laborie & part of Choiseul (4)	6,931	1s
	Micoud, Praslin & Dennery (5)	18,140	2s
Total		46,932	

1850	Castries & Anse la Raye (1)	41,000	2s
	Gros Islet & Dauphin (2)	5,500	1s 8d
	Soufrière, Canaries & Choiseul (3)	6,200	10d
	Vieux Fort, Laborie & part of Choiseul (4)	3,600	1s 6d
	Micoud, Praslin & Dennery (5)	47,700	2s
Total		104,000	
1851	Castries & Anse la Raye (1)	16,024	1s
	Gros Islet, Dauphin & Dennery (2)	6,850	1s to 1s 4d
	Choiseul & part Laborie (3)	7,143	1s
	Vieux Fort, Laborie & Micoud (4)	15,041	2s 6d
Total		45,058	
1852	Castries & Anse la Raye (1)	19,964	10d
	Gros Islet, Dauphin & Dennery (2)	18,837½	10d to 1s
	Choiseul & part Laborie (3)	11,252	1s 6d
	Vieux Fort, Laborie & Micoud (4)	16,875	8d to 10d
Total		66,928½	
1853	Castries & Anse la Raye (1)	15,070	1s 4d to 1s 6d
	Gros Islet, Dauphin & Dennery (2)	7,155	8d to 1s 4d
	Choiseul & part Laborie (3)	10,996	3s 4d
	Vieux Fort, Laborie & Micoud (4)	24,226½	1s 3d
Total		58,347½	
1854	Castries & Anse la Raye (1)	26,687	1s 5d
	Gros Islet, Dauphin & Dennery (2)	11,385	1s 3d to 2s
	Choiseul & part Laborie (3)	14,587	3s 6d
	Vieux Fort, Laborie & Micoud (4)	25,092	1s 6d
Total		77,751	
1855	Castries & Anse la Raye (1)	19,685	2s
	Gros Islet, Dauphin & Dennery (2)	16,081	1s 6d to 2s
	Choiseul & part Laborie (3)	19,250	2s
	Vieux Fort, Laborie & Micoud (4)	20,359	1s 6d to 2s
Total		45,373	

1856	Castries & Anse la Raye (1)	6,267	1s 6d to 2s
	Gros Islet, Dauphin & Dennery (2)	21,360	2s to 2s 6d
	Choiseul & part Laborie (3)	38,950	1s 6d to 2s
	Vieux Fort, Laborie & Micoud (4)	19,015	1s 4d
Total		*86,052*	
1857	Castries & Anse la Raye (1)	6,446	2s
	Gros Islet, Dauphin & Dennery (2)	6,035	2s
	Choiseul & part Laborie (3)	25,337	1s 6d to 1s 8d
	Vieux Fort, Laborie & Micoud (4)	11,239	1s 6d
Total		*49,957*	
1858	Castries & Anse la Raye (1)	13,238	2s
	Gros Islet, Dauphin & Dennery (2)	11,398	1s 10d
	Choiseul & part Laborie (3)	36,916	1s 6d
	Vieux Fort, Laborie & Micoud (4)	19,314	1s 6d
Total		*80,860*	
1859	Castries & Anse la Raye (1)	2,790	1s 3d to 1s 9d
	Gros Islet, Dauphin & Dennery (2)	12,061	1s 4d
	Choiseul & part Laborie (3)	33,941	1s 4d
	Vieux Fort, Laborie & Micoud (4)	14,741	1s 3d to 1s 5d
Total		*63,533*	
1860	Castries & Anse la Raye (1)	12,882	1s
	Gros Islet, Dauphin & Dennery (2)	NR	1s
	Choiseul & part Laborie (3)	27,421	1s 4d
	Vieux Fort, Laborie & Micoud (4)	14,498	1s to 1s 6d
Total		*54,801*	
1861	Castries & Anse la Raye (1)	10,509	1s
	Gros Islet, Dauphin & Dennery (2)	1,114	1s
	Choiseul & part Laborie (3)	36,174	3s 4d
	Vieux Fort, Laborie & Micoud (4)	9,246	1s 6d
Total		*46,048*	

1862	Castries & Anse la Raye (1)	10,460	1s
	Gros Islet, Dauphin & Dennery (2)	NR	1s
	Choiseul & part Laborie (3)	20,950	3s 4d
	Vieux Fort, Laborie & Micoud (4)	10,691	1s to 1s 11d
Total		**42,101**	
1863	Castries & Anse la Raye (1)	10,288	11d
	Gros Islet, Dauphin & Dennery (2)	15,000	1s
	Choiseul & part Laborie (3)	25,104	1s 6d to 1s 8d
	Vieux Fort, Laborie & Micoud (4)	10,674	10d to 1s
Total		**61,066**	
1864	Castries & Anse la Raye (1)	12,240	1s
	Gros Islet, Dauphin & Dennery (2)	4,000	1s
	Choiseul & part Laborie (3)	23,378	3s to 3s 6d
	Vieux Fort, Laborie & Micoud (4)	16,930	1s 4d to 2s
Total		**40,308**	
1865	Castries, Gros Islet, Dauphin & Dennery (1)	27,240	1s
	Anse la Raye, Choiseul & Soufrière (2)	22,441	1s 8d
	Vieux Fort, Laborie, Praslin & Micoud (3)	8,921	10d to 1s
Total		**58,602**	
1866	Castries, Gros Islet, Dauphin & Dennery (1)	27,640	1s
	Anse la Raye, Choiseul & Soufrière (2)	13,923	1s 4d
	Vieux Fort, Laborie, Praslin & Micoud (3)	13,448	10d
Total		**55,011**	
1867	Castries, Gros Islet, Dauphin & Dennery (1)	9,462	NR
	Anse la Raye, Choiseul & Soufrière (2)	14,188	1s 4d to 1s 8d
	Vieux Fort, Laborie, Praslin & Micoud (3)	12,845	10d to 1s
Total		**36,495**	
1868	Castries, Gros Islet, Dauphin & Dennery (1)	13,069	NR
	Anse la Raye, Choiseul & Soufrière (2)	14,224	1s 2d to 1s 4d
	Vieux Fort, Laborie, Praslin & Micoud (3)	8,102	10d
Total		**35,395**	

1869	Castries, Gros Islet, Dauphin & Dennery (1)	26,947	1s
	Anse la Raye, Choiseul & Soufrière (2)	13,712	1s
	Vieux Fort, Laborie, Praslin & Micoud (3)	10,468	1s
Total		51,127	
1870	Castries, Gros Islet, Dauphin & Dennery (1)	23,577	NR
	Anse la Raye, Choiseul & Soufrière (2)	21,306	NR
	Vieux Fort, Laborie, Praslin & Micoud (3)	11,841	NR
Total		56,724	

Between 1871 and 1877, the Colony Report stated that "there being no means of obtaining the information required under this form the blanks have not been filled, it estimates by officers not possessing special knowledge are necessarily unreliable".

1878	Castries, Gros Islet, Dauphin & Dennery (1)	NR	NR
	Anse la Raye, Choiseul & Soufrière (2)	25,000	4s
	Vieux Fort, Laborie, Praslin & Micoud (3)	NR	NR
Total		25,000	
1879	Castries, Gros Islet, Dauphin & Dennery (1)	NR	4s
	Anse la Raye, Choiseul & Soufrière (2)	NR	4s
	Vieux Fort, Laborie, Praslin & Micoud (3)	NR	4s
Total		NR	
1880	Castries, Gros Islet, Dauphin & Dennery (1)	NR	NR
	Anse la Raye, Choiseul & Soufrière (2)	25,000	4s
	Vieux Fort, Laborie, Praslin & Micoud (3)	NR	4s
Total		25,000	

Between 1881 and 1883, there were no records of agriculture within the Colony Reports.
From 1884, the records were no longer listed by district names, but as a total figure of all districts combined.

Year	Rum Produced (gal)	Price per Gallon (£sd)
1884	365,900	1s 4d
1885	86,143	1s 4d
1886	69,900	1s
1887	29,289	1s
1888	60,134	1s
1889	43,310	2s
1890	83,046	1s
1891	70,282	NR
1892	40,732	NR
1893	1,706	NR
1894	1,420	NR
1895	9,918	NR
1896	1,280½	NR
1897	10,107¼	NR
1898	1,005,181	1s 2d
1899	62,351	5½d
1900	72,910	1s 2d
1901	85,712	1s 6d
1902	89,362	1s 6d
1903	72,470	1s 6d
1904	57,429	1s 6d
1905	56,150	1s 6d
1906	49,533	1s 6d
1907	57,213	1s 2d
1908	23,440	1s 2d
1909	71,419	1s 2d
1910	46,131	1s 2d
1911	62,471	1s 2d
1912	59,014	1s 2d
1913	51,188	1s 2d
1914	42,879	1s 2d
1915	48,259	2s
1916	63,213.19	2s

1917	NR	5s
1918	NR	5s

Year	Rum Produced (gal)	Total Value (£)
1919	365,900	7,561
1920	51,957	9,039
1921	51,385	10,277
1922	54,484.4	10,891
1923	53,338.7	NR
1924	39,081	NR
1925	45,762.2	NR
1926	34,161.3	NR
1927	1,700	212
1928	1,323	218
1929	2,013	339
1930	29,918	NR
1931	31,003	NR
1932	30,485	NR
1933	28,440	NR
1934	NR	NR
1935	NR [2]	NR
1936 - 1938	NR	NR

[2] *The Colony Report 1935 mentions that there was difficulty in disposing of the factory molasses, with only a proportion being used for the manufacture of rum for local use.*

CHAPTER 13.2

Number of Rum Distilleries

Year	Parish Name and District Number	Number of Rum Distilleries
1851	*Vieux Fort, Laborie & Micoud (4)*	*10*
1885	*Total Number Across Saint Lucia*	*8*
1886	*Total Number Across Saint Lucia*	*9*
1887- 1889	*Castries, Dennery and Gros-Islet (1)*	*2*
	Soufrière, Choiseul, Anse la Raye (2)	*5*
	Vieux Fort, Laborie & Micoud (3)	*-*
Total		*7*
1890- 1891	*Castries, Dennery and Gros-Islet (1)*	*2*
	Soufrière, Choiseul, Anse la Raye (2)	*6*
	Vieux Fort, Laborie & Micoud (3)	*-*
Total		*8*
1892	*Castries, Dennery and Gros-Islet (1)*	*2*
	Soufrière, Choiseul, Anse la Raye (2)	*4*
	Vieux Fort, Laborie & Micoud (3)	*-*
Total		*6*

1893-1895	Castries, Dennery and Gros-Islet (1)	2
	Soufrière, Choiseul, Anse la Raye (2)	3
	Vieux Fort, Laborie & Micoud (3)	-
Total		**5**
1896	Castries, Dennery and Gros-Islet (1)	2
	Soufrière, Choiseul, Anse la Raye (2)	2
	Vieux Fort, Laborie & Micoud (3)	-
Total		**4**
1897	Castries, Dennery and Gros-Islet (1)	1
	Soufrière, Choiseul, Anse la Raye (2)	2
	Vieux Fort, Laborie & Micoud (3)	-
Total		**3**
1898	Castries, Dennery and Gros-Islet (1)	1
	Soufrière, Choiseul, Anse la Raye (2)	1
	Vieux Fort, Laborie & Micoud (3)	-
Total		**2**
1899- 1901	Castries, Dennery and Gros-Islet (1)	1
	Soufrière, Choiseul, Anse la Raye (2)	-
	Vieux Fort, Laborie & Micoud (3)	-
Total		**1**

Year	District Number	Number of Rum Distilleries & Name
1902- 1916	Castries & Anse la Raye (1)	1 (Cul de Sac)
	Vieux Fort, Laborie & Micoud (3)	1 (Troumassee)
Total		**2**
1917	Castries & Anse la Raye (1)	1 (Cul de Sac)
	Vieux Fort, Laborie & Micoud (3)	1 (Troumassee – closed September 1917)
Total		**2**
1918- 1920	Castries & Anse la Raye (1)	1 (Cul de Sac)
Total		**1**

1921-1930	Castries & Anse la Raye (1)	1 (Cul de Sac)
	Vieux Fort, Laborie & Micoud (3)	3 Vieux Fort / Troumassee) / Beauchamp)
Total		*4*
1931-1942	Castries & Anse la Raye (1)	2 (Cul de Sac / Dennery)
	Vieux Fort, Laborie & Micoud (3)	1 (Vieux Fort)
Total		*3*
1943-1944	Castries & Anse la Raye (1)	2 (Cul de Sac / Dennery)
Total		*2*
1945-1960	Castries & Anse la Raye (1)	2 (Cul de Sac / Dennery / Roseau)
Total		*3*
1961-1972	Castries & Anse la Raye (1)	2 (Dennery / Roseau)
Total		*2*
1973-	Castries & Anse la Raye (1)	1 (Roseau)
Total		*1*

CHAPTER 13.3

Number of Cane Fields (Carrés)

Key:

Carrés – square, equivalent to about 3 ⅓ acre
Hectare – equivalent to 2.47105 acre

Year	Area Under Cultivation *(hectares)*
1765	18
1767	53
1769	166
1771	5,901,040
1773	1,456
1775	1,759
1777	2,003
1779	2,214
1780	2,297
1784	3,271
1785	3,871
1786	2,936
1787	2,870
1788	2,019
1789	1,902

Year	Parish Name and District Number	No. of Cane Fields (acres)
1828	Castries (1)	738
	Gros Islet (1)	609
	Anse la Raye (1)	560
	Soufrière & Choiseul (2)	1,107
	Laborie (2)	720
	Vieux Fort (3)	744
	Micoud & Praslin (3)	592
	Dennery (3)	520
	Dauphin (3)	225
Total		5,845
1829	No Record	
1830	Castries (1)	740
	Gros Islet (1)	585
	Anse la Raye (1)	560
	Soufrière & Choiseul (2)	1,107
	Laborie (2)	589
	Vieux Fort (3)	779
	Micoud & Praslin (3)	667
	Dennery (3)	520
	Dauphin (3)	210
Total		5,757

1831	Castries (1)	672
	Gros Islet (1)	233
	Anse la Raye (1)	759
	Soufrière (2)	786
	Choiseul (2)	173
	Laborie (2)	330
	Vieux Fort (3)	540
	Micoud & Praslin (3)	655
	Dennery (3)	338
	Dauphin (3)	240
Total		**4,752**
1832	Castries (1)	600
	Gros Islet (1)	296
	Anse la Raye (1)	256
	Soufrière (2)	633
	Choiseul (2)	291
	Laborie (2)	93
	Vieux Fort (3)	505
	Micoud & Praslin (3)	582
	Dennery (3)	195
	Dauphin (3)	190
Total		**3,641**
1833	Castries (1)	630
	Gros Islet (1)	333
	Anse la Raye (1)	200
	Soufriere (2)	224
	Choiseul (2)	120
	Laborie (2)	570
	Vieux Fort (3)	500
	Micoud & Praslin (3)	522
	Dennery (3)	101
	Dauphin (3)	190
Total		**3,390**

1834	Castries (1)	630
	Gros Islet (1)	311
	Anse la Raye (1)	216
	Soufrière (2)	636
	Choiseul (2)	180
	Laborie (2)	683
	Vieux Fort (3)	570
	Micoud & Praslin (3)	548
	Dennery (3)	275
	Dauphin (3)	119
Total		**4,239**
1835	Castries (1)	990
	Gros Islet (1)	222
	Anse la Raye (1)	250
	Soufrière (2)	576
	Choiseul (2)	210
	Laborie (2)	489
	Vieux Fort (3)	387
	Micoud & Praslin (3)	510
	Dennery (3)	273
	Dauphin (3)	180
Total		**4,087**
1836	Castries (1)	917
	Gros Islet (1)	218
	Anse la Raye (1)	250
	Soufrière (2)	295
	Choiseul (2)	190
	Laborie (2)	621
	Vieux Fort (3)	150
	Micoud & Praslin (3)	266
	Dennery (3)	418
	Dauphin (3)	112
Total		**3,442**

1837	Castries & Anse la Raye (1)	1,256
	Gros Islet & Dauphin (2)	586
	Soufrière & Choiseul (3)	830
	Vieux Fort & Laborie (4)	620
	Micoud, Praslin & Dennery (5)	832
Total		4,124
1838	Castries & Anse la Raye (1)	449
	Gros Islet & Dauphin (2)	486
	Soufrière & Choiseul (3)	756
	Vieux Fort & Laborie (4)	400
	Micoud, Praslin & Dennery (5)	1,038
Total		3,129
1839	Castries & Anse la Raye (1)	386
	Gros Islet & Dauphin (2)	405
	Soufrière & Choiseul (3)	466
	Vieux Fort & Laborie (4)	468
	Micoud, Praslin & Dennery (5)	59
Total		1,764
1840	Castries & Anse la Raye (1)	400
	Gros Islet & Dauphin (2)	633
	Soufrière & Choiseul (3)	660
	Vieux Fort & Laborie (4)	362
	Micoud, Praslin & Dennery (5)	421
Total		2,476
1841	Castries & Anse la Raye (1)	450
	Gros Islet & Dauphin (2)	629
	Soufrière & Choiseul (3)	689
	Vieux Fort & Laborie (4)	529
	Micoud, Praslin & Dennery (5)	540
Total		2,837

1842	Castries & Anse la Raye (1)	653
	Gros Islet & Dauphin (2)	697
	Soufrière & Choiseul (3)	800
	Vieux Fort & Laborie (4)	539
	Micoud, Praslin & Dennery (5)	551
Total		**3,240**
1843	Castries & Anse la Raye (1)	759
	Gros Islet & Dauphin (2)	723
	Soufrière & Choiseul (3)	604
	Vieux Fort & Laborie (4)	651
	Micoud, Praslin & Dennery (5)	602
Total		**3,339**
1844	Castries & Anse la Raye (1)	2,125
	Gros Islet & Dauphin (2)	2,640
	Soufrière & Choiseul (3)	1,320
	Vieux Fort & Laborie (4)	896
	Micoud, Praslin & Dennery (5)	1,166
Total		**8,147**
1845	Castries & Anse la Raye (1)	629
	Gros Islet & Dauphin (2)	762
	Soufrière, Canaries & Choiseul (3)	1,046
	Vieux Fort, Laborie & part of Choiseul (4)	660
	Micoud, Praslin & Dennery (5)	713
Total		**3,810**
1846	Castries & Anse la Raye (1)	735
	Gros Islet & Dauphin (2)	752
	Soufrière, Canaries & Choiseul (3)	1,082
	Vieux Fort, Laborie & part of Choiseul (4)	638
	Micoud, Praslin & Dennery (5)	730
Total		**3,937**

1847	*Castries & Anse la Raye (1)*	*745*
	Gros Islet & Dauphin (2)	*678*
	Soufrière, Canaries & Choiseul (3)	*1,212*
	Vieux Fort, Laborie & part of Choiseul (4)	*657*
	Micoud, Praslin & Dennery (5)	*700*
Total		*3,992*
1848	*Castries & Anse la Raye (1)*	*705*
	Gros Islet & Dauphin (2)	*792*
	Soufrière, Canaries & Choiseul (3)	*1,050*
	Vieux Fort, Laborie & part of Choiseul (4)	*608*
	Micoud, Praslin & Dennery (5)	*621*
Total		*3,776*
1849	*Castries & Anse la Raye (1)*	*567*
	Gros Islet & Dauphin (2)	*552*
	Soufrière, Canaries & Choiseul (3)	*1,100*
	Vieux Fort, Laborie & part of Choiseul (4)	*667*
	Micoud, Praslin & Dennery (5)	*640*
Total		*3,526*
1850	*Castries & Anse la Raye (1)*	*500*
	Gros Islet & Dauphin (2)	*468*
	Soufrière, Canaries & Choiseul (3)	*1,393*
	Vieux Fort, Laborie & part of Choiseul (4)	*597*
	Micoud, Praslin & Dennery (5)	*617*
Total		*3,575*
1851	*Castries & Anse la Raye (1)*	*691*
	Gros Islet, Dauphin & Dennery (2)	*620*
	Choiseul & part Laborie (3)	*1,013*
	Vieux Fort, Laborie & Micoud (4)	*691*
Total		*3,015*
1852	*Castries & Anse la Raye (1)*	*703*
	Gros Islet, Dauphin & Dennery (2)	*786*
	Choiseul & part Laborie (3)	*1,296*
	Vieux Fort, Laborie & Micoud (4)	*776*
Total		*3,563*

1853	Castries & Anse la Raye (1)	789
	Gros Islet, Dauphin & Dennery (2)	822
	Choiseul & part Laborie (3)	952
	Vieux Fort, Laborie & Micoud (4)	926
Total		**3,489**
1854	Castries & Anse la Raye (1)	709
	Gros Islet, Dauphin & Dennery (2)	745.5
	Choiseul & part Laborie (3)	1,007
	Vieux Fort, Laborie & Micoud (4)	829
Total		**3,290.5**
1855	Castries & Anse la Raye (1)	696
	Gros Islet, Dauphin & Dennery (2)	790
	Choiseul & part Laborie (3)	1,002
	Vieux Fort, Laborie & Micoud (4)	765
Total		**3,253**
1856	Castries & Anse la Raye (1)	784
	Gros Islet, Dauphin & Dennery (2)	879
	Choiseul & part Laborie (3)	1,214
	Vieux Fort, Laborie & Micoud (4)	723
Total		**3,600**
1857	Castries & Anse la Raye (1)	674
	Gros Islet, Dauphin & Dennery (2)	578
	Choiseul & part Laborie (3)	408
	Vieux Fort, Laborie & Micoud (4)	751
Total		**3,411**
1858	Castries & Anse la Raye (1)	780
	Gros Islet, Dauphin & Dennery (2)	633
	Choiseul & part Laborie (3)	1,275
	Vieux Fort, Laborie & Micoud (4)	856
Total		**3,544**

1859	Castries & Anse la Raye (1)	833
	Gros Islet, Dauphin & Dennery (2)	682
	Choiseul & part Laborie (3)	1,485
	Vieux Fort, Laborie & Micoud (4)	895
Total		**3,895**
1860	Castries & Anse la Raye (1)	862
	Gros Islet, Dauphin & Dennery (2)	692
	Choiseul & part Laborie (3)	1,670
	Vieux Fort, Laborie & Micoud (4)	841
Total		**4,065**
1861	Castries & Anse la Raye (1)	862.5
	Gros Islet, Dauphin & Dennery (2)	720
	Choiseul & part Laborie (3)	1,946
	Vieux Fort, Laborie & Micoud (4)	951
Total		**4,479.5**
1862	Castries & Anse la Raye (1)	864
	Gros Islet, Dauphin & Dennery (2)	989
	Choiseul & part Laborie (3)	1,908
	Vieux Fort, Laborie & Micoud (4)	951
Total		**4,712**
1863	Castries & Anse la Raye (1)	859
	Gros Islet, Dauphin & Dennery (2)	995
	Choiseul & part Laborie (3)	1,718
	Vieux Fort, Laborie & Micoud (4)	1,045
Total		**4,617**
1864	Castries & Anse la Raye (1)	870
	Gros Islet, Dauphin & Dennery (2)	1,030
	Choiseul & part Laborie (3)	1,801
	Vieux Fort, Laborie & Micoud (4)	1,100½
Total		**4,801½**
1865	Castries, Gros Islet, Dauphin & Dennery (1)	1,845
	Anse la Raye, Choiseul & Soufrière (2)	1,884
	Vieux Fort, Laborie, Praslin & Micoud (3)	1,171
Total		**4,856**

1866	Castries, Gros Islet, Dauphin & Dennery (1)	1,890
	Anse la Raye, Choiseul & Soufrière (2)	2,110
	Vieux Fort, Laborie, Praslin & Micoud (3)	127½
Total		**5,277½**
1867	Castries, Gros Islet, Dauphin & Dennery (1)	988½
	Anse la Raye, Choiseul & Soufrière (2)	2,218
	Vieux Fort, Laborie, Praslin & Micoud (3)	1,552
Total		**4,758½**
1868	Castries, Gros Islet, Dauphin & Dennery (1)	1,267
	Anse la Raye, Choiseul & Soufrière (2)	2,282
	Vieux Fort, Laborie, Praslin & Micoud (3)	1,672
Total		**5,221**
1869	Castries, Gros Islet, Dauphin & Dennery (1)	1,099
	Anse la Raye, Choiseul & Soufrière (2)	3,305
	Vieux Fort, Laborie, Praslin & Micoud (3)	1,584
Total		**5,988**
1870	Castries, Gros Islet, Dauphin & Dennery (1)	887
	Anse la Raye, Choiseul & Soufrière (2)	2,536
	Vieux Fort, Laborie, Praslin & Micoud (3)	1,609
Total		**5,032**

Between 1871 and 1876, the Colony Report stated that "there being no means of obtaining the information required under this form the blanks have not been filled, it estimates by officers not possessing special knowledge are necessarily unreliable".

1877	Castries, Gros Islet, Dauphin & Dennery (1)	20,000
	Anse la Raye, Choiseul & Soufrière (2)	2,300
	Vieux Fort, Laborie, Praslin & Micoud (3)	13,700
Total		**36,000**
1878	Castries, Gros Islet, Dauphin & Dennery (1)	NR
	Anse la Raye, Choiseul & Soufrière (2)	2,500
	Vieux Fort, Laborie, Praslin & Micoud (3)	1,370
Total		**3,870**

1879	Castries, Gros Islet, Dauphin & Dennery (1)	NR
	Anse la Raye, Choiseul & Soufrière (2)	3,000
	Vieux Fort, Laborie, Praslin & Micoud (3)	1,370
Total		4,370
1880	Castries, Gros Islet, Dauphin & Dennery (1)	NR
	Anse la Raye, Choiseul & Soufrière (2)	2,500
	Vieux Fort, Laborie, Praslin & Micoud (3)	1,370
Total		3,870

Between 1881 and 1883, there were no records of agriculture within the Colony Reports.
In 1884, the records were no longer listed by district names, but as a total figure of all districts combined.

Year	No. of Cane Fields (acres)
1884	5,600

Between 1885 and 1896, there were no records of number of cane fields within the Colony Reports.

Year	Parish Name & District Number	No. of Cane Fields (acres)
1897-1904	Castries (1)	1,126
	Dennery (1)	785
	Gros Islet (1)	100
	Soufriere (2)	263
	Choiseul (2)	424
	Anse la Raye (2)	543
	Vieux Fort (3)	1,298
	Laborie (3)	490
	Micoud (3)	205
Total		5,234

Between 1905 and 1947, there were no records of number of cane fields within the Colony Reports.

Year	No. of Cane Fields *(acres)*
1948	2,083
1951	2,940
1952	3,400

Between 1949 and 1950, there were no records of number of cane fields within the Colony Reports.

CHAPTER 13.4

Number of Sugar Estates

The year stated is the number of sugar estates noted for that year, it does not reflect the growth or reduction of working estates from years surrounding such due to lack of records available.
Source is predominantly from R, Renard 1982a, p.16. "Statistics for the economic history of St. Lucia (1763-1769)".

Year	No. Sugar Estates
1767	5
1768	10
1769	16
1771	33
1773	39
1775	41
1777	53
1778	44
1779	44
1780	28
1784	73
1785	83
1786	73
1787	62
1788	46
1789	42
1819	102
1843	81

Year	District Number	No. Sugar Estates
1848 – 1850 [3]	*1*	*12*
	2	*12*
	3	*24*
	4	*_ [6]*
	5	*13*
Total		*61*
1851 [4]	*1*	*16*
	2	*12*
	3	*-*
	4	*-*
Total		*28*
1852-54 [4]	*1*	*16*
	2	*13*
	3	*-*
	4	*-*
Total		*29*
1855 [4]	*1*	*16*
	2	*12*
	3	*-*
	4	*-*
Total		*28*
1856 [4]	*1*	*30*
	2	*12*
	3	*35*
	4	*-*
Total		*77* [7]
1857 [4]	*1*	*32*
	2	*12*
	3	*41*
	4	*-*
Total		*85*

1858[4]	*1*	*41*
	2	*12*
	3	*62*
	4	*22*
Total		*137*
1859[4]	*1*	*85*
	2	*13*
	3	*75*
	4	*32*
Total		*205*
1860[4]	*1*	*51*
	2	*19*
	3	*75*
	4	*32*
Total		*177*
1861[4]	*1*	*30*
	2	*19*
	3	*75*
	4	*22*
Total		*146*
1862[4]	*1*	*30*
	2	*19*
	3	*79*
	4	*29*
Total		*157*
1863 - 1864[4]	*1*	*30*
	2	*"13 large & 6 small"*
	3	*80*
	4	*29*
Total		*158*
1865[5]	*1*	*44*
	2	*84*
	3	*29*
Total		*157*

1866 [5]	*1*	*54*
	2	*83*
	3	*29*
Total		*166*
1867 [5]	*1*	*43*
	2	*83*
	3	*31*
Total		*159*
1868 [5]	*1*	*43*
	2	*85*
	3	*33*
Total		*161*
1869 [5]	*1*	*43*
	2	*76*
	3	*25*
Total		*144*
1870 [5]	*1*	*43*
	2	*83*
	3	*25*
Total		*151*
1871 [5]	*1*	*43*
	2	*54*
	3	*32*
Total		*129*
1872 [5]	*1*	*45*
	2	*60*
	3	*33*
Total		*138*
1873 [5]	*1*	*31*
	2	*60*
	3	*33*
Total		*124*

1874 [5]	1	31
	2	74
	3	33
Total		138
1875 - 1876 [5]	1	33
	2	74
	3	33
Total		140
1877 [5]	1	50
	2	100
	3	37
Total		187
1878 [5]	1	91
	2	64
	3	37
Total		192
1878 [5]	1	91
	2	64
	3	37
Total		192
1879 [8]	1	214
1880 - 1883 [3]	1	89
	2	88
	3	37
Total		214
1884		NR

[3] Districts were defined as 1 (Castries and Anse la Raye), 2 (Gros Islet and Dauphine), 3 (Canaries and part of Choiseul), 4 (Vieux Fort and part of Choiseul) and 5 (Dennery and Micoud).

[4] Districts were defined as 1 (Castries and Anse la Raye), 2 (Gros Islet, Dauphin and Dennery), 3 (Soufrière, Choiseul and part of Laborie), 4 (Vieux Fort, part of Laborie and Micoud).

[5] Districts were defined as 1 (Castrie, Gros Islet, Dauphin & Dennery), 2 (Anse la Raye, Choiseul & Soufrière) and 3 (Vieux Fort, Laborie, Micoud & Praslin).

[6] Recorded as "each having a building for manufacturing purposes"

[7] Additional note was recorded as "plus 14 small sugar estates with cattle & water mills"

[8] Recorded as "total colony"

CHAPTER 13.5

Sugar Mills and Type

Year	District	No. Sugar Mills	Steam	Water	Cattle	Wind	Steam & Wind	Water & Cattle
1848	1 [9]	12	7	4	1	-	-	-
	2	12	7	3	2	-	-	-
	3	24	-	19	5	-	-	-
	4	0	-	12	1	5	-	-
	5	13	2	10	1	-	-	-
Total		**61**	**16**	**48**	**10**	**5**	**0**	**0**
1849	1 [9]	12	7	4	1	-	-	-
	2	12	9	3	1	-	-	-
	3	24	1	18	5	-	-	-
	4	0	-	12	1	5	-	-
	5	13	1	10	1	-	1	-
Total		**61**	**18**	**47**	**9**	**5**	**1**	**0**
1850	1 [9]	12	7	4	1	-	-	-
	2	12	9	1	1	-	1	-
	3	24	-	17	5	-	1	1
	4	0	-	12	2	-	-	-
	5	13	2	10	1	-	-	-
Total		**61**	**17**	**44**	**10**	**0**	**2**	**1**
1851	1 [10]	16	9	4	3	-	-	-
	2	12	8	3	1	-	-	-
	3	0	1	28	6	-	-	-
	4	0	-	15	2	3	-	-
Total		**28**	**18**	**59**	**12**	**3**	**0**	**0**

Year	District							
1852	1 [10]	16	9	4	3	-	-	-
	2	13	9	3	1	-	-	-
	3	0	1	28	6	-	-	-
	4	0	2	18	2	3	-	-
Total		**29**	**21**	**53**	**12**	**3**	**0**	**0**
1853	1 [10]	16	9	4	3	-	-	-
	2	13	9	3	1	-	-	-
	3	0	1	27	6	-	-	-
	4	0	2	18	2	3	-	-
Total		**29**	**21**	**52**	**12**	**3**	**0**	**0**
1854	1 [10]	16	9	4	3	-	-	-
	2	13	9	3	1	-	-	-
	3	0	1	28	6	-	-	-
	4	0	2	18	2	3	-	-
Total		**29**	**21**	**53**	**12**	**3**	**0**	**0**
1855	1 [10]	16	9	4	3	-	-	-
	2	12	8	4	0	-	-	-
	3	0	1	28	6	-	-	-
	4	0	2	15	1	4	-	-
Total		**28**	**20**	**51**	**10**	**4**	**0**	**0**

[9] *Districts were defined as 1 (Castries and Anse la Raye), 2 (Gros Islet and Dauphine), 3 (Canaries and part of Choiseul), 4 (Vieux Fort and part of Choiseul) and 5 (Dennery and Micoud).*

[10] *Districts were defined as 1 (Castries and Anse la Raye), 2 (Gros Islet, Dauphin and Dennery), 3 (Soufrière, Choiseul and part of Laborie), 4 (Vieux Fort, part of Laborie and Micoud).*

Year	District	No. Sugar Mills	Steam	Water	Cattle	Wind	Steam and Wind	Hand Powered	No Manufacture	Steam and Cattle	Steam and Water
1856	1[10]	30	7	4	13	-	1	2	2	-	-
	2	12	8	4	-	-	-	-	-	-	-
	3	35	1	28	6	-	-	-	-	-	-
	4	0	2	15	1	4	-	-	-	-	-
	Total	77	18	51	20	4	1	2	2	0	0
1857	1[10]	32	6	4	14	-	-	-[12]	-	3	-
	2	12	9	3	-[13]	-	-	-	-	-	-
	3	41	1	26	9	5	-	-	-	-	-
	4	0	2	15	1	4	-	-	-	-	-
	Total	85	18	48	24	9	0	0	0	3	0
1858	1[10]	41	6	4	14	1	-	-[14]	-	-	3
	2	12	9	3	-[15]	-	-	-	-	-	-
	3	62	2	26	34	-	-	-	-	-	-
	4	22	3	15	-	4	-	-	-	-	-
	Total	137	20	48	48	5	0	0	0	0	3
1859	1[10]	85	6	4	14	2	-	-	-	-	8
	2	13	9	3	1	-	-	-	-	-	-
	3	75	4	25	38	8	-	-	-	-	-
	4	32	3	15	-	4	-	-	-	-	-
	Total	205	22	47	53	14	0	0	0	0	8
1860	1[10]	51	7	4	35	5	-	-	-	-	-
	2	19	9	3	7	-	-	-	-	-	-
	3	75	4	25	38	8	-	-	-	-	-
	4	32	3	15	-	4	-	-	-	-	-
	Total	177	23	47	80	17	0	0	0	0	0

Year	District										
1861	1[10]	30	7	3	17	2	-	-	-	-	1
	2	19	9	3	7	-	-	-	-	-	-
	3	75	14	25	35	14	-	-	-	-	-
	4	22	3	15	-	4	-	-	-	-	-
Total		**146**	**33**	**46**	**59**	**20**	**0**	**0**	**0**	**0**	**1**
1862 - 1863	1[10]	30	7	5	17	3	-	-	-	-	1
	2	19	9	3	7	-	-	-	-	-	-
	3	79	4	25	36	14	-	-	-	-	-
	4	29	5	15	5	4	-	-	-	-	-
Total		**157**	**25**	**48**	**65**	**21**	**0**	**0**	**0**	**0**	**1**
1864	1[10]	30	7	3	17	2	-	-	-	-	1
	2	19	9	3	7	-	-	-	-	-	-
	3	80	4	26	36	14	-	-	-	-	-
	4	29	5	15	5	4	-	-	-	-	-
Total		**158**	**25**	**47**	**65**	**20**	**0**	**0**	**0**	**0**	**1**

[10] Districts were defined as 1 (Castries and Anse la Raye), 2 (Gros Islet, Dauphin and Dennery), 3 (Soufrière, Choiseul and part of Laborie), 4 (Vieux Fort, part of Laborie and Micoud).

[12] Recorded as "several by hand"

[13] Recorded as "several smaller sugar estates in the quarter having cattle mills"

[14] Recorded as "others by hand" – no number was recorded.

[15] Recorded as " several smaller estates with cattle mills"

Year	District	No. Sugar Mills	Steam	Water	Cattle	Wind
1865	1[11]	44	14	9	21	-
	2	84	5	29	36	14
	3	29	5	15	5	4
Total		**157**	**24**	**53**	**62**	**18**
1866	1[11]	54[16]	14	9	1	-
	2	83	6	29	34	14
	3	29	5	15	5	4
Total		**166**	**24**	**53**	**62**	**18**

1867	1[11]	43	14	9	20	-
	2	83	6	29	34	14
	3	31	6	15	5	5
Total		157	24	53	62	18
1868	1[11]	43	14	9	20	-
	2	85	7	25	38	15
	3	33	7	15	6	7
Total		161	28	49	64	22
1869	1[11]	43	14	9	20	-
	2	76	7	50	4	16
	3	25	7	12	5	1
Total		144	28	71	29	17
1870	1[11]	43	14	9	20	-
	2	83	12	52	4	15
	3	25	4	11	5	-
Total		151	30	72	29	15
1871	1[11]	43	14	9	20	-
	2	54	12	22	12	-
	3	32	-	11	9	10
Total		129	28	42	41	10
1872	1[11]	45	15	9	20	1
	2	60	15	20	17	8
	3	33	7	11	9	6
Total		138	37	40	46	15
1873	1[11]	31	16	2	12	1
	2	60	15	20	17	8
	3	33	7	11	9	6
Total		124	38	33	38	15
1874	1[11]	31	16	2	12	1
	2	74	17	24	20	13
	3	33	7	11	9	6
Total		138	40	37	41	20

1875 - 1876	1 [11]	33	17	2	13	1
	2	74	17	24	20	13
	3	33	7	11	9	6
Total		**140**	**41**	**37**	**42**	**20**
1877	1 [11]	50	19	2	28	1
	2	100	16	24	30	30
	3	37	9	10	11	7
Total		**187**	**44**	**36**	**69**	**38**
1878	1 [11]	91	22	3	65	1
	2	64	19	25	15	25
	3	37	9	10	11	7
Total		**192**	**50**	**38** [17]	**91** [17]	**33**
1879	1 [18]	214	50	38	90	36
Total		**214**	**50**	**38**	**90**	**36**
1880-1883	1 [11]	89	22	3	63	1
	2	88	19	25	16	28
	3	37	9	10	11	7
Total		**214**	**50**	**38**	**91**	**33**

[16] Recorded as "30 small" but does not state type of mill power used.
[17] A note was recorded as "the 'cattle' and 'wind' power mills are, as a rule, in very small estates or holdings of from 3 to 30 acres in cane cultivation"
[18] Recorded as island wide instead of individual Quarters.

CHAPTER 13.6

Number of Sugar Usines

Year	District Number	No. Sugar Usines
1885	*No Record*	*5*
1886	*No Record*	*4*
1887 – 1901 [19]	*1*	*3*
	2	*-*
	3	*1*
Total		*4*

[19] Districts were defined as 1 (Castries, Dennery and Gros-Islet), 2 (Soufriere, Choiseul, Anse-le-Ray) and 3 (Vieux Fort, Laborie, Micoud).

Year	District Number [2]	No. Sugar Usines & Name
1902 – 1943 [20]	*1*	*3* *(Cul de Sac / Roseau / Dennery)*
	2	*-*
	3	*1* *(Vieux Fort)*
Total		*4*
1944 – 1958 [20]	*1*	*3* *(Cul de Sac / Roseau / Dennery)*
	2	*-*
	3	*-*
Total		*3*
1959 – 1963 [20]	*1*	*1* *(Roseau)*
	2	*-*
	3	*-*
Total		*1*

[20] Districts were defined as 1 (Castries, Dennery and Gros-Islet), 2 (Soufrière, Choiseul, Anse-le-Ray) and 3 (Vieux Fort, Laborie, Micoud).

CHAPTER 13.7

Sugar Usine Production

The following shows the production quantities for sugar from the sugar factories (the French naming being *sugar usine*).

In 1884, the records were no longer listed by district names, but as a total figure of all districts combined.

Key:

t – tonne
lbs – pound
NR – no record available

Year	Usine Sugar Cultivated	Price per Ton (£)
1884	1,400 t	20
1885	2,200 t	18
1886	2,650 t	16
1887	6,295,646 lbs	16
1888	6,289,700 lbs	16
1889	6,127,000 lbs	19
1890	7,890,000 lbs	16
1891	7,057,400 lbs	NR
1892	10,346,300 lbs	NR
1893	8,011,200 lbs	NR
1894	7,668,400 lbs	NR
1895	7,362,200 lbs	NR
1896	6,843,920 lbs	NR

Key:

t – tonne
lbs – pound
d – pence
NR – no record available

Year	Usine Sugar Cultivated	Price per lbs (d)
1897	7,616,332 lbs	NR
1898	7,722,800 lbs	3d for white / 2d for brown
1899	8,834,424 lbs	3d for white / 2d for brown
1900	8,612,320 lbs	3d for white / 2d for brown
1901	9,934,000 lbs	2½d for white / 2d for brown
1902	8,253,484 lbs	2½d for white / 2d for brown
1903	7,727,400 lbs	2½d for white / 2d for brown
1904	9,893,184 lbs	2½d for white / 2d for brown
1905	3,721 t	2½d for white / 2d for brown
1906	5,441 t	2½d for white / 2d for brown
1907	5,302 t	2½d
1908	4,481 t	2d
1909	5,360 t	2d
1910	5,199 t	2d
1911-1913	NR	2d
1914	NR	2½d
1915	NR	3d to 4½d
1916	NR	4d to 5d
1917	NR	3½d
1918	NR	3½d to 4½d
1919	NR	3½d

Key:

t – tonne
SM – Sugar Manufacturers Ltd (both factories combined)
CFC- Cane Farmer Contributions

The below table also features records of quantity of farmers' canes reaped and supplied to the two active sugar companies during the sugar cane seasons (labelled CFC).

Sugar Cane Year or Season	Sugar Manufacturers Ltd (Roseau Factory) (t)	Sugar Manufacturers Ltd (Cul-de-Sac Factory) (t)	Dennery Factory Co. Ltd (t)	Total (t)
1948	Not Recorded			5,000
1949/50	Not Recorded			8,500
1951	Not Recorded			100,084
1952	Not Recorded			95,817
1953-54	6,838	4,702	7,747	SM: 11,540 Total: 19,287
1954-55	7,965	4,368	7,333	SM: 12,333 Total: 19,666
1955-56	9,648	6,299	8,365	SM: 15,947 Total: 24,312
1956	Not Recorded			10,873
1957	Not Recorded			Factories: 7,850 CFC:11,317
1958	Not Recorded			Factories: 6,975 CFC: 10,317
1959-1960	Not Recorded			5,498
1961-1962	Not Recorded			3,880

CHAPTER 13.8

'Sugar' Cultivation

Key:

s - shilling
d – pence
lbs – pounds
NR – no record available

Year	Parish Name and District Number	Sugar Cultivated (lbs)	Price per Cart (£sd)
1828	Castries (1)	1,285,000	18s 6d
	Gros Islet (1)	1,132,900	
	Anse la Raye (1)	940,000	
	Soufrière & Choiseul (2)	1,983,000	
	Laborie (2)	835,000	
	Vieux Fort (3)	1,243,000	
	Micoud & Praslin (3)	1,320,000	
	Dennery (3)	960,000	
	Dauphin (3)	581,600	
Total		**10,380,500**	
1829	No Record		

1830	Castries (1)	1,337,000	18s
	Gros Islet (1)	1,170,000	
	Anse la Raye (1)	940,000	
	Soufrière & Choiseul (2)	1,983,000	
	Laborie (2)	636,000	
	Vieux Fort (3)	853,000	
	Micoud & Praslin (3)	1,43,700	
	Dennery (3)	96,000	
	Dauphin (3)	410,000	
Total		**7,962,000**	
1831	Castries (1)	830,000	12s
	Gros Islet (1)	553,000	
	Anse la Raye (1)	432,815	
	Soufrière (2)	1,076,000	
	Choiseul (2)	192,000	
	Laborie (2)	422,000	
	Vieux Fort (3)	880,000	
	Micoud & Praslin (3)	130,000	
	Dennery (3)	536,000	
	Dauphin (3)	570,000	
Total		**5,561,815**	
1832	Castries (1)	600,000	15s 6d
	Gros Islet (1)	553,000	
	Anse la Raye (1)	428.500	
	Soufrière (2)	691,500	
	Choiseul (2)	146,600	
	Laborie (2)	48,000	
	Vieux Fort (3)	679,900	
	Micoud & Praslin (3)	1,092,000	
	Dennery (3)	504,000	
	Dauphin (3)	320,000	
Total		**5,061,500**	

1833	Castries (1)	700,000	16s
	Gros Islet (1)	416,500	
	Anse la Raye (1)	441,000	
	Soufrière (2)	719,571	
	Choiseul (2)	162,000	
	Laborie (2)	42,000	
	Vieux Fort (3)	668,000	
	Micoud & Praslin (3)	1, 027,088	
	Dennery (3)	380,184	
	Dauphin (3)	439,600	
Total		**5,365,943**	
1834	Castries (1)	750,000	NR
	Gros Islet (1)	573,000	
	Anse la Raye (1)	532,000	
	Soufrière (2)	979,700	
	Choiseul (2)	292,350	
	Laborie (2)	661,200	
	Vieux Fort (3)	654,000	
	Micoud & Praslin (3)	1,109,000	
	Dennery (3)	690,388	
	Dauphin (3)	428,000	
Total		**6,530,638**	
1835	Castries (1)	650,000	NR
	Gros Islet (1)	768,000	
	Anse la Raye (1)	435,000	
	Soufrière (2)	784,800	
	Choiseul (2)	200,000	
	Laborie (2)	537,000	
	Vieux Fort (3)	771,200	
	Micoud & Praslin (3)	841,000	
	Dennery (3)	474,379	
	Dauphin (3)	400,000	
Total		**5,861,379**	

1836	Castries (1)	537,000	NR
	Gros Islet (1)	336,000	
	Anse la Raye (1)	284,000	
	Soufriere (2)	370,000	
	Choiseul (2)	370,000	
	Laborie (2)	665,000	
	Vieux Fort (3)	165,000	
	Micoud & Praslin (3)	191,000	
	Dennery (3)	564,000	
	Dauphin (3)	835,400	
Total		**4,318,010**	
1837	Castries & Anse la Raye (1)	660,400	48s
	Gros Islet & Dauphin (2)	1,104,000	
	Soufrière & Choiseul (3)	826,000	
	Vieux Fort & Laborie (4)	730,000	
	Micoud, Praslin & Dennery (5)	1,343,500	
Total		**4,663,900**	
1838	Castries & Anse la Raye (1)	809,000	17s
	Gros Islet & Dauphin (2)	883,000	21s
	Soufrière & Choiseul (3)	1,160,000	21s 8d
	Vieux Fort & Laborie (4)	1,200,000	NR
	Micoud, Praslin & Dennery (5)	1,770,000	20s
Total		**5,822,999**	
1839	Castries & Anse la Raye (1)	947,000	£60
	Gros Islet & Dauphin (2)	771,000	
	Soufrière & Choiseul (3)	756,003	
	Vieux Fort & Laborie (4)	1,198,300	
	Micoud, Praslin & Dennery (5)	123,000	
Total		**3,795,303**	

1840	Castries & Anse la Raye (1)	1,600,000	£1.8 to 1.12
	Gros Islet & Dauphin (2)	975,433	£1.5
	Soufrière & Choiseul (3)	736,600	£1.5
	Vieux Fort & Laborie (4)	444,000	NR
	Micoud, Praslin & Dennery (5)	697,000	NR
Total		**4,453,033**	
1841	Castries & Anse la Raye (1)	2,000.000	25s to 30s
	Gros Islet & Dauphin (2)	1,054,000	
	Soufrière & Choiseul (3)	1,165,690	
	Vieux Fort & Laborie (4)	715,000	
	Micoud, Praslin & Dennery (5)	101,600	
Total		**5,036,290**	
1842	Castries & Anse la Raye (1)	1,678,800	£1.4
	Gros Islet & Dauphin (2)	1,389,000	£1.4
	Soufrière & Choiseul (3)	175,700	18s 3d
	Vieux Fort & Laborie (4)	915,410	£1.0
	Micoud, Praslin & Dennery (5)	1,104,000	£1.0
Total		**5,262,910**	
1843	Castries & Anse la Raye (1)	1,055,600	16s to £1.4
	Gros Islet & Dauphin (2)	943,130	18s to 20s
	Soufrière & Choiseul (3)	1,182,500	16s
	Vieux Fort & Laborie (4)	909,500	14s
	Micoud, Praslin & Dennery (5)	999,400	£1
Total		**5,090,130**	
1844	Castries & Anse la Raye (1)	1,800,000	15s to 24s
	Gros Islet & Dauphin (2)	150,800	18s
	Soufrière & Choiseul (3)	1,292,770	18s
	Vieux Fort & Laborie (4)	1,436,000	16s
	Micoud, Praslin & Dennery (5)	1,457,200	16s
Total		**6,136,770**	

1845	Castries & Anse la Raye (1)	949,300	15s to 24s
	Gros Islet & Dauphin (2)	1,659,510	18s
	Soufrière, Canaries & Choiseul (3)	2,071,860	14s to 16s
	Vieux Fort, Laborie & part of Choiseul (4)	1,600,000	16s
	Micoud, Praslin & Dennery (5)	1,499,600	16s
Total		**7,780,270**	
1846	Castries & Anse la Raye (1)	852,200	15s to 24s
	Gros Islet & Dauphin (2)	1,309,840	16s
	Soufrière, Canaries & Choiseul (3)	1,316,000	16s
	Vieux Fort, Laborie & part of Choiseul (4)	1,248,500	16s
	Micoud, Praslin & Dennery (5)	1,422,200	16s
Total		**6,148,740**	
1847	Castries & Anse la Raye (1)	953,329	15s to 24s
	Gros Islet & Dauphin (2)	1,904,325	12s
	Soufrière, Canaries & Choiseul (3)	2,120,320	12s to 16s
	Vieux Fort, Laborie & part of Choiseul (4)	1,718,200	12s
	Micoud, Praslin & Dennery (5)	1,988,100	12s
Total		**8684,265**	
1848	Castries & Anse la Raye (1)	1,347,500	12s
	Gros Islet & Dauphin (2)	1,168,000	12s
	Soufrière, Canaries & Choiseul (3)	1,160,400	10s to 12s
	Vieux Fort, Laborie & part of Choiseul (4)	1,007,200	12s
	Micoud, Praslin & Dennery (5)	1,538,400	10s
Total		**6,221,500**	
1849	Castries & Anse la Raye (1)	1,033,352	NR
	Gros Islet & Dauphin (2)	838,700	12s
	Soufrière, Canaries & Choiseul (3)	1,460,800	10s to 12s
	Vieux Fort, Laborie & part of Choiseul (4)	1,239,000	10s to 12s
	Micoud, Praslin & Dennery (5)	1,565,500	12s
Total		**6,157,352**	

1850	Castries & Anse la Raye (1)	606,800	15s
	Gros Islet & Dauphin (2)	985,700	10s to 15s
	Soufrière, Canaries & Choiseul (3)	1,550,000	10s to 16s
	Vieux Fort, Laborie & part of Choiseul (4)	1,002,500	8s to 10s
	Micoud, Praslin & Dennery (5)	1,292,912	14s
Total		5,527,912	
1851	Castries & Anse la Raye (1)	1,344,200	12s
	Gros Islet, Dauphin & Dennery (2)	1,207,700	10s to 12s
	Choiseul & part Laborie (3)	2,530,600	10s
	Vieux Fort, Laborie & Micoud (4)	1,615,300	8s
Total		6,691,800	
1852	Castries & Anse la Raye (1)	1,364,000	10s
	Gros Islet, Dauphin & Dennery (2)	1,326,060	8s
	Choiseul & part Laborie (3)	2,464,400	10s
	Vieux Fort, Laborie & Micoud (4)	1,976,100	8s to 9s
Total		7,130,560	
1853	Castries & Anse la Raye (1)	1,175,800	12s
	Gros Islet, Dauphin & Dennery (2)	1,336,100	12s to 15s
	Choiseul & part Laborie (3)	2,372,000	12s
	Vieux Fort, Laborie & Micoud (4)	1,898,800	10s
Total		6,782,900	
1854	Castries & Anse la Raye (1)	1,674,400	9s
	Gros Islet, Dauphin & Dennery (2)	1,313,700	9s to 12s
	Choiseul & part Laborie (3)	2,539,700	10s
	Vieux Fort, Laborie & Micoud (4)	1,886,300	8s
Total		7,414,100	
1855	Castries & Anse la Raye (1)	1,160,776	9s
	Gros Islet, Dauphin & Dennery (2)	1,280,600	7s to 8s
	Choiseul & part Laborie (3)	2,471,000	10s
	Vieux Fort, Laborie & Micoud (4)	1,771,491	10s to 11s
Total		6,683,867	

1856	Castries & Anse la Raye (1)	763,800	18s to 20s
	Gros Islet, Dauphin & Dennery (2)	1,442,000	14s
	Choiseul & part Laborie (3)	2,487,900	25s
	Vieux Fort, Laborie & Micoud (4)	1,591,560	12s to 14s
Total		**6,285,600**	
1857	Castries & Anse la Raye (1)	741,151	20s to 30s
	Gros Islet, Dauphin & Dennery (2)	1,022,800	20s to 28s
	Choiseul & part Laborie (3)	2,666,644	20s
	Vieux Fort, Laborie & Micoud (4)	1,831,500	16s to 20s
Total		**6,262,000**	
1858	Castries & Anse la Raye (1)	779,548	12s to 15s
	Gros Islet, Dauphin & Dennery (2)	1,091,500	12s to 14s
	Choiseul & part Laborie (3)	3,483,520	12s to 14s
	Vieux Fort, Laborie & Micoud (4)	1,886,100	12s to 14s
Total		**7,240,668**	
1859	Castries & Anse la Raye (1)	1,097,322	10s to 14s
	Gros Islet, Dauphin & Dennery (2)	1,241,650	14s
	Choiseul & part Laborie (3)	2,974,265	10s to 14s
	Vieux Fort, Laborie & Micoud (4)	1,899,700	10s to 13s
Total		**7,212,937**	
1860	Castries & Anse la Raye (1)	1,315,563	12s to 16s
	Gros Islet, Dauphin & Dennery (2)	1,289,668	14s
	Choiseul & part Laborie (3)	3,331,720	10s to 12s
	Vieux Fort, Laborie & Micoud (4)	1,851,100	12s to 15s
Total		**7,788,051**	
1861	Castries & Anse la Raye (1)	1,361,008	12s
	Gros Islet, Dauphin & Dennery (2)	1,303,500	14s
	Choiseul & part Laborie (3)	4,065,600	15s
	Vieux Fort, Laborie & Micoud (4)	1,985,820	16s
Total		**8,715,928**	

1862	Castries & Anse la Raye (1)	1,270,007	12s
	Gros Islet, Dauphin & Dennery (2)	1,775,900	12s
	Choiseul & part Laborie (3)	3,716,042	12s
	Vieux Fort, Laborie & Micoud (4)	2,008,225	10s to 12s
Total		**8,770,174**	
1863	Castries & Anse la Raye (1)	1,216,094	11s
	Gros Islet, Dauphin & Dennery (2)	1,786,900	14s
	Choiseul & part Laborie (3)	4,574,231	NR
	Vieux Fort, Laborie & Micoud (4)	1,950,523	12s to 12s 6d
Total		**9,527,748**	
1864	Castries & Anse la Raye (1)	1,217,071	10s
	Gros Islet, Dauphin & Dennery (2)	1,167,000	10s
	Choiseul & part Laborie (3)	3,724,860	14s to 18s
	Vieux Fort, Laborie & Micoud (4)	1,730,830	12s to 18s
Total		**8,342,761**	
1865	Castries, Gros Islet, Dauphin & Dennery (1)	3,003,971	10s
	Anse la Raye, Choiseul & Soufrière (2)	3,779,650	10s to 14s
	Vieux Fort, Laborie, Praslin & Micoud (3)	2,407,780	12s to 18s
Total		**9,191,401**	
1866	Castries, Gros Islet, Dauphin & Dennery (1)	3,006,464	10s
	Anse la Raye, Choiseul & Soufrière (2)	4,648,058	12s
	Vieux Fort, Laborie, Praslin & Micoud (3)	2,972,400	12s
Total		**10,627,422**	
1867	Castries, Gros Islet, Dauphin & Dennery (1)	1,210,760	10s to 20s
	Anse la Raye, Choiseul & Soufrière (2)	4,518,352	13s to 14s 6d
	Vieux Fort, Laborie, Praslin & Micoud (3)	3,047,420	12s
Total		**8,776,512**	
1868	Castries, Gros Islet, Dauphin & Dennery (1)	2,262,560	10s to 13s
	Anse la Raye, Choiseul & Soufrière (2)	5,072,865	12s to 14s
	Vieux Fort, Laborie, Praslin & Micoud (3)	3,067,473	12s
Total		**10,402,898**	

1869	Castries, Gros Islet, Dauphin & Dennery (1)	1,503,484	10s to 13s
	Anse la Raye, Choiseul & Soufrière (2)	6,547,006	12s to 14s
	Vieux Fort, Laborie, Praslin & Micoud (3)	2,716,100	12s to 13s
Total		10,766,590	
1870	Castries, Gros Islet, Dauphin & Dennery (1)	2,144,091	NR
	Anse la Raye, Choiseul & Soufrière (2)	6,320,988	NR
	Vieux Fort, Laborie, Praslin & Micoud (3)	397,905	NR
Total		12,444,136	

Between 1871 and 1876, the Colony Report stated that "there being no means of obtaining the information required under this form the blanks have not been filled, it estimates by officers not possessing special knowledge are necessarily unreliable".

1877	Castries, Gros Islet, Dauphin & Dennery (1)	3,575,000	12s to 15s
	Anse la Raye, Choiseul & Soufrière (2)	4,500,000	12s to 15s
	Vieux Fort, Laborie, Praslin & Micoud (3)	3,584,000	12s to 15s
Total		11,659,000	
1878	Castries, Gros Islet, Dauphin & Dennery (1)	NR	NR
	Anse la Raye, Choiseul & Soufrière (2)	5,000,000	10s
	Vieux Fort, Laborie, Praslin & Micoud (3)	3,232,320	NR
Total		8,232,320	
1879	Castries, Gros Islet, Dauphin & Dennery (1)	NR	10s
	Anse la Raye, Choiseul & Soufrière (2)	NR	10s
	Vieux Fort, Laborie, Praslin & Micoud (3)	NR	10s
Total		8,232,320	
1880	Castries, Gros Islet, Dauphin & Dennery (1)	NR	NR
	Anse la Raye, Choiseul & Soufrière (2)	5,000,000	12s
	Vieux Fort, Laborie, Praslin & Micoud (3)	38,860	12s
Total		5,038,860	

CHAPTER 13.9

Molasses Produced

Key:

s - shilling
d – pence
gal – gallon
NR – no record available

Year	Parish Name and District Number	Molasses Produced (gal)	Price Per Gallon (£sd)
1828	Castries (1)	36,000	9d
	Gros Islet (1)	56,450	
	Anse la Raye (1)	10,550	
	Soufrière & Choiseul (2)	39,802	
	Laborie (2)	21,300	
	Vieux Fort (3)	52,300	
	Micoud & Praslin (3)	37,230	
	Dennery (3)	30,760	
	Dauphin (3)	9,490	
Total		**290,822**	
1829	No Record		

1830	Castries (1)	36,440	7½d
	Gros Islet (1)	43,130	
	Anse la Raye (1)	10,550	
	Soufrière & Choiseul (2)	39,802	
	Laborie (2)	20,000	
	Vieux Fort (3)	40,000	
	Micoud & Praslin (3)	107,300	
	Dennery (3)	30,700	
	Dauphin (3)	600	
Total		**238,522**	
1831	Castries (1)	21,291	6d
	Gros Islet (1)	25,050	
	Anse la Raye (1)	10,282	
	Soufrière (2)	23,350	
	Choiseul (2)	3,800	
	Laborie (2)	8,467	
	Vieux Fort (3)	70,000	
	Micoud & Praslin (3)	25,300	
	Dennery (3)	20,150	
	Dauphin (3)	17,000	
Total		**224,690**	
1832	Castries (1)	17,900	8d
	Gros Islet (1)	12,550	
	Anse la Raye (1)	25,000	
	Soufrière (2)	14,250	
	Choiseul (2)	3,272	
	Laborie (2)	1,220	
	Vieux Fort (3)	21,800	
	Micoud & Praslin (3)	21,700	
	Dennery (3)	13,500	
	Dauphin (3)	4,500	
Total		**135,692**	

1833	Castries (1)	18,500	9d
	Gros Islet (1)	13,150	
	Anse la Raye (1)	18,300	
	Soufrière (2)	17,150	
	Choiseul (2)	4,160	
	Laborie (2)	16,189	
	Vieux Fort (3)	27,657	
	Micoud & Praslin (3)	22,500	
	Dennery (3)	17,053	
	Dauphin (3)	7,500	
Total		**162,159**	
1834	Castries (1)	30,000	NR
	Gros Islet (1)	35,000	
	Anse la Raye (1)	13,137	
	Soufrière (2)	20,750	
	Choiseul (2)	1,000	
	Laborie (2)	20,700	
	Vieux Fort (3)	26,400	
	Micoud & Praslin (3)	27,090	
	Dennery (3)	16,320	
	Dauphin (3)	2,600	
Total		**192,997**	
1835	Castries (1)	19,900	7½d
	Gros Islet (1)	12,900	
	Anse la Raye (1)	2,800	
	Soufrière (2)	15,726	
	Choiseul (2)	6,000	
	Laborie (2)	16,266	
	Vieux Fort (3)	33,467	
	Micoud & Praslin (3)	25,000	
	Dennery (3)	9,825	
	Dauphin (3)	2,800	
Total		**144,684**	

1836	Castries (1)	17,200	NR
	Gros Islet (1)	4,200	
	Anse la Raye (1)	1,500	
	Soufrière (2)	7,400	
	Choiseul (2)	3,000	
	Laborie (2)	7,540	
	Vieux Fort (3)	1,800	
	Micoud & Praslin (3)	7,100	
	Dennery (3)	15,640	
	Dauphin (3)	24,675	
Total		*74,955*	
1837	Castries & Anse la Raye (1)	28,573	7½d
	Gros Islet & Dauphin (2)	25,700	
	Soufrière & Choiseul (3)	8,000	
	Vieux Fort & Laborie (4)	7,000	
	Micoud, Praslin & Dennery (5)	35,500	
Total		*104,773*	
1838	Castries & Anse la Raye (1)	10,500	8d
	Gros Islet & Dauphin (2)	35,000	11d
	Soufrière & Choiseul (3)	20,860	1s
	Vieux Fort & Laborie (4)	0	0
	Micoud, Praslin & Dennery (5)	70,000	7s 2d
Total		*136,360*	
1839	Castries & Anse la Raye (1)	34,200	NR
	Gros Islet & Dauphin (2)	7,720	
	Soufrière & Choiseul (3)	13,000	
	Vieux Fort & Laborie (4)	35,140	
	Micoud, Praslin & Dennery (5)	21,600	
Total		*111,600*	

1840	Castries & Anse la Raye (1)	22,300	11¼d
	Gros Islet & Dauphin (2)	10,000	10d
	Soufrière & Choiseul (3)	5,164	10d
	Vieux Fort & Laborie (4)	12,730	NR
	Micoud, Praslin & Dennery (5)	19,600	NR
Total		**69,794**	
1841	Castries & Anse la Raye (1)	23,500	1s
	Gros Islet & Dauphin (2)	17,800	6d
	Soufrière & Choiseul (3)	23,690	1s to 1s 6d
	Vieux Fort & Laborie (4)	29,383	NR
	Micoud, Praslin & Dennery (5)	25,700	NR
Total		**120,073**	
1842	Castries & Anse la Raye (1)	90,720	7d
	Gros Islet & Dauphin (2)	25,346	7d
	Soufrière & Choiseul (3)	30,000	6d
	Vieux Fort & Laborie (4)	44,560	6d
	Micoud, Praslin & Dennery (5)	26,200	6d
Total		**214,826**	
1843	Castries & Anse la Raye (1)	18,000	6d to 7d
	Gros Islet & Dauphin (2)	18,720	6d
	Soufriere & Choiseul (3)	30,880	7½d
	Vieux Fort & Laborie (4)	28,400	6d
	Micoud, Praslin & Dennery (5)	35,576	6½d
Total		**131,576**	
1844	Castries & Anse la Raye (1)	48,000	6d
	Gros Islet & Dauphin (2)	24,040	10d
	Soufrière & Choiseul (3)	30,470	1s
	Vieux Fort & Laborie (4)	48,000	6s 2d
	Micoud, Praslin & Dennery (5)	35,000	6s 2d
Total		**185,510**	

1845	*Castries & Anse la Raye (1)*	*14,920*	*8d*
	Gros Islet & Dauphin (2)	*31,000*	*7d*
	Soufrière, Canaries & Choiseul (3)	*68,653*	*5d*
	Vieux Fort, Laborie & part of Choiseul (4)	*43,900*	*6d*
	Micoud, Praslin & Dennery (5)	*24,600*	*6d*
Total		*183,073*	
1846	*Castries & Anse la Raye (1)*	*16,000*	*8d to 1s*
	Gros Islet & Dauphin (2)	*27,700*	*8d*
	Soufrière, Canaries & Choiseul (3)	*41,148*	*2½d*
	Vieux Fort, Laborie & part of Choiseul (4)	*32,684*	*6d*
	Micoud, Praslin & Dennery (5)	*21,000*	*6d*
Total		*138,532*	
1847	*Castries & Anse la Raye (1)*	*17,000*	*8d to 1s*
	Gros Islet & Dauphin (2)	*16,600*	*6d*
	Soufriere, Canaries & Choiseul (3)	*30,389*	*6d*
	Vieux Fort, Laborie & part of Choiseul (4)	*43,370*	*5d*
	Micoud, Praslin & Dennery (5)	*14,900*	*5d*
Total		*122,259*	
1848	*Castries & Anse la Raye (1)*	*31,335*	*4d*
	Gros Islet & Dauphin (2)	*24,240*	*2d*
	Soufriere, Canaries & Choiseul (3)	*16,000*	*5d to 6d*
	Vieux Fort, Laborie & part of Choiseul (4)	*28,850*	*NR*
	Micoud, Praslin & Dennery (5)	*36,100*	*5d*
Total		*136,525*	
1849	*Castries & Anse la Raye (1)*	*29,480*	*6d*
	Gros Islet & Dauphin (2)	*78,550*	*6d*
	Soufrière, Canaries & Choiseul (3)	*18,000*	*5d to 6d*
	Vieux Fort, Laborie & part of Choiseul (4)	*39,300*	*5d to 6d*
	Micoud, Praslin & Dennery (5)	*27,650*	*5d*
Total		*192,980*	

1850	Castries & Anse la Raye (1)	14,830	5d
	Gros Islet & Dauphin (2)	24,740	6d
	Soufrière, Canaries & Choiseul (3)	30,000	6d
	Vieux Fort, Laborie & part of Choiseul (4)	38,800	6d
	Micoud, Praslin & Dennery (5)	31,910	5d
Total		**140,280**	
1851	Castries & Anse la Raye (1)	40,320	5d
	Gros Islet, Dauphin & Dennery (2)	2,473	4d to 6d
	Choiseul & part Laborie (3)	79,300	5d
	Vieux Fort, Laborie & Micoud (4)	37,447	5d
Total		**159,540**	
1852	Castries & Anse la Raye (1)	18,538	4d
	Gros Islet, Dauphin & Dennery (2)	32,345	3d to 4d
	Choiseul & part Laborie (3)	104, 000	3d
	Vieux Fort, Laborie & Micoud (4)	50,912	3d to 4d
Total		**206,695**	
1853	Castries & Anse la Raye (1)	24,800	4d
	Gros Islet, Dauphin & Dennery (2)	43,935	2d to 4d
	Choiseul & part Laborie (3)	66,800	4d
	Vieux Fort, Laborie & Micoud (4)	79,177	4d
Total		**214,712**	
1854	Castries & Anse la Raye (1)	39,995	4d
	Gros Islet, Dauphin & Dennery (2)	40,034	3d to 5d
	Choiseul & part Laborie (3)	70,985	5d
	Vieux Fort, Laborie & Micoud (4)	60,611	4d
Total		**208,625**	
1855	Castries & Anse la Raye (1)	32,402	6d
	Gros Islet, Dauphin & Dennery (2)	26,916	3d to 5d
	Choiseul & part Laborie (3)	66,601	6d
	Vieux Fort, Laborie & Micoud (4)	50,232	4d to 5d
Total		**176,157**	

1856	*Castries & Anse la Raye (1)*	*15,960*	*5d to 1s*
	Gros Islet, Dauphin & Dennery (2)	*39,080*	*16d*
	Choiseul & part Laborie (3)	*73,842*	*10d to 1s*
	Vieux Fort, Laborie & Micoud (4)	*54,839*	*6½d*
Total		*1,183,721*	
1857	*Castries & Anse la Raye (1)*	*16,579*	*10d to 1s 2d*
	Gros Islet, Dauphin & Dennery (2)	*26,415*	*NR*
	Choiseul & part Laborie (3)	*79,622*	*1d to 1s*
	Vieux Fort, Laborie & Micoud (4)	*50,879*	*NR*
Total		*173,435*	
1858	*Castries & Anse la Raye (1)*	*22,964*	*4d to 6d*
	Gros Islet, Dauphin & Dennery (2)	*23,695*	*4d to 5d*
	Choiseul & part Laborie (3)	*68,843*	*6d*
	Vieux Fort, Laborie & Micoud (4)	*50,940*	*6d*
Total		*166,442*	
1859	*Castries & Anse la Raye (1)*	*37,417*	*4d to 5d*
	Gros Islet, Dauphin & Dennery (2)	*33,172*	*5d*
	Choiseul & part Laborie (3)	*90,028*	*6d*
	Vieux Fort, Laborie & Micoud (4)	*47,322*	*4d to 5d*
Total		*207,939*	
1860	*Castries & Anse la Raye (1)*	*114,340*	*5d to 10d*
	Gros Islet, Dauphin & Dennery (2)	*35,940*	*6d*
	Choiseul & part Laborie (3)	*89,548*	*6d*
	Vieux Fort, Laborie & Micoud (4)	*44,576*	*5d to 6d*
Total		*284,404*	
1861	*Castries & Anse la Raye (1)*	*22,866*	*6d*
	Gros Islet, Dauphin & Dennery (2)	*21,664*	*6d*
	Choiseul & part Laborie (3)	*88,876*	*6d*
	Vieux Fort, Laborie & Micoud (4)	*29,794*	*6d*
Total		*62,700*	

1862	Castries & Anse la Raye (1)	21,608	4½d
	Gros Islet, Dauphin & Dennery (2)	NR	4d
	Choiseul & part Laborie (3)	91,594	1d
	Vieux Fort, Laborie & Micoud (4)	35,666	2d to 5d
Total		148,868	
1863	Castries & Anse la Raye (1)	30,526	4d
	Gros Islet, Dauphin & Dennery (2)	39,450	5d
	Choiseul & part Laborie (3)	NR	6d
	Vieux Fort, Laborie & Micoud (4)	44,480	4d to 5d
Total		114,456	
1864	Castries & Anse la Raye (1)	30,000	5d
	Gros Islet, Dauphin & Dennery (2)	22,500	5d
	Choiseul & part Laborie (3)	84,520	6d to 8d
	Vieux Fort, Laborie & Micoud (4)	54,928	5d to 8d
Total		191,948	
1865	Castries, Gros Islet, Dauphin & Dennery (1)	69,450	6d
	Anse la Raye, Choiseul & Soufrière (2)	91,990	5d to 6d
	Vieux Fort, Laborie, Praslin & Micoud (3)	31,513	4½d to 5d
Total		192,843	
1866	Castries, Gros Islet, Dauphin & Dennery (1)	69,470	NR
	Anse la Raye, Choiseul & Soufrière (2)	301,079	NR
	Vieux Fort, Laborie, Praslin & Micoud (3)	67,225	NR
Total		437,774	
1867	Castries, Gros Islet, Dauphin & Dennery (1)	45,450	4d to 4d½
	Anse la Raye, Choiseul & Soufrière (2)	318,254	5d to 6d
	Vieux Fort, Laborie, Praslin & Micoud (3)	67,106	5d
Total		420,810	
1868	Castries, Gros Islet, Dauphin & Dennery (1)	64,910	NR
	Anse la Raye, Choiseul & Soufrière (2)	301,834	5d to 6d
	Vieux Fort, Laborie, Praslin & Micoud (3)	68,206	5d
Total		434,950	

1869	Castries, Gros Islet, Dauphin & Dennery (1)	31,342	6d
	Anse la Raye, Choiseul & Soufrière (2)	44,972	6d
	Vieux Fort, Laborie, Praslin & Micoud (3)	67,744	6d
Total		**144,058**	
1870	Castries, Gros Islet, Dauphin & Dennery (1)	26,362	NR
	Anse la Raye, Choiseul & Soufrière (2)	77,804	NR
	Vieux Fort, Laborie, Praslin & Micoud (3)	48,922	NR
Total		**153,088**	

Between 1871 and 1876, the Colony Report stated that "there being no means of obtaining the information required under this form the blanks have not been filled, it estimates by officers not possessing special knowledge are necessarily unreliable".

1877	Castries, Gros Islet, Dauphin & Dennery (1)	NR	8d to 1s
	Anse la Raye, Choiseul & Soufrière (2)	106,000	8d to 1s
	Vieux Fort, Laborie, Praslin & Micoud (3)	30,000	8d to 1s
Total		**136,000**	
1878	Castries, Gros Islet, Dauphin & Dennery (1)	NR	NR
	Anse la Raye, Choiseul & Soufrière (2)	110,000	6d
	Vieux Fort, Laborie, Praslin & Micoud (3)	36,000	6d
Total		**146,000**	
1879	Castries, Gros Islet, Dauphin & Dennery (1)	NR	6d
	Anse la Raye, Choiseul & Soufrière (2)	NR	6d
	Vieux Fort, Laborie, Praslin & Micoud (3)	NR	6d
Total		**NR**	
1880	Castries, Gros Islet, Dauphin & Dennery (1)	NR	NR
	Anse la Raye, Choiseul & Soufrière (2)	100,000	6d
	Vieux Fort, Laborie, Praslin & Micoud (3)	36,000	6d
Total		**136,000**	

Between 1881 and 1883, there were no records of agriculture within the Colony Reports. In 1884, the records were no longer listed by district names, but as a total figure of all districts combined.

Year	Molasses Produced (gal unless stated)	Price per Gallon (£sd)
1884	381,500	4d
1885	215,804	4d
1886	414,160	4d
1887	NR	4d
1888	346,300	7d
1889	634,492	4d
1890	213,360	NR
1891	330,780	NR
1892	253,680	NR
1893	223,320	NR
1894	279,402	NR
1895	105,000	NR
1896	381,500	4d
1897	3,520	NR
1898	162,670	3d
1899	62,500	3d
1900	57,960	3d
1901	7,780	3d
1902	5,640	3d
1903	59,570	3d
1904	NR	3d
1905	424 p	3d
1906	11 p	3d
1907	NR	NR
1908	NR	NR
1909	60,099	NR
1910	95,222	NR
1911-1934	NR	NR

Year	Molasses Produced (gal)	Value (£)
1935	168,903	2,401
1936	107,128	1,132
1937	144,016	3,201
1938	150,278	3,086
1939	128,389	3,027
1940	128,945	2,485
1941-1950	NR	NR
1951	403,961	NR
1952	467,500	NR

CHAPTER 13.10

Muscovado Production and Number of Sugar Works

Key:

cwt – hundredweight
lbs – pound
t - tonne
NR – no record available

In 1884, the records were no longer listed by district names, but as a total figure of all districts combined.

Year	Muscovado Produced	Price per Ton (£)
1884	4,540 cwt	13
1885	4,100 cwt	10
1886	1,678 cwt	11
1887	3,623,600 lbs	11
1888	2,441,300 lbs	11
1889	2,553,800 lbs	13
1890	3,274,000 lbs	11
1891	2,755,200 lbs	NR
1892	2,525,300 lbs	NR
1893	1,928,400 lbs	NR
1894	2,377,800 lbs	NR
1895	763,700 lbs	NR
1896	1,105,608 lbs	NR
1897	1,025,360 lbs	NR
1898	680,900 lbs	NR
1899	101,200 lbs	NR
1900	387,600 lbs	1d
1901	945,800 lbs	1d

1902	*1,329,480 lbs*	*1d*
1903	*85,200 lbs*	*1d*
1904	*425,020 lbs*	*1d*
1905	*792 t*	*1d per lbs*
1906	*230 t*	*1d per lbs*
1907	*62 1/20ᵗʰ t*	*1d per lbs*
1908	*101 3/56ᵗʰ t*	*1½d per lbs*
1909	*160 t*	*1½d per lbs*
1910	*76 t*	*1½d per lbs*
1911-1914	*NR*	*1½d per lbs*
1915	*NR*	*2d to 3d per lbs*
1916	*NR*	*2½d to 3d per lbs*
1917	*NR*	*2½d per lbs*
1918	*NR*	*2½d to 3d per lbs*
1919	*NR*	*2½d per lbs*

Year	*Number of Muscovado Sugar Works*
1886	*Approx. 115*
1887-1891	*Approx. 100*
1892-1901	*No Record*
1902-1920	*Recorded as* *"There are a few sugar mills at work, as to which there is no reliable information"*

There's no mention of muscovado sugar works from 1921-1963.

CHAPTER 13.11

Malhado Production

Key:

lbs – pound
NR – no record available

Year	Melhado Produced	Price
1903	889,056 lbs	NR
1904	1,233 lbs	NR
1905	803 casks	NR
1906	313 casks	NR

CHAPTER 13.12

Molasquit Production

Key:

s – shilling
t - tonne
NR – no record available

Year	Molasquit Produced	Price per Bag (s)
1906	1,517 bags	NR
1907	3,700 bags	5
1908	7 t	5

CHAPTER 14

Saint Lucia Export Figures

The following tables of records have been adapted from numerous Saint Lucia Colony Reports (also known as Colonial Blue Books), courtesy of the *British Online Archives* and *The National Archives* in London. These Colony Reports were a yearly record of a colony's taxes, duties and other sources of revenue, military expenditure, legislation, laws, and proclamations, and import and export statistics amongst many others.

As a colony, Saint Lucia has had a record of such, dating back from 1821 to 1963, and adapting where possible, as well as deciphering from the handwritten inputs, you can find an insight into the manufacturing and export figures of sugar and its different varietals, plus rum, as well as the agricultural figures from the sugar cane estates and appropriate connections to such. Please note, there is a lack of consistency of certain weights and measures as the years go on, so each record has been adapted as seen. Any missing years are either mentioned and noted, or the records of such were no longer present due to the format of the Colony Reports at that time. For example, the first year of 1821 has no records at all regarding exports, production or acreage of cane. Please refer to each table key for guidance where needed.

Currency values stated as £sd and written as *Pound. Shilling. Pence (for example, £97,046, 11 shilling and 0 pence is formatted as 97,046.11.0)* until 1947 when the local currency changed to US$ on the Colony Reports.

CHAPTER 14.2

Rum Export

Key:

bbl – barrel
t – tonne
hhd – hogshead
quarter – quarter cask
pipe – pipe barrel
dp – puncheon
gal – gallon
W.I – West Indies
N.A.B.C – North American British Colonies

Year	Total Qty.	Total Value (£sd)
1822	*NR*	*4,786.17.2*
1823	*31,950 gal*	*3,993.15.0*
1824-1827	*No Record*	
1828	*304 p / 47 hhd*	*2,659.0.0*
1829	*653 p*	*4,334.0.0*
1830	*274 p / 19 cask / 1 pipe / 11 hhd*	*1,553.0.0*
1831	*421 p / 2 pipes / 6 Quarter / 35 hhd*	*NR*
1832	*2 pipes*	*NR*
1833	*133 p / 4 hhd / 22 casks / 11 demijohn*	*NR*
1834	*57 p / 3 Quarter*	*NR*
1835	*No Record*	
1836	*1 hhd / 1 Quarter / 1 demijohn*	*15.17.0*
1837	*90 p*	*547.0.0*
1838	*60 / 41 p / 21 bbl*	*1,374.7.0*
1839	*120 p*	*1,540.10.0*
1840	*129 p / 10 Quarter*	*1,560.0.0*
1841	*123 p*	*680.0.0*
1842	*67 p*	*710.0.0*
1843	*21 p / 4 casks*	*222.0.0*

1844	1,121 p	1,257.0.0
1845	170 p	1,946.5.1
1846	3,559 gal	355.18.0
1847	43,418 gal / 332 p / 25 hhd / 24 casks	4,034.15.6
1848	13,921 gal / 119 p / 1 hhd / 162 casks	1,033.14.0
1849	5,391 gal	271.12.6
1850	840 gal	42.0.0
1851	958 gal	65.4.6
1852	3,400 gal / 31p / 2 hhd / 2 casks	170.0.0
1853	2,800 gal / 21 p / 6 hhd	216.0.0
1854	14,364 gal / 115 p / 1 hhd / 29 casks	1,428.3.0
1855	38,848 gal	6,893.16.0

Between 1824 and 1827, the Colony Report stated that "This information could not be obtained".

Year	1856	1857	1858	1859
Great Britain (gal)	5,461	60 p / 7,071	13,006	8,752
N.A.B.C (gal)	10 p / 12,000	-	3,045	4,935
Dutch W.I (gal)	-	3 p / 340	-	-
French W.I (gal)	-	-	48	26
United States (gal)	-	-	2,268	1,680
British W.I (gal)	-	-	-	871
Total Qty. (gal)	10 p / 17,461	63 p / 7,411	18,367	16,264
Total Value (£sd)	566.9.6	823.9.7	1,788.17.0	1,081.6.0

Year	1860	1861	1862	1863	1864
Great Britain (gal)	16,516	7,320	478	6,192	805
N.A.B.C (gal)	4,400	2,760	-	7,057	-
Barbados (gal)	1,230	-	-	-	720
United States (gal)	6,610	-	2,413	-	-
Swedish W.I (gal)	465	-	2,391	-	-
Dominica (gal)	-	480	-	-	-
Danish W.I (gal)	-	480	-	-	-
British W.I (gal)	-	-	120	-	-
Trinidad & Tobago (gal)	-	-	186	-	-
French W.I (gal)	-	-	2,687	96	75
Venezuela (gal)	-	-	-	1,954	-
St. Vincent (gal)	-	-	-	-	470
Total Qty. (gal)	29,221	11,040	8,275	15,299	2,070
Total Value (£sd)	2,400.0.0	847.18.0	442.18.0	844.7.0	138.15.0

Year	1865	1866	1867	1868	1869	1870
Great Britain (gal)	12,892	3,533	7,076	-	-	-
N.A.B.C (gal)	2,884	114	28	-	-	-
Barbados (gal)	-	-	-	-	36	2,102
United States (gal)	-	-	1,728	-	-	-
New Grenada (gal)	-	-	36	-	-	-
Dominica (gal)	-	-	-	-	118	-
Dutch W.I (gal)	-	-	-	-	560	-
British W.I (gal)	-	-	-	1,861	-	-
French W.I (gal)	862	2,334	1,234	197	1,126	359
Total Qty. (gal)	16,638	5,981	10,102	2,058	1,840	2,461
Total Value (£sd)	844.5.0	360.0.0	515.2.0	122.0.0	186.0.0	168.0.0

Year	1871	1872	1873	1874	1875
Great Britain (gal)	930	1,379	220	5,756	4,170
Barbados (gal)	1,124	542	400	-	-
Danish W.I (gal)	-	-	126	-	-
French W.I (gal)	7,262	802	135	208	140
Total Qty. (gal)	9,316	2,723	881	5,973	4,310
Total Value (£sd)	593.13.4	272.2.0	100.10.0	473.6.8	452.16.0

Year	1876	1877	1878	1879	1880
Great Britain (gal)	41,409	25,558	15,272	7,470	-
French W.I (gal)	107 ¼	39	619	72	195
St. Vincent (gal)	18	-	-	-	-
France (gal)	-	-	56	-	-
Total Qty. (gal)	41,534 ¼	25,597	15,949	7,542	195
Total Value (£sd)	4,403.27.0	1,932.3.0	1,292.15.0	572.19.6	39.0.0

Year	1881	1882	1883	1884	1885
Great Britain (gal)	-	-	10	-	10,041
French W.I (gal)	62	90	1,596	11,790	508
Dominica (gal)	-	-	3	-	-
France (gal)	-	-	49	60	10,115
United States (gal)	-	-	-	1,860	-
Barbados (gal)	-	-	-	90	-
Spanish W.I (gal)	-	-	-	-	384
Colon (gal)	-	-	-	-	1,118
Total Qty. (gal)	62	90	1,658	13,8000	22,166
Total Value (£sd)	15.10.0	45.0.0	331.12.0	920.0.0	1,293.0.4

Year	1886	1887	1888	1889	1890
United Kingdom *(gal)*	-	-	-	-	126
French W.I *(gal)*	-	384	-	-	-
France *(gal)*	796	6,976	115	355	2,408
Barbados *(gal)*	492	-	-	-	-
Colon *(gal)*	1,138	509	1,423	-	-
Total Qty. *(gal)*	2,426	7,869	1,538	355	2,534
Total Value *(£sd)*	121.6.0	393.9.0	153.16.0	35.10.0	253.8.0

Year	1891	1892	1893	1894	1895
Canada *(gal)*	-	-	-	188	-
French W.I *(gal)*	36	-	-	-	-
Germany *(gal)*	-	-	-	22	-
France *(gal)*	452	4,071	1,687	1,165	9,899 ¾
United States *(gal)*	387	-	-	-	-
Barbados *(gal)*	-	2.5	-	-	-
St. Martins *(gal)*	-	-	-	45	-
Antigua *(gal)*	-	-	-	-	18
Total Qty. *(gal)*	875	4,073.5	1,687	1,420	9,917 ¾
Total Value *(£sd)*	87.10.0	407.7.0	112.9.4	106.10.0	1,033.2.0

Year	1896	1897	1898	1899	1900
United Kingdom *(gal)*	-	7,116 ¼	9,577	-	10,989
French W.I *(gal)*	187	366	196	2,655	289
Germany *(gal)*	-	746	-	-	-
France *(gal)*	1,093.5	1,879	4,829	1,690	642
Barbados *(gal)*	-	-	16	-	-
Danish W.I *(gal)*	-	-	-	653	-
Dominica *(gal)*	-	-	-	1,232	1,542
Total Qty. *(gal)*	1,280.5	10,107 ¼	14,618	6,229	13,462
Total Value *(£sd)*	91.15.4	588.10.8	916.13.4 ¾	381.10.7	897.9.4

Year	1901	1902	1903	1904
United Kingdom (gal)	18,054	21,229	13,808	3,268
Canada (gal)	2,135	2,280	321	-
Germany (gal)	-	-	-	32
France (gal)	1,351	958	2,123	2,384
Dominica (gal)	1,298	-	-	-
Total Qty. (gal)	22,838	24,467	16,252	5,684
Total Value (£sd)	1,332.4.4	1,019.9.2	812.12.0	236.16.8

Year	1905	1906	1907	1908	1909
United Kingdom (gal)	5,780	-	8	12,938	14,231
Canada (gal)	-	-	18	-	-
French W.I (gal)	-	-		124	-
France (gal)	2,094	6,086	3,237	10,378	13,082
Dominica (gal)	621	190	-	-	570
Total Qty. (gal)	8,495	6,276	3,263	23,440	27,883
Total Value (£sd)	424.15.0	316.2.0	163.3.0	1,367.6.8	2,323.11.0

Year	1910	1911	1912	1913	1914
United Kingdom (gal)	3,471	-	36,925	4,667	6,463
Belgium (gal)	776	-	-	-	-
St. Vincent (gal)	-	-	91	1,674	-
France (gal)	183	12,410	-	7,683 ⅖	13,181
Dominica (gal)	232	-	-	-	-
Venezuela (gal)	-	-	1,572	-	-
Ships' Stores (gal)	-	-	466 ¼	116	-
Grenada (gal)	-	-	-	3,620	-
Total Qty. (gal)	4,692	12,410	39,054 ¼	17,760 ⅖	19,644
Total Value (£sd)	391.0.0	1,034.3.4	2,603.12.4	2,032.16.10	1,796.6.0

Year	1915	1916	1917	1918 - 1921
United Kingdom (gal)	24,708	8,042.4	-	No Record
Ships' Stores (gal)	65	-	-	
Martinique (gal)	-	7,733.6	-	
France (gal)	61	-	-	
Dominica (gal)	1,285	2,238.5	477.1	
Total Qty. (gal)	26,219	18,014.5	477.1	
Total Value (£sd)	2,717.26.1	1,801.8.6	66.2.11	

Year	1922	1923	1924	1925	1926	1927	1928
United Kingdom (gal)	-	-	-	-	-	1,700	1,303
Antigua (gal)	361	433	-	-	-	-	-
Bermuda (gal)	-	50	-	-	-	-	-
Montserrat (gal)	-	166	-	2	-	-	-
Ships' Stores (gal)	-	-	95 ¾	61	37	-	20
Total Qty. (gal)	361	649	95 ¾	63	37	1,700	1,323
Total Value (£)	63	64	29	25	11	212	218

Year	1929	1930	1931 - 1935	1936	1937	1938
United Kingdom (gal)	2,013	1,583.9	No Record	4,091.4	2,427	10,251
Ships' Stores (gal)	-	13		-	-	-
Total Qty. (gal)	2,013	1,596.9		4,091.4	2,427	10,251
Total Value (£)	339	288		649	243	1,186

Year	1939	1940	1941 - 1946	1947	1948 - 1960
United Kingdom (gal)	6,097.7	25,307	21	13,431	No Record
Total Qty. (gal)	6,097.7	25,307		13,431	
Total Value	£684	£3,727		$8,985	

[21] The Series of Colonial Annual Reports, which was re-introduced for the year 1946-47 (after suspension in 1940 due to World War 2) was then continued with those relating to 1946-47.

Year	1961	1962
Total Qty. (gal)	22,709	15,578
Total Value ($)	34	21

CHAPTER 14.2

'Sugar' Export

Export areas for 1823-1855 are recorded together and stated as 'Great Britain, British West Indies, British North America Colonies, United States of America and Foreign States'. The records defined them as such but only attributed a value to each with no individual quantity recorded.

Export areas for the below are stated within the note identifiers. The records defined them as such but only attributed a value to each with no quantity recorded.

Key:

bbl – barrel
t – tonne
hhd – hogshead
lbs – pounds
pcs – pieces
NR – no record available

Year	Quantity of Sugar and Unit	Total Value (£sd)
1823	*6,061,702 hhd*	*136,388.5.9¾*
1828	*6,634 hhd / 1,319 bbl / 1,375 t*	*101,378.6.0*
1829	*6,388 hhd / 1,074 bbl*	*88,286.0.0*
1830	*6,064 hhd / 1,401 bbl / 1,049 pcs*	*105,128.7.0*
1831	*5,263 hhd / 1,229 bbl / 1,082 pieces / 2½ pcs*	*NR*
1832	*37 demijohns / 156 furkins*	*NR*
1833	*2,979 hhd / 862 bbl*	*NR*
1834	*4,162 hhd / 1,414 bbl / 2½ bbl / 1,096 pcs / 18½ pcs*	*87,136.15.3*
1835	*3,668 hhd / 1,198 bbl / 944 t / 2 half bbl's*	*54,714.0.0*
1836	*2,688 hhd / 454 t / 844 bbl*	*45,875.5.0*
1837	*3,407 hhd / 1,167 bbl*	*51,540.0.0*
1839	*No Record*	
1839	*2,343 hhd / 415 t / 1,068 bbl*	*59,485.20.0*

1840	*2,589 hhd / 216 t / 759 bbl*	*58,243.0.0*
1841	*3,356 hhd / 1,073 bbl*	*119,284.16.0*
1842	*4,450 hhd / 1,584 bbl*	*89,111.10.0*
1844	*4,490 hhd / 1,734 bbl*	*90,805.16.0*
1849	*4,548 hhd / 213 t / 2,184½ bbl*	*46,984.0.0*
1850	*3,754 hhd / 178 t / 2,059 bbl*	*38,442.1.6*
1851	*4,807 hhd / 275 t / 3,074 bbl*	*43,090.18.0*
1855	*4,656 hhd / 255 t / 2,250 bbl*	*42,819,12.9*
1856	*No Record*	

The table below represents the total pounds (lbs) of shipments within the total quantity column, with the breakdown of types of measures produced labelled within the brackets.

Year	1857	1858	1859
Great Britain *(£sd)*	*788,422.0.0*	*73,292.15.0*	*91,910.0.0*
British N.A *(£sd)*	-	-	*298.0.0*
British W.I *(£sd)*	*34.0.0*	*8.0.0*	*7.0.0*
Danish Colonies *(£sd)*	*17.0.0*	-	-
Total Qty.	*6,259,475 lbs (4,511 hhd / 250 t / 2,857 bbl / 23 ½ bbl)*	*7,347,125 lbs (5,086 hhd / 388 t / 3,537 bbl / 31 ½ bbl)*	*7,966,785 lbs (5,397 hhd / 423 t / 4,728 bbl / 104 ½ bbl)*
Total Value *(£sd)*	*788.473.0.0*	*73,300.15.0*	*92,215.0.0*

CHAPTER 14.3

Sugar Cane Pieces Export

Year	Total Qty.	Great Britain (£sd)	West Indies (£sd)	Total Value (£sd)
1837	728 Sticks	-	66.0.0	66.0.0
1848	25 Sticks	0.5.0	-	0.5.0

CHAPTER 14.4

Sugar Refined Export

Key:

p - puncheon
t – tonne
hhd – hogshead
lbs – pounds

Year	Total Quantity	Great Britain (£sd)	West Indies (£sd)	Grenada (££sd)	Trinidad & Tobago (£sd)	Foreign States (£sd)	Total Value (£sd)
1836	2 p	-	60.0.0	-	-	-	60.0.0
1838	2 p	-	19.0.0	-	-	-	19.0.0
1840	10 (unit not recorded)	-	60.0.0	-	-	-	60.0.0
1843	92 Packs	397.6.9	155.11.0	-	-	2.0.0	554.17.9
1843	3 hhd	-	19.4.0	-	-	-	19.4.0
1845	4 Packs	-	22.10.0	-	-	1.16.0	24.6.0
1846	61.0.15 (unit not recorded)	-	168.5.4	-	-	-	168.5.4
1849	19 hhd / 3 t	-	54.11.6	-	-	-	54.11.6
1873	320 lbs	-	-	10.8.4	-	-	10.8.4
1885	612 lbs	-	-	10.4.0	-	-	10.4.0
1886	2,900 lbs	-	-	-	37.12.4	-	37.12.4

CHAPTER 14.5

Muscovado Sugar Export

Export areas for the below included Great Britain, West Indies, North American British Colonies, United States and Foreign States. The records defined them as such but only attributed a total value to each with no quantity recorded.

Key:

bbl – barrel
t – tonne
hhd – hogshead
lbs – pound
t - tonne
cwt - hundredweight
NR – no record available
British N.A – British North American
W.I – West Indies

Year	Total Quantity	Total Value (£sd)
1822	*280 hhd / 476 bbl*	*4,978.5.2*
1838	*3,974 hhd / 1,011 bbl*	*NR*
1843	*3,797 hhd / 1,960 bbl*	*68,670.0.0*
1845	*5,038 hhd*	*85,271.13.6*
1846	*46,650.0.7* *(unit not recorded)*	*70,930.10.0*
1848	*4,089 hhd / 78 t*	*38,101.4.0*
1852	*5,121 hhd / 269 t*	*44,462.0.0*
1853	*5,050 hhd / 212 t*	*43,015.6.10*
1854	*4,812 hhd / 245 t*	*41,468.1.5*

Year	1860	1861	1862	1863
Great Britain *(lbs)*	7,877,665	9,582,000	8,707,340	8,401,200
Barbados *(lbs)*	10,000	12,000	48,875	39,750
United States *(lbs)*	70,500	-	-	-
British N.A *(lbs)*	-	-	6,200	41,000
Bahamas *(lbs)*	-	-	-	4,800
Total Qty. *(lbs)*	7,958,165	9,594,000	8,762,415	8,725,125
Total Value *(£sd)*	91,813.0.0	80,027.0.0	76,714.0.0	69,480.0.0

Year	1864	1865	1866	1867
Great Britain *(lbs)*	8,080,525	8,526,946	10,840,438	9,513,705
British N.A *(lbs)*	-	25,300	-	-
French W.I *(lbs)*	-	-	48,800	31,900
United States *(lbs)*	29,500	27,000	53,500	9,200
Barbados *(lbs)*	-	-	-	4,000
St. Vincent *(lbs)*	-	-	-	60,975
Danish W.I *(lbs)*	-	-	-	400
Newfoundland *(lbs)*	-	-	-	200
Total Qty.	8,110,025 lbs (5,534 hhd / 265 t / 5,308 bbl)	8,579,146 lbs (5,918 hhd / 529 t / 5,038 bbl)	10,942,738 lbs (7,176 hhd / 1,345 t / 6,528 bbl)	9,626,380 lbs (6,356 hhd / 990 t / 5,445 bbl)
Total Value *(£sd)*	95,700.0.0	92,404.0.0	89,360.0.0	77,556.13.4

Year	1868	1869	1870	1871
Great Britain (lbs)	11,053,929	10,244,425	12,520,903	12,326,810
Danish W.I (lbs)	-	6,400	-	-
United States (lbs)	24,800	-	1,300	15,400
Dutch W.I (lbs)	40,300	-	-	-
French W.I (lbs)	-	266,400	291,200	500,750
Trinidad & Tobago (lbs)	-	-	57,800	-
British N.A (lbs)	-	-	-	16,000
Total Qty.	11,119,029 lbs (7,434 hhd / 1,042 t / 7,502 bbl)	10,571,325 lbs (7,108 hhd / 928 t / 5,914 bbl)	12,865,103 lbs (9,154 hhd / 1,132 t / 5,654 bbl)	12,918,960 lbs (9,160 hhd / 1,076 t / 5,464 bbl)
Total Value (£sd)	103,937.0.0	102,700.0.0	133,275.10.0	150,816.0.0

Year	1872	1873	1874
Great Britain (lbs)	13,390,450	11,948,700	13,197,060
French W.I (lbs)	102,000	127,800	79,400
Barbados (lbs)	18,400	-	15,600
United States (lbs)	-	-	8,200
Total Qty.	13,510,850 lbs (9,348 hhd / 1,146 t / 6,620 bbl)	12,076,500 lbs (8,257 hhd / 972 t / 5,534 bbl)	13,374,060 lbs (8,770 hhd / 1,312 t / 4,783 bbl)
Total Value (£sd)	165,360.0.0	135,338.0.0	127,712.10.0

Year	1875	1876	1877
Great Britain (lbs)	14,730,300	9,802,100	9,943,800
French W.I (lbs)	20,100	-	19,800
United States (lbs)	31,400	16,600	691,800
St. Vincent (lbs)	57,100	-	-
Total Qty.	14,832,900 lbs (10,333 hhd / 1,388 t / 5,044 bbl)	9,818,700 lbs (6,643 hhd / 893 t / 3,873½ bbl)	10,655,400 lbs (7,275 hhd / 895 t / 4,922 bbl)
Total Value (£sd)	131,879.0.0	92,832.0.0	127,615.0.0

Year	1878	1879	1880
Great Britain (lbs)	11,286,900	15,386,300	13,239,500
French W.I (lbs)	-	6,400	27,500
United States (lbs)	-	-	65,800
Total Qty.	11,286,900 lbs (7,074 hhd / 887 t / 5,531 bbl)	15,392,900 lbs	13,332,800 lbs (8,642 hhd / 1,063 t / 6,499 bbl)
Total Value (£sd)	97,050.0.0	148,608.0.0	143,584.0.0

Year	1881	1882	1883	1884
Great Britain (lbs)	9,414,450	12,628,700	9,989,100	14,501
French W.I (lbs)	-	65,000	-	19
United States (lbs)	66,800	280,000	3,823,100	126,996
St. Vincent (lbs)	-	800	-	-
Total Qty. (lbs)	9,481,250	12,974,500	13,812,200	141,516
Total Value (£sd)	107,295.0.0	145,071.0.0	150,276.0.0	91,985.8.0

Year	1885	1886	1887	1888
Great Britain (lbs)	8,710,400	200	-	118,000
United States (lbs)	5,307,700	3,685,900	3,620,500	2,321,700
Grenada (lbs)	-	3,000	400	-
St. Vincent (lbs)	-	400	600	1,200
French W.I (lbs)	500	200	-	-
Colon (lbs)	-	2,000	2,000	400
Total Qty. (lbs)	9,018,600	3,690,700	3,623,500	2,441,300
Total Value (£sd)	56,366.5.0	18,947.15.10	20,220.8.6	22,231.14.10

Year	1889	1890	1891	1892
Great Britain (lbs)	116,100	142,700	136,400	908,500
United States (lbs)	2,437,300	3,101,600	2,619,800	1,593,100
St. Vincent (lbs)	400	-	-	700
French W.I (lbs)	-	28,800	-	-
Colon (lbs)	-	600	-	-
Dutch W.I (lbs)	-	200	-	-
France (lbs)	-	-	-	21,200
Grenada (lbs)	-	-	-	1,000
Danish W.I (lbs)	-	-	-	800
Total Qty (lbs)	2,553,800	3,273,900	2,756,200	2,525,300
Total Value (£sd)	22,231.14.10	20,466.17.6	18,253.4.0	14,655.15.3

Year	1893	1894	1895	1896
United Kingdom (lbs)	316,200	254,100	12,200	239,000
France (lbs)	-	-	43,600	15,600
United States (lbs)	1,340,900	1,103,200	501,000	692,700
Grenada (lbs)	-	2,200	400	-
St. Vincent (lbs)	-	3,200	600	-
Dutch W.I (lbs)	-	-	-	200
Canada (lbs)	241,500	1,015,100	205,700	155,800
French W.I (lbs)	-	-	-	1,000
Total Qty (lbs)	1,928,400	2,377,800	763,700	1,104,300
Total Value (£sd)	14,463.0.0	12,483.9.0	3,341.3.9	5,852.15.9

Year	1897	1898	1899	1900
United Kingdom (lbs)	279,200	188,100	76,600	184,400
United States (lbs)	651,800	324,600	-	177,600
Dutch W.I (lbs)	-	-	-	-
Canada (lbs)	89,700	167,000	-	18,400
French W.I (lbs)	4,660	1,000	-	200
Trinidad & Tobago (lbs)	-	200	-	-
Halifax (lbs)	-	-	8,000	-
Havre (lbs)	-	-	16,600	-
St. Kitts (lbs)	-	-	-	7,000
Total Qty (lbs)	1,025,360	680,900	101,200	387,600
Total Value (£sd)	3,899.19.10	3,197.15.11	474.7.5	1,903.7.8

Year	1901	1902	1903	1904
United Kingdom (lbs)	338,200	1,314,480	85,200	235,516
Canada (lbs)	7,000	15,000	-	189,504
United States (lbs)	580,200	-	-	-
French W.I (lbs)	19,200	-	-	-
Grenada (lbs)	800	-	-	-
St. Vincent (lbs)	400	-	-	-
Total Qty (lbs)	945,800	1,329,480	85,200	425,020
Total Value (£sd)	3,166.14.10	2,967.12.1	266.5.0	1,517.18.7

Year	1905	1906	1907	1908	1909
United Kingdom (t)	162	170	60 $421/1120^{th}$	95	157 ¼
Canada (t)	630	60	1 $151/224^{th}$	-	-
Montserrat (t)	-	-	-	$1/8^{th}$	-
Dominica (t)	-	-	-	$3/7^{th}$	2 $3/7^{th}$
France (t)	-	-	-	5½	-
Total Qty (t)	792	230	62 $1/20^{th}$	101 $3/56^{th}$	159 $27/28^{th}$
Total Value (£sd)	5,544.0.0	1,610.0.0	403.6.6	707.7.6	1,139.14.10

Year	1910	1911	1912
United Kingdom	76 t	166 $67/140^{th}$ t	3,017.64 cwt
Canada	-	4 $19/28^{th}$ t	200.100 cwt
St. Vincent	-	-	4.26 cwt
Dominica	-	1 $3/5^{th}$ t	-
Total Qty.	76 t	172 $53/70^{th}$ t	3,222.78 cwt
Total Value (£sd)	760.0.0	1,534.16.3	1,608.13.0

Year	1913	1914	1915	1916	1917
United Kingdom *(cwt)*	503.88	994.60	8,155.80	14,379.10	538.36
Canada *(cwt)*	-	-	239.74	915.94	-
United States *(cwt)*	-	112	104.50	-	-
Martinique *(cwt)*	-	203.62	-	196.93	3,418.83
Grenada *(cwt)*	-	21.48	-	-	-
Bermuda *(cwt)*	-	-	-	-	28.79
Total Qty. *(cwt)*	503.88	1,331.58	8,499.82	15,492.58	3,985.86
Total Value *(£sd)*	291.5.0	644.3.4	4,851.15.8	9,213.12.8	3,309.15.10

Year	1918	1919	1920	1921	1922
United Kingdom	-	39,254.75 cwt	5,750 cwt	265 t	152.5 t
Bermuda	4 cwt	-	-	-	-
Ships Stores	-	2 cwt	-	-	-
United States	-	-	-	1 t	25.12 t
Barbados	-	-	2 cwt	-	-
Canada	-	-	17.14 cwt	1 t	0.8 t
Antigua	40 cwt	-	-	-	-
Barbados	590 cwt	-	-	-	-
Montserrat	4 cwt	-	-	-	-
Total Qty.	678.57 cwt	39,256.75 cwt	5,769.14 cwt	267 t	178.42 t
Total Value *(£sd)*	800.13.0	61,101.4.5	5,190.0.0	3,872.0.0	782.0.0

Year	1923	1924	1925	1926	1927	1928-1936	1937
United Kingdom *(t)*	120	483	430.7	456.9	178	No Record	2
United States *(t)*	10	-	-	-	-		-
Antigua *(t)*	6	14	-	-	-		-
Total Qty. *(t)*	136	497	430.7	456.9	178		2
Total Value *(£)*	2,161	9,508	4,774	5,414	2,235		20

CHAPTER 14.6

Usine Sugar Export

Key:

bbl – barrel
t – tonne
hhd – hogshead
lbs – pound
t - tonne
cwt - hundredweight
NR – no record available
British N.A – British North American
W.I – West Indies

Year	1876	1877	1878	1879
Great Britain	*760 t 14 cwt*	*702 t*	*640 t*	*880 t*
Barbados	-	-	-	*5 t*
Total Qty.	*760 t 14 cwt*	*702 t*	*640 t*	*886 t 6 cwt*
Total Value (£sd)	*18,256.16.0*	*18,252.0.0*	*14,080.0.0*	*1 t 6 cwt*

Year	1880	1881	1882	1883	1884
Great Britain	*629 t*	*820 t*	*1,714 t*	*1,453 t*	*865 t*
United States	-	-	-	*4 t*	*530 t*
French W. I	-	-	-	*4 t*	-
St. Vincent	*10 cwt*	-	-	*1 t*	-
Total Qty.	*629 t 10 cwt*	*820 t*	*1,714 t*	*1,462 t*	*1,395 t*
Total Value (£sd)	*15,737.10.0*	*22,960.0.0*	*47,892.0.0*	*38,915.0.0*	*27,900.0.0*

Year	1885	1886	1887	1888
Great Britain (lbs)	4,346,200	2,644,600	1,805,000	3,852,800
United States (lbs)	405,200	3,093,900	4,151,800	420,200
Grenada (lbs)	24,200	14,000	8,200	12,000
Dominica (lbs)	400	-	200	900
St. Vincent (lbs)	2,000	600	246	3,000
Antigua (lbs)	1,000	-	-	-
Montserrat (lbs)	-	1,218	-	-
Dutch W.I (lbs)	-	200	-	-
Colon (lbs)	-	200	5,000	600
France (lbs)	-	-	200	-
Barbados (lbs)	-	114,600	25,000	-
French W.I (lbs)	-	-	-	200
Total Qty. (lbs)	4,779,000	5,869,318	6,295,646	6,289,700
Total Value (£sd)	40,223.5.0	41,923.14.0	45,671.10.9	50,542.4.8

Year	1889	1890	1891	1892
United Kingdom (lbs)	5,998,800	4,214,200	2,447,600	3,944.800
United States (lbs)	88,800	3,654,000	4,605,400	6,401,800
Grenada (lbs)	5,000	10,600	4,000	-
Dominica (lbs)	400	-	-	-
St. Vincent (lbs)	-	103	400	-
Barbados (lbs)	-	10,000	-	-
Total Qty. (lbs)	6,093,000	7,888,900	7,054,400	10,346,600
Total Value (£sd)	63,922.2.0	63,111.4.0	60,890.1.6	76,213.15.11

Year	1893	1894	1895	1896
United Kingdom (lbs)	2,202,600	3,354,200	1,670,800	1,623,400
United States (lbs)	5,804,600	4,314,200	5,690,600	5,220,200
French W.I (lbs)	-	-	-	320
St. Vincent (lbs)	-	-	800	-
Canada (lbs)	4,000	-	-	-
Total Qty. (lbs)	8,011,200	7,668,400	7,362,200	6,843,920
Total Value (£sd)	76,106.8.0	53,678.16.0	46,013.15.0	56,095.14.0

Year	1897	1898	1899	1900
United Kingdom (lbs)	26,000	140,400	508,600	2,140,000
United States (lbs)	7,582,000	7,434,000	8,314,800	6,459,800
French W.I (lbs)	1,560	2,800	424	2,320
St. Vincent (lbs)	2,100	1,600	10,600	200
Barbados (lbs)	5,672	3,000	-	-
France (lbs)	-	141,000	-	-
Grenada (lbs)	-	-	-	10,000
Total Qty. (lbs)	7,617,332	7,722,800	8,834,424	8,612,320
Total Value (£sd)	55,497.14.0	49,370.15.1 ½	56,319.9.1	51,673.18.5

Year	1901	1902	1903	1904
United Kingdom (lbs)	2,220,400	1,225,384	6,217,000	7,932,288
United States (lbs)	7,713,600	6,834.700	1,507,600	-
French W.I (lbs)	-	-	200	-
St. Vincent (lbs)	-	1,000	600	672
Canada (lbs)	-	192,400	-	1,958,432
Dominica (lbs)	-	-	2,000	1,792
Total Qty. (lbs)	9,934,000	8,253,484	7,727,400	9,893,184
Total Value (£sd)	44,348.4.4	23,029.5.3	32,772.7.0	48,582.12.0

Year	***1905***	***1906***	***1907***	***1908***
***United Kingdom** (t)*	*3,599*	*4,459*	*4,468 ¾*	*4,118 ½*
***Canada** (t)*	*122*	*980 ⅗*	*833 ¼*	*740*
***Montserrat** (t)*	-	-	-	*2 ½*
***Dominica** (t)*	-	-	-	*8 ½*
***St. Vincent** (t)*	-	-	-	*11*
***Grenada** (t)*	-	*1 ⅖*	-	-
***Total Qty.** (t)*	***3,721***	***5,441***	***5,302***	***4,881***
***Total Value** (£sd)*	***37,210.0.0***	***51,689.10.0***	***53,020.0.0***	***53,691.0.0***

Year	***1909***	***1910***	***1911***	***1912-1918***	***1919***
United Kingdom	*4,616 ½ t*	*4,488 9/10th t*	*3,665 t*	*No Record*	*34,178 cwt*
Canada	*702 3/10th t*	*705 t*	*620 t*		-
Montserrat	*1 ⅗ t*	-	-		-
Dominica	*16 5/7th t*	*4 ½ t*	*2 ⅖ t*		-
St. Vincent	*22 4/7th t*	*3/10th t*	*1 t*		*50 cwt*
Grenada	*⅒ t*	*3/10th t*	*⅕ t*		*20 cwt*
Barbados	-	-	-		*54 cwt*
Bermuda	-	-	-		*212.53 cwt*
Total Qty.	***5,359 11/14th t***	***5,199 t***	***4,288 ⅗ t***		***34,514.53 cwt***
***Total Value** (£sd)*	***59,627.12.3***	***64,987.10.0***	***52,535.7.0***		***46,720.8.5***

CHAPTER 14.7

Sugar Syrup Export

Key:

gal – gallon
W.I – West Indies

Year	Total Qty. (gal)	French W.I (gal)	Grenada (gal)	Total Value (£sd)
1895	345	-	345	9.16.0
1886	100	100	-	5.10.0
1897	455	455	-	23.17.19

CHAPTER 14.8

Malhado Sugar Export

Year	Total Qty. (casks)	United Kingdom (casks)	Total Value (£sd)
1903	882 casks	882 casks	1,984.10.0
1905	803 casks	803 casks	2,049.0.0
1906	313 casks	313 casks	939.0.0

CHAPTER 14.9

Sugar Casks Export

Year	Total Qty. (casks)	United Kingdom (casks)	Total Value (£sd)
1904	1,233	1,233	3,699.0.0

CHAPTER 14.10

Molascuit Sugar Export

Key:

t – tonne

Year	1906	1907	1908	1909
United Kingdom	1,517 bags	1,927 bags	2,446 bags	-
France	-	1,725 bags	-	-
Barbados	-	12 bags	-	-
Grenada	-	36 bags	128 bags	7 t
Total Qty.	1,517 bags	3,700 bags	2,594 bags	7 t
Total Value (£sd)	379.5.0	925.0.0	648.10.0	21.0.0

CHAPTER 14.11

Molasses Sugar Export

Export areas for the below included Great Britain, West Indies, North American British Colonies, United States and Foreign States.

Key:

t – tonne
gal – gallon
p – puncheon
hhd – hogshead
bbl – barrel
NR – no record available

Year	Total Qty.	Total Value (£sd)
1822	NR	6,730.8.1
1823	199,300 gal	14,947.10.0
1828	2,631 p	12,249.0.0
1829	2,227 p / 40 hhd / 11 bbl	9,353.0.0
1830	1,623 p	4,846.0.0
1831	51 casks / 1,951 p	NR
1832	1,529 p / 6 bbl / 51 casks	NR
1833	1,312 p	NR
1835	1,531 p	6,128.0.0
1836	805 p	4,206.10.0
1837	1,179 p	5,644.5.0
1839	1,228 p	3,347.0.0
1840	670 p	5,119.0.0
1841	1,013 p	8,105.0.0
1842	1,015 p	3,141.0.0
1843	1,333 p	6,906.0.0
1844	1,178 p	4,539.0.0
1845	1,488 p	4,455.18.0

1846	197,420 gal	4,877.0.0
1847	1,456 p	6,025.5.0
1848	1,121 p	3,542.15.10
1849	1,323 p	4,181.11.8
1850	105,774 gal	3,159.2.10
1851	112,158 gal	3,477.7.0
1852	1,260 p	3,778.5.0
1853	1,485 p	4,180.10.0
1854	1,040 p	2,934.0.0
1855	102,835 gal	2,031.12.0
1856	48,920 gal / 347 p	2,198.0.0
1857	803 p / 85,695 gal [22]	6,231.0.0
1857	71 p / 7,800 gal [24]	578.0.0
1857	227 p / 24,970 gal [25]	1,816.0.0
1857	10 p / 1,005 gal [26]	120.0.0
1858	21,535 gal [22]	912.17.0
1858	36,453 gal [23]	822.13.0
1858	26,929 gal [25]	1,000.0.0
1859	4,047 gal [22]	102.8.6
1859	61,900 gal [23]	1,481.5.0
1859	17,460 gal [24]	811.10.0
1859	1,210 gal [25]	44.0.0

[22] Export to Great Britain
[23] Export to British North American Colonies
[24] Export to British West Indies Colonies
[25] Export to U.S.A
[26] Export to Danish Colonies

Year	1860	1861	1862	1863	1864
Great Britain (gal)	26,500	51,360	33,800	43,200	51,400
British W.I (gal)	26,400	63,840	68,600	-	-
Barbados (gal)	3,600	-	2,400	-	14,100
United States (gal)	65,700	-	-	-	17,000
Danish W.I (gal)	200	480	-	-	-
British N.A (gal)	-	-	-	68,000	39,400
Total Qty. (gal)	122,400	115,680	104,800	111,200	126,900
Total Value (£sd)	5,012.0.0	3,711.0.0	3,668.0.0	3,436.0.0	3,807.0.0

Year	1865	1866	1867	1868	1869
Great Britain (gal)	23,300	10,400	83,000	119,200	187,900
British N.A (gal)	41,300	23,100	2,400	-	-
Barbados (gal)	22,200	17,500	7,700	3,100	3,500
United States (gal)	33,100	9,600	29,200	35,800	-
St. Kitts (gal)	-	200	-	-	-
Dutch W.I (gal)	-	-	-	33,300	-
Dominica (gal)	-	-	-	-	200
British Guiana (gal)	-	-	-	-	300
French W.I (gal)	-	-	508,000	-	13,400
Total Qty. (gal)	119,900	147,200	175,100	191,400	205,300
Total Value (£sd)	2,997.0.0	4,316.0.0	3,253.0.0	7,656.0.0	8,212.0.0

Year	1870	1871	1872	1873	1874
Great Britain (gal)	69,500	77,900	193,270	1,700	2,000
British N.A (gal)	7,900	32,200	-	-	-
Barbados (gal)	5,600	-	-	-	-
United States (gal)	1,500	31,800	-	-	100,100
French W.I (gal)	68,200	42,600	63,745	163,100	130,200
Granada (gal)	-	-	-	6,000	-
St. Vincent (gal)	300	300	-	6,000	-
Total Qty. (gal)	153,000	234,800	257,015	176,800	232,300
Total Value (£sd)	6,120.0.0	9,392.0.0	9,346.0.0	7,072.0.0	9292.0.0

Year	1875	1876	1877	1878	1879
Great Britain (gal)	122,200	3,800	2,900	-	3,310
Barbados (gal)	1,700	-	3,600	-	-
United States (gal)	130,100	34,800	5,7100	43,230	-
French W.I (gal)	41,500	72,500	66,700	119,160	322,110
Danish W.I (gal)	-	-	-	270	-
Grenada (gal)	-	-	-	990	-
Swedish W.I (gal)	1,300	-	-	-	-
St. Kitts (gal)	-	-	-	-	886
Total Qty. (gal)	296,800	111,100	156,700	163,650	326,200
Total Value (£sd)	11,872.0.0	4,444.0.0	6,268.0.0	5,947.10.0	8,880.0.0

Year	1880	1881	1882	1883	1884
Great Britain (gal)	3,300	23,400	-	-	-
Barbados (gal)	-	6,000	4,000	-	-
United States (gal)	-	6,000	-	34,600	-
French W.I (gal)	246,900	191,400	300,500	174,600	-
St. Vincent (gal)	-	-	-	50	-
Martinique (gal)	-	-	-	-	335,900
Total Qty. (gal)	250,200	226,80	304,50	209,250	335,900
Total Value (£sd)	10,008.0.0	10,206.0.0	13,703.0.0	8,370.0.0	8,397.10.0

Year	1885	1886	1887	1888	1889
United Kingdom (gal)	2,158	-	2,600	86,730	14,100
Barbados (gal)	-	-	-	10	-
French W.I (gal)	379,249	215,804	204,480	108,247 (sic)	170,091
Total Qty. (gal)	381,407	215,804	207,080	144,987	181,191
Total Value (£sd)	6,356.15.8	3,596.14.8	3,451.6.8	2,416.9.0	5,372.4.9

Year	1890	1891	1892	1893	1894
United Kingdom (gal)	10,800	1,560	-	8,520	-
Martinique (gal)	-	-	-	245,160	-
French W.I (gal)	333,031	211,800	330,780	-	223,320
Total Qty. (gal)	343,831	213,360	330,780	253,680	223,320
Total Value (£sd)	8,595.15.6	5,334.0.0	7,580.7.6	4,756.10.0	3,722.0.0

Year	1895	1896	1897	1898	1899
United Kingdom (gal)	-	-	67,080	-	-
Barbados (gal)	23,640	-	-	-	-
French W.I (gal)	256,320	105,000	68,040	160,580	62,500
St. Vincent (gal)	-	-	-	2,090	-
Total Qty. (gal)	279,960	105,000	135,120	162,670	62,500
Total Value (£sd)	3,499.10.0	1,443.15.0	1,857.18.0	2,236.14.3	859.7.6

Year	1900	1901	1902	1903	1904
United Kingdom (gal)	-	-	1,920	58,400	No Record
Canada (gal)	-	6,460	2,040	50	
French W.I (gal)	57,960	-	-	-	
Grenada (gal)	-	1,320	1,680	-	
France (gal)	-	-	-	6,000	
Dominica (gal)	-	-	-	120	
Total Qty. (gal)	57,960	7,780	5,640	59,570	
Total Value (£sd)	1,086.15.0	81.0.10	94.0.0	992.16.8	

Year	1905	1906	1907	1908	1909
United Kingdom	20 p	-	-	-	-
Canada	-	11 casks	47 casks	-	26,549 gal
St. Martin	-	-	2 casks	-	-
Barbados	402 p	-	-	60 casks	33,550 gal
Dominica	2 p	-	-	-	-
Total Qty.	424 p	11 casks	49 casks	60 casks	60,099 gal
Total Value (£sd)	848.0.0	16.0.0	103.14.0	90.0.0	1,103.15.5

Year	1910	1911	1912	1913	1914
Canada (gal)	95,220	74,306	12,541	6,135	3,902 ½
Cayenne (gal)	-	-	4	-	-
Grenada (gal)	-	-	-	-	2,400
Martinique (gal)	-	-	-	-	23,844
Total Qty. (gal)	95,220	74,306	12,545	6,135	30,146 ½
Total Value (£sd)	1,914.7.3	1,400.2.1	507.12.6	155.0.0	443.6.9

Year	1915	1916	1917	1918	1919
United Kingdom (gal)	-	-	40	-	-
Canada (gal)	-	350	4,560	14,345	62,924
St. Vincent (gal)	-	-	-	2,040	-
Dominica (gal)	-	40	-	-	-
Martinique (gal)	17,000	105,474	73,710	-	-
Grenada (gal)	-	-	-	27,055	5,400
Total Qty. (gal)	17,000	105,864	78,310	43,440	68,324
Total Value (£sd)	214.2.0	2,215.0.10	2,542.8.11	2,178.0.11	4974.15.4

Year	1920	1921
Dominica (gal)	-	140
Grenada (gal)	10,240	2,824
Total Qty. (gal)	10,240	2,964
Total Value (£sd)	272.0.0	112.0.0

From 1921 onwards, the Colony Reports start to refer to molasses as 'fancy molasses', a lighter, sweeter, and milder-flavoured type of molasses which is extracted earlier in the sugar refining process.

Year	1921	1922	1923	1924	1925
United Kingdom (gal)	-	10	-	-	-
Canada (gal)	98,629	149,854	83,194	136,207	105,855
Barbados (gal)	200	-	-	-	-
Dominica (gal)	1,683	-	-	-	-
United States (gal)	200	680	29,102	23,378	17,200
St. Martin (gal)	-	172	72	-	-
Antigua (gal)	-	2,760	-	-	-
St. Vincent (gal)	-	-	-	-	51
Total Qty. (gal)	100,71	153,476	112,368	159,589	153,413
Total Value (£)	5,213	8,108	7,783	12,323	7,818

Year	1926	1927	1928	1929	1930	1931
Canada (gal)	121,779	87,541	65,225	44,786	36,736	9,136
Barbados (gal)	24	-	-	-	-	-
Bermuda (gal)	-	-	-	-	38	10
United States (gal)	34,621	66,024	12,000	3,602	2,620	11,367
Total Qty. (gal)	156,424	153,610	77,225	48,388	39,394	20,513
Total Value (£)	8,659	7,582	3,518	2,467	2,272	1,140

Year	1932	1933	1934	1935	1936	1937
Canada (gal)	18,059	30,131	23,080	16,916	24,602	32,009
Newfoundland (gal)	-	-	-	-	-	5,433
Bermuda (gal)	56	44	-	44	-	-
United States (gal)	2,280	-	-	11,296	-	9,439
Total Qty. (gal)	20,395	30,175	23,080	28,264	24,602	46,881
Total Value (£)	1,349	1,329	1,431	1,380	522	2,347

Year	1938	1939
Canada (gal)	-	31,626
Newfoundland (gal)	27,254	7,439
Bermuda (gal)	40	12
Total Qty. (gal)	27,294	39,077
Total Value (£)	1,723	2,229

From 1940, the Colony Records no longer mention the export markets.

Year	Total Qty. (gal)	Total Value ($)
1940	128,945	2,485
1947	10	33
1948	160,891	29,918
1949	10,369	1,607
1950	160,625	15,548
1951	218,891	46,460
1952	81,167	24,153
1953	220,579	27,108
1954	190,520	18,946
1955	40,541	3,648
1956	133,297	15,182
1957	49,000	5,880
1958	58,840	7,438
1959	40,000	4,800

CHAPTER 14.12

Vacuum Pan Sugar Export

Key:

t – tonne
cwt – hundredweight
lbs – pounds

Year	1912	1913	1914	1915
United Kingdom	*72,518 cwt*	*75,534 cwt*	*58,418 cwt 96 lbs*	*83,772 cwt*
Canada	*12,340 cwt*	*14,600 cwt*	*16,200 cwt*	*-*
Dominica	*40 cwt 32 lbs*	*-*	*2 cwt*	*20 cwt*
St. Vincent	*11 cwt 50 lbs*	*30 cwt 28 lbs*	*32 cwt 26 lbs*	*4 cwt*
Grenada	*12 cwt*	*400 cwt*	*-*	*1 cwt*
Curacao	*-*	*10 cwt*	*-*	*-*
Martinique	*-*	*973 cwt 40 lbs*	*-*	*261 cwt 81 lbs*
Bermuda	*-*	*-*	*-*	*18 cwt*
Total Qty.	*84,921 cwt 82 lbs*	*91,547 cwt 68 lbs*	*74,653 cwt 10 lbs*	*84,076 cwt 81 lbs*
Total Value (£sd)	*48,829.19.11*	*65,221.7.0*	*43,396.17.0*	*81,889.9.0*

Year	1916	1917	1918	1919	1920
United Kingdom	58,583 cwt 16 lbs	60,596 cwt	58,197 cwt 73 lbs	No Record	72,779 cwt 109 lbs
Canada	12,058 cwt	18,000 cwt	167 cwt 54 lbs		-
Dominica	3 cwt 88 lbs	60 cwt	-		-
St. Vincent	14 cwt 100 lbs	-	-		-
United States	-	2 cwt	-		2,000 cwt
Martinique	3,310 cwt 32 lbs	1,612 cwt	-		-
Bermuda	12 cwt 85 lbs	-	-		-
Montserrat	32 cwt	-	-		-
Ships' Stores	-	-	20 cwt 62 lbs		-
Total Qty.	74,011 cwt 9 lbs	80,270 cwt	58,365 cwt 15 lbs		74,779 cwt 109 lbs
Total Value (£sd)	81,464.16.9	72,715.17.10	73,766.16.0		141,125.0.0

Year	1921	1922	1923	1924	1925	1926
United Kingdom (t)	962	3,211.6	1,798	3,133	4,888 ½	2,877
Canada (t)	-	576	1,295	435	1/10	1,879 8/10
Dominica (t)	-	20.10	33	20	-	
Antigua (t)	-	23.8	13	-	-	-
Grenada (t)	-	1	-	-	-	-
United States (t)	2,004	-	-	-	-	-
St. Maarten (t)	-	-	-	-	-	1/10
Bermuda (t)	5	6.8	-	-	-	-
Total Qty. (t)	2,967	5,829.2	3,147	3,588	4,888 ⅗	4,757
Total Value (£)	76,937	66,741	75,304	87,987	72,559	65,444

Year	1927	1928	1929	1930	1931
United Kingdom (t)	1,031	1,949 3/10	1,649 ⅕	3,928 4/5	346
Canada (t)	3,400	2,149 7/10	2,886 4/5	638 4/5	3,627
Montserrat (t)	-	1	-	-	-
Trinidad (t)	1	-	-	-	-
Total Qty. (t)	4,432	4,100	4,536	4,567 ⅗	3,973
Total Value (£)	74,200	63,050	51,237	45,289	35,554

Year	1932	1933	1934	1935	1936	1937
United Kingdom (t)	3,091	4,441	2,505	1,660	5,307	7,225
Canada (t)	1,899	499	2,225	4,400	2,400	-
Total Qty. (t)	4,900	4,940	4,730	6,080	7,707	7,225
Total Value (£)	46,466	46,493	39,396	48,377	60,358	60,358

Year	1938	1939
United Kingdom (t)	3,308	4,882
Canada (t)	4,498	2,300
Total Qty. (t)	7,806	7,182
Total Value (£)	64,711	64,237

There were no records mentioned between 1940 and 1947.

Year	Total Qty.	Total Value ($)
1947	4,615 t	477,305
1948	6,568 t	659,031
1949	7,516 t	819,462
1950	8,629 t	1,137,119
1951	8,017 t	1,137,380
1952	7,538 t	1,257,032
1953	8,712 t	1,598,431
1954	7,301 t	1,309,899
1955	9,053 t	1,559,090
1956	9,125 t	1,598,687
1957	5,884 t	1,421,526
1958	6,270 t	1,112,482
1959	5,006 t	996,528
1960	78,825 lbs	690
1961	79,608 lbs	707
1962	4,057 lbs	366

BIBLIOGRAPHY:

Books, articles and pamphlets:

Breen, Henry H. 1844. Republished 2017. *St. Lucia: Historical, Statistical, and Descriptive*. London: Andesite Press

Campbell, John. 1763 (re-published 2015). *Candid and Impartial Considerations on the Nature of the Sugar Trade; the Comparative Importance of the British and French Islands in the West-Indies: . of St. Lucia and Granada, Truly Stated*. London: FB&C Limited

Harmsen, Jolien, Guy Ellis and Robert Devaux. 2012. *A History of St Lucia*. St Lucia: Lighthouse Road Publications

Harmsen, Jolien. 1999. *Sugar, slavery and settlement: A social history of Vieux Fort St. Lucia, from the Amerindians to the present*. St. Lucia: Saint Lucia National Trust

Hutchinson, Primus J, Patrish Lionel, Stanislaus Albert, Margaret Lubrin Aoki, Francis S. Leonce, Fr. Lambert St. Rose and Bryan Auguste. 2024. *Stories of Roseau Valley*. Saint Lucia: Jako Productions.

Morne Coubaril History, courtesy of Morne Coubaril Historical Adventure Park, Saint Lucia.

Rollinson, David. 2001. *Railways of the Caribbean*. London and Oxford: Macmillan Education Ltd.

Shingleton-Smith, Louise. 2001. *Mamiku: The Tale of an 18th Century Sugar Plantation in St. Lucia*. St Lucia: Mamiku Gardens Ltd

Reports, letter and other documents:

Companies and Intellectual Property in Saint Lucia via Saint Lucia Government Gazette. August 5, 2024, page 1048 to 1063.

British Online Archives, West Yorkshire, UK: *The following records contributed by British Foreign & Commonwealth Office.*

Saint Lucian Blue Books, 1828-1836. Identifier:73235N-01
Saint Lucian Blue Books, 1838-1844. Identifier:73235N-02
Saint Lucian Blue Books, 1845-1849. Identifier:73235N-03
Saint Lucian Blue Books, 1850-1854. Identifier:73235N-04
Saint Lucian Blue Books, 1855-1861. Identifier:73235N-05
Saint Lucian Blue Books, 1873-1876. Identifier:73235N-06

Saint Lucian Blue Books, 1877-1880. Identifier:73235N-07
Saint Lucian Blue Books, 1881-1885. Identifier:73235N-08
Saint Lucian Blue Books, 1886-1889. Identifier:73235N-09
Saint Lucian Blue Books, 1890-1892. Identifier:73235N-10
Saint Lucian Blue Books, 1893-1895. Identifier:73235N-11
Saint Lucian Blue Books, 1896-1899. Identifier:73235N-12
Saint Lucian Blue Books, 1900-1903. Identifier:73235N-13
Saint Lucian Blue Books, 1904-1906. Identifier:73235N-14
Saint Lucian Blue Books, 1907-1909. Identifier:73235N-15
Saint Lucian Blue Books, 1910-1913. Identifier:73235N-16
Saint Lucian Blue Books, 1913-1916. Identifier:73235N-17
Saint Lucian Blue Books, 1916-1919. Identifier:73235N-18
Saint Lucian Blue Books, 1919-1922. Identifier:73235N-19
Saint Lucian Blue Books, 1923-1926. Identifier:73235N-20
Saint Lucian Blue Books, 1927-1930. Identifier:73235N-21
Saint Lucian Blue Books, 1931-1933. Identifier:73235N-22
Saint Lucian Blue Books, 1934-1936. Identifier:73235N-23
Saint Lucian Blue Books, 1937-1938. Identifier:73235N-24
Bristol Shipping Records: Imports and Exports, 1805. Identifier:72948-C-06

National Archives (formerly Public Record Office), Kew, London

CO 258/18 : Blue books of statistics, etc. 1821
CO 258/19 : Blue books of statistics, etc. 1822
CO 258/20 : Blue books of statistics, etc. 1823
CO 258/21 : Blue books of statistics, etc. 1824
CO 258/22 : Blue books of statistics, etc. 1825
CO 258/23 : Blue books of statistics, etc. 1826
CO 258/25 : Blue books of statistics, etc. 1829
CO 258/33 : Blue books of statistics, etc. 1837
CO 258/51 : Blue books of statistics, etc. 1855
CO 258/52 : Blue books of statistics, etc. 1856
CO 258/53 : Blue books of statistics, etc. 1857
CO 258/54 : Blue books of statistics, etc. 1858
CO 258/58 : Blue books of statistics, etc. 1862
CO 258/59 : Blue books of statistics, etc. 1863
CO 258/60 : Blue books of statistics, etc. 1864
CO 258/61 : Blue books of statistics, etc. 1865
CO 258/62 : Blue books of statistics, etc. 1866
CO 258/63 : Blue books of statistics, etc. 1867
CO 258/64 : Blue books of statistics, etc. 1868
CO 258/65 : Blue books of statistics, etc. 1869
CO 258/66 : Blue books of statistics, etc. 1870
CO 258/67 : Blue books of statistics, etc. 1871
CO 258/68 : Blue books of statistics, etc. 1872
CO 258/70 : Blue books of statistics, etc. 1874
CO 258/71 : Blue books of statistics, etc. 1875

CO 258/75 : Blue books of statistics, etc. 1879
CO 258/77 : Blue books of statistics, etc. 1881
CO 258/78 : Blue books of statistics, etc. 1882
CO 258/79 : Blue books of statistics, etc. 1883
CO 258/135 : Blue books of statistics, etc. 1939
CO 258/136 : Blue books of statistics, etc. 1940

The Library of the University of Texas: Colonial Report St Lucia 1948-62. Call number: 972.98 SA24R. Publisher: London: H.M.S.O.

St. Lucia 1963 and 1964: London: H.M.S.O.

R, Renard 1982a, p.16. *"Statistics for the economic history of St. Lucia"* (1763-1769).

Credit to the following sources for the re-publication of imagery:

Belle Portwe Studio: page 104.
Berry Bros. & Rudd: page 110.
BritishEmpire: page 94.
Elements 8: page 110.
Hamilton, Ed: page 110.
Joseph, Tony: page 97.
Mike Veissid and Scripoworld.com: page 95.
Numista: page 95.
Planteray: page 110.
Sasu Postcardman: page 96.
St. Lucia Distillers Ltd: pages 102, 106-110.
TortoisePath: page 97.
TuesdayPints: page 105.
WorthPoint: page 96.

INDEX:

These do not include data from the production or export records.

1931 Rum – 60, 109, 140-142
1979 Ruby Reserve Rum – 143
Abolition of slavery – 7, 27, 33, 34
  Slave Trade Act 1807 - 29
  Emancipation Act – 8, 34
  Amelioration laws – 29, 33
  metayage and métayer – 36
Admiral Rodney Rum – 58, 59, 105, 106, 125-128
Africa – 18
aging – 119
Alan Lang – 59
Andre Winter – 61
Andrew Edward – 58
Angostura Ltd – 59, 139
Anse Ger River – 21
Anse la Raye – 20, 24, 26, 46
Antigua – 6, 18, 35, 47, 78
Antigua Syndicate Estate Ltd – 56
Arpenteur Générale Jean François Lefort de Latour – 23-26
Aupicon – 10
B. 2935 Cane – 49
B. 3013 Cane - 49
B. 3439 Cane - 49
B. 35187 Cane – 49
BH10(12) Cane – 49
Bahamas – 76
bananas – 31, 50, 55, 56
Battles and Wars
  American War of Independence – 22
  Battle of the Saints – 7
  First Brigand War – 27, 29
  French Revolution – 7
  Grand Battle of Cul de Sac – 22
  Second Brigand War – 28, 29
  Second French Revolution - 27
  Seven-Year-War – 9
  World War One – 8
  World War Two – 30, 51
Barbados – 6, 8, 15, 18, 33, 35, 39, 47, 50, 51, 57, 60, 76, 80-84
Barbados Land Settlement Scheme – 49
Barbados Settlement Company – 51
  L.A. Chase - 51
Barbay Limited – 59

Beane Field – 8
Beausejour – 10
Berry Bros. & Rudd – 110, 150
Bermuda – 80, 83
Bexon – 54
Blackadder – 151
blending – 119
boiling house – 15-16
Bonpland – 151
Bourbon Cane – 49
Brazil – 15, 35
Brigands – 27, 28, 29
Bristol, United Kingdom – 75
British Guiana – 35, 81
Bruce Perry – 61
Buccaneer Rum – 58, 108, 144
Cadenhead – 152
carrés or hectares – 10-12, 14, 19-22
Cayenne (French Guiana) – 47
Canada – 77, 78, 79, 82, 84
Canaries River – 20
Cane Farmers Association – 54
cane trash – 14
Caribs and Carib Indians – 5, 6, 21
Castries – 19, 20, 23, 26, 35, 46, 48
Castries Crème – 152
Castries fire 1805 – 34
Castries fire 1813 – 34
Castries Harbour – 7
Cellar Master – 61
Chairman's Reserve Rum – 59, 60, 106, 128-136
Choc/Marisule – 20
Choiseul – 15, 20, 21, 24, 26, 32, 91
Ciceron – 54
Clarke Street (see Malgrétoute-Micoud Road)
CL Financial – 59
CLICO Holdings Barbados Limited (CHBL) – 59
coal – 8, 47
cocoa – 8, 9, 18, 19, 25, 31, 41, 50
coconuts – 31, 50
coffee – 8, 9, 12, 14, 18, 19, 30, 41
coffey still – *see McMillan Ltd Coffey Column*
Colon, Panama – 77
Compagnie des Indes – 152
Companies and Intellectual Property in Saint Lucia – 61
cotton – 8, 9, 18, 19, 25, 41
Crème la Caye – 107, 138

Creole, planters – 10, 28
Crystal Lime Rum Liqueur - 122
Crystal White Rum – 106, 122
Cuba – 35, 39
curing house – 16
Cul de Sac – 23, 37, 48
Cul de Sac cane juice rum – 49
Cyril Mangal – 61
de Nozière – 21
de Tascher – 21
Danish West Indies – 76, 81
Dauphin – 22, 25, 26, 41
Dennery – 21, 25, 26, 37, 40, 48, 54
Denros Bounty Rum and Bounty Rum – 58-59, 105, 121-125
Denros Strong Rum – 122
Deny Duplessis – 61
Des Blanchard – 21
distillery – 16
Distillery Manager – 61
Dominica – 55, 78, 80-81, 84
D.W.D. Comins – 40, 41
Duncans Gin – 58
Duncan Taylor – 152
Dutch West Indies – 78
East Caribbean Distillers Ltd – 58
Elements 8 Rum – 110, 145-146
energy – 116
Evanius Harris – 61
Factory Ordinance No.8 1943 – 53
Famille Ricci – 152-153
fancy molasses – 82
fermentation – 116
Five Blondes Rum – 58, 144
Fort Rodney and Pigeon Island – 23
France – 78, 79, 82, 84
French Government, Royals and Generals
  Cardinal Richelieu – 5
  d'Esnambuc – 5
  du Parquet – 5
  Duke of Orleans – 6
  King Louis XVI – 27
  Marechal D'Estrees – 6
  Marquis de Champigny – 6
  Napoleon Bonaparte – 32
  Robespierre – 27
  Victor Hugues – 7, 27
French West Indies – 77, 80-81

G&P Dormoy – 58
Geest Industries Ltd – 39, 56, 58
  John van Geest - 55
Geographical Indication (GI) – 61
ginger – 9
Governors & Administrators of Saint Lucia
  Brigadier-General John Moore – 28
  Chief Justice John Jeremie – 33
  Colonel Thorn – 50
  D.G. Garraway – 45
  d'Estaing – 7
  de Gimat – 26
  de Laborie – 23, 33
  de Longueville – 6, 9
  de Micoud – 19, 26, 33, 85
  de Ricard – 26
  D.G. Garraway – 45
  Goyrand – 26, 28
  John Compton – 54
  Karl LaCorbinière – 54
  Lieutenant-Governor Charles Henry Darling – 36
  Major Judge – 5
  Rousselan – 5
  Sir Harry Langhorne Thompson – 47
Great Britain and United Kingdom Government, Royals and Generals
  Charles I – 5-6
  Duke of Montagu – 6
  Earl of Carlisle – 5
  Earl of Sandwich – 7
  Francis Lord Willoughby – 5
  General Abercrombie – 7
Grenada – 8, 10, 18, 55, 78-79, 82, 84
Gros Islet – 10, 21, 25-26, 35, 41, 48
Groupe Bernard Hayot – 60
Guadeloupe – 6, 7, 27-29, 38, 56
Halifax, Nova Scotia – 77
Hamilton Rum – 110, 146-148
hand mills – 41
harvest and season – 14, 15, 23
Harvey Nichols – 155-156
Havre, France – 77, 78
Hayman's – 59
Henry Hegart Breen – 9, 35
Hewanorra International Airport – 8
Hogsheads – 16, 34
Hotel Chocolat – 155
hurricane – 22, 23, 26, 32

Ian John – 61
International Sugar Agreement – 51
Javalatté – 138
John Dore 1 Pot Still – 117, 145
John Dore 2 Pot Still – 118, 145
Koko-nut Rum – 107, 138
kola nut – 41
Krimshaya Vodka – 58
Kwèyòl Spiced Rum – 106, 123
L'Ivrogne river – 20
La Ressource – 10
La Belle Creole – 59, 110, 139
La Maison du Rhum – 150-151
Lavelle Brandy – 58
Le Chemin Royal (also known as Royal Road and le Grand Chemin) – 10
Le Petit Carenage – 7
Laborie – 21, 24, 26, 41, 46, 90
Lennox Wilson – 61
Loic Leger – 60
limes – 50
Louisiana U.S.A – 35
Malgrétoute-Micoud Road – 37
malhado sugar – 83
Margaret Monplaisir – 60
Marigot – 23
Marigot Bay Rum Cream – 107, 136-138
Martinique – 6, 9, 10-11, 18, 23, 27, 33, 38, 47, 60, 82, 84
Master Blender – 61
Master Distiller – 61
McMillan Ltd Coffey Column – 118, 145
Mervin Charles – 61
Mezan – 153
Michael Speakman – 61
Micoud – 10, 19, 21, 25, 26, 48, 91
molascuit sugar – 84
molasses – 15, 16, 41, 74, 80, 81, 82, 115
Montserrat – 6, 78, 80
Moon Import – 153
Morne Fortune – 7
Mount Gay Rum – 59
muscovado – 14, 47, 74, 76, 77, 78
National Convention in Paris – 27
Navigation Acts – 35
Nevis – 6
Newfoundland – 76, 83
Nobikis – 153
Nutz' n Rum – 108, 138

Old Fort Rum – 108, 144
Ordinance 6 of 18th April 1874 – 37
ox cart – 14
Pais-Bouche – 23
Piton – 155
Plantation / Planteray Rum – 110, 148-150
Planters, Plantations and Factories
 Anse Canot Estate – 42
 Anse Mahaut Estate – 42
 Anse Galet Estate – 42
 Anse Mamin Estate – 42, 93
 Anse la Raye Estate – 42
 Anse Noire Estate – 38, 42
 Balembouche Estate – 42, 90, 91, 98, 99, 100
  Uta and daughters Verena and Anitanja Lawaetz – 91
 Beauchamp Estate – 42
  Beauchamp Distillery – 50, 113
 Beauséjours Estate - 42
 Beausejour & Au Repos Estate – 42
 Bellefond or Belfond Estate
  Henry Devaux de Bellefond (son of Jean-Baptiste de Vaux) – see Devaux
 Belle Vue Estate – 38, 42
 Belisle Cornibert du Boulay – *see Soufrière Estate*
 Belle Plaine Estate – 42
 Bellairs Estate (Roseau) – 41
 Bernard (Dauphin) – 22
 Black Bay Estate (Vieux Fort) – 38, 42
 Blancherot (Dauphin) - 22
 Bois d'Orange Estate – 42
 Boniface Gaud (Dauphin) – 22
 Bonne Fortune Estate – 42
 Bonne Terre Estate – 42
 Budin (Soufrière) – 20
 C. Belair Estate – 42
 Canaries Estate – 42
 Canelles Estate – 38, 42
 Cap Estate – 42
 Charles Dada (Dauphin) – 22
 Charlotte (Castries) – 20
 Clauzel (Soufrière) – 30
 Colas Dada (Dauphin) – 22
 Compagnie de Pichery Estate – 19
  Nouet – 19
 Corinthe Estate – 42
 Crown Lands Estate – 54
 Cul de Sac Central Sugar Factory – 37, 39, 45, 47, 49, 50, 53-54, 56-57, 90, 96
 Cul de Sac Co. Ltd – 37, 53

Dauphin Estate – 42
Dennery & Co – 39
Dennery Central Sugar Factory – 37, 39, 45-47, 49, 50, 53, 55, 77, 90
    Barnard Family – 38
       Craig Barnard – 59
       Denis Barnard – 50, 54, 55, 58
       Laurie Barnard - 58, 59, 60, 115
       Dennery Distillery – 50, 113
Dennery Factory Co. Ltd – 54, 56
Desgatieres Estate – 43
Desruisseaux Estate – 41
Dezincher Estate – 19
    Dubuq Letang – 19
Diamond Estate – 42
Drake & Co – 45
    Henry Hales – 45
Duc (Soufrière) – 20
Dubernay (Dauphin) – 22
Dubuq Letang – *see Dezincher Estate*
Dugue (Castries) – 20
Dugue de la Touche – 20
Duhamal (Dauphin) – 22
Elisabeth Brisefer (Gros Islet) – 21
Emmanuel and Theophine DuBoulay – *see St. Lucia Central Sugar Factory Company Ltd*
Entrepot Estate – 43
Esperance Estate – 43
Ferret Marnoux (Soufrière) – 20
Ferol Lacour (Dauphin) - 22
Fond d'Or Estate – 43, 92
Fond Doux Estate – 43
Fond Estate – 43
Frambourg (Dauphin) – 22
Francois (Dennery) – 21
Francois (Soufrière) – 20
Francois Grand Champ (Dauphin) - 22
Grandase Estate – 43
H. Todd – *see Soufrière Estate*
Henri Loyo – *see Soufreuse Estate*
Hope Estate – 43
Incommode Estate – 43
Jalouise Estate – 43, 93, 101
Jeanne d'Arc Estate – 31
    John Devaux – see Devaux
Joseph DuBoulay – 50
L'Orangerie Estate – 43
La Caye Estate – 43, 53

La Diorant (Dauphin) – 22
la Garde (Dennery) – 21
La Norrat (Dauphin) – 22
La Pointe Estate – 43
La Resource Estate – 43
La Riche Estate – 43
le Bond (Vieux Fort) – 10
Le Parc Estate – 43
Levacher (Vieux Fort) – 10
Lizoni (Choiseul) – 20-21
Louise Soyer (Dauphin) - 22
Louison (Dennery) – 21
M. d'Or Estate – 43
M. Courbaril Estate – 43, 92, 102
M. Lezard Estate – 43
M. Plaisant Estate – 43
Madame Dubuc Roche – 10
Malgrétoute Estate – 42, 43
Mamiku Estate – 33, 85-89, 91
Marie-Anne de Vaux, also named Madame de Micoud – *13, 85*
Marie Magdeleine (Dauphin) – 22
Marie Rose (Choiseul) – 20, 21
Marie Rose and Francois Martininq (Gros Islet) – 21
Marigot Estate – 43
Marquis Estate – 43, 48
Martin (Soufrière) – 20
Mimy Ridier (Gros Islet) – 21
Mon Repos Estate – 38
Mon Repos Sugar Mill – *92, 97*
Mondesir Estate – 43
Mont d'Or Estate (Roseau) – 41
Morne Coubaril Estate – 11-12, 14, 29-32
Morne Coubaril Historical Adventure Park – 11
Devaux – 11
Edward Devaux - *32*
Emile Devaux – *31-32*
Gabriel Devaux – *32*
Guillaume-Andre de Vaux des Rivieres – *11-12*
Irma de Gaillard de Laubenque – *31*
Jean-Baptiste de Vaux – *13*
Henry de Vaux de Bellefond – *11-13, 30*
Henry Devaux de Bellefond (son of Jean-Baptiste de Vaux) – *13*
John Devaux – *32*
Philippe de Vaux – *11-12, 14, 30*
Philippe-Henry – *13, 30*
Reginald Devaux – *3*
Nouet – *see Compagnie de Pichery Estate*

Palmiste Estate – 44
Pearl Estate – 30, 43
Perou Estate – 43
Peru Estate (Roseau) – 41
Pointe Sable Estate– 38, 44
Prevost (Soufrière) – 20
Providence Estate – 43
Pt. Caraibe Estate – 44
Rabaca, Zabeth and Marianne (Choiseul) – 20-21
Rabat Estate – 44
Ravine Claire Estate – 44
Rayne Estate – 44
Reduit Estate – 44
Remond Dampierre (Dauphin) – 22
Ressource Estate – 44
Retraite Estate – 38, 44
Reunion Estate – 44
Richeford Estate – 44
Rigout (Gros Islet) – 21
River Doree Estate – 43
    Riviere Doree Sugar Mill – 91
Roseau Central Sugar Factory – 37, 39, 41, 45-49, 53-54, 56-57, 77
Roseau Estate – 41, 44, 58
    Geest Industries Ltd – 39, 56, 58
    John van Geest – 55
    St. Lucia Distillers Ltd – 39, 58, 59, 60, 61, 102, 103, 104-109, 114
Roseau Co. Ltd – 54
Ruby Estate – 44
Saint-Philippe Estate – 30
    Philippe-Henry – see Devaux
    Vittet (Soufrière) – 30
Saphir Estate – 44
Sans Soucis Estate – 44
Savannes Estate – 44
Soucis Estate – 43, 44
Soufreuse Estate / Terre Blanche Estate – 12-13, 44
    Guillaume-Andre de Vaux des Rivieres - see Devaux
    Henri Loyo – 13
Soufrière Estate – 12, 30, 44, 92
    Belisle Cornibert du Boulay – 13
    Marie-Anne de Vaux - see Mamiku Estate
    G. H. Todd – 13
    Henry de Vaux de Bellefond - see Devaux
    Widow Izaac – 13
St. Lucia Central Sugar Factory Company Ltd – 37-38, 40, 45, 95
    Emmanuel and Theophine DuBoulay – 37, 40
St Lucia Usines and Estates Company – 40, 45-46, 48

St Remy Estate – 44
St Urbain Estate – 44
Stanislas (Soufrière) – 20
Stonefield Estate – 32
  Gabriel Devaux – see Devaux
Sugar Manufacturers Ltd – 54, 56
  Abel Ghirawoo – 54
  Francis Carasco – 54
  Harold Devaux – 49, 54
  Sir Garnet Gordon – 54
Terre Blanche Estate - *see Soufreuse Estate*
Toc Estate – 42
Tourny Estate – 38, 44
Toussaint Blancherot (Dauphin) – 22
Troumassée Estate – 44, 48-49, 97
  Troumassée Distillery – 49-50, 113
Union Estate – 44
Union Praslin Estate – 44
Union Vale Estate – 44
Valet Estate – 44
Vide Bouteille Estate – 44
Vieux Fort Central Sugar Factory – 37, 39, 45, 47-48, 50, 77, 90, 96
  Vieux Fort Distillery – 114
Vieux Fort Sugar Company – 50-51
Vittet (Soufrière) – *see Saint-Philippe Estate*
Widow Izaac – *see Soufrière Estate*
Pointe Caraïbe – 20
Pontinus Clery – 61
pot still – *see John Dore and Vendôme*
Praslin – 10, 19, 21, 25, 26, 33
Quality Assurance – 61
railways – 39, 49-51
Rameau/Latille – 21
Renegade – 153
Rhum Ste. Lucie – 154
Rivière de La Brelotte – 23
Rodney Bay – 20
Roger Miller – 61
RomDeLuxe – 153
Ron D'Oro Rum – 58, 110, 144
Roseau – 23, 37
Roseau Cane – 49
Roseau River - 115
rum – 15, 16, 46, 57, 58, 59, 89, 111
rum licence – 41
S.B.S – 154
Saint Lucia Labour Party – 54

John Compton – 54
Sales and Marketing Director – 61
Sergin David – 61
Ships, Commanders and Captains
Admiral Jarvis – 7
Captain Hervey – 7
Captain Nicholas St. John – 5
Colonel Carew – 6
François Joseph Paul De Grasse – 7
Lord Admiral George Rodney – 7, 23
Nathanial Uring – 6
Olive Branch – 5
Sir Ralph Abercrombie – 28
Silver Seal – 154
Soufrière – 11-15, 20, 24, 26, 28, 30, 31-32, 35
Slaves and Slavery – 14, 15, 18, 19, 22, 23, 24, 25, 26, 32, 34, 85-89
Smuggler's Rum Punch – 144
St. Christopher – 6
St. Kitts – 35, 81
St Lucia Banana Growers Association – 55
St. Lucia Distillers Ltd – 39, 58, 59-61, 102-104-109, 114
St Lucia Jacobin Club – 27
St Lucia Workers Co-operative Union – 54
  George Charles – 54
  J. Burke King – 54
  Martin JnBaptiste – 54
St. Martin – 47, 83
St Urbain – 10
St. Vincent – 6, 8, 10, 18, 28, 47, 55, 76, 78, 79, 81, 83-84
sugar casks – 83
Sugar Duties Act 1846 – 35
sugar syrup – 46, 83
Sugar Labour Welfare Fund Committee – 54
sugarloaf – 74
sucrérie or plantation – 9-10, 14-15, 18-19, 23-25, 27, 33, 38, 41, 74
The Royal Cane Cask Company – 154
The Secret Treasures – 154-155
Ti Tasse Coffee Liqueur – 139
Ti Rocher – 21
tobacco – 9
Tobago – 8
Toz Rum – 109, 140
trash house – 16
Treasure Bay Caribbean Rum Punch – 144
Treaties and Agreements
  Aix la Chapelle – 6, 9
  Anglo-American agreement – 8

Saint Lucia Independence – 8
Treaty of Amiens – 8, 32
Treaty of Paris – 7-8, 10
Treaty of Versailles – 7, 23
Trinidad – 35, 39, 50
Trinidad & Tobago – 77
Troumassee Rum – 49
United States of America- 8, 76-78, 81, 83
United States Virgin Islands Sugar Corporation – 56
usine – 41, 47, 79
vacuum pan sugar – 46, 84
Velier – 155
Vendôme Pot Still – 118, 145
Victory '24 Rum – 143
Vieux Fort – 10, 15, 21, 24, 26, 28, 35, 37, 41, 46, 49, 50
wages – 46, 50
water source – 114
water wheel – 25
West Indian Liqueur Company (WILCO) – 59. 137
West Indies Breeding Station – 60
Windward Islands – 8
wind mills – 15, 46